MW00788356

Lyndon Johnson, Vietnam, and the Presidency

Kenneth E. Montague Presidential Rhetoric Series

Lyndon Johnson, Vietnam, and the Presidency

The Speech of March 31, 1968

David Zarefsky

TEXAS A&M UNIVERSITY PRESS
COLLEGE STATION

Library of Congress Cataloging-in-Publication Data
Names: Zarefsky, David, author.
Title: Lyndon Johnson, Vietnam, and the presidency : the speech of March
    31, 1968 / David Zarefsky.
Other titles: Kenneth E. Montague presidential rhetoric series.
Description: First edition. | College Station : Texas A&M University Press,
    [2021] | Series: Kenneth E. Montague presidential rhetoric series |
    Includes bibliographical references and index.
Identifiers: LCCN 2020051977 | ISBN 9781623499365 (hardcover) | ISBN
    9781623499372 (ebook)
Subjects: LCSH: Johnson, Lyndon B. (Lyndon Baines), 1908–1973. | Vietnam
    War, 1961–1975—Participation, American—Political aspects. | Tet
    Offensive, 1968. | Presidents—United States—Election—1968. | United
    States—Politics and government—1963–1969.
Classification: LCC E846 .Z37 2021 | DDC 973.923092—dc23
LC record available at https://lccn.loc.gov/2020051977

For my grandchildren Ella, Marni, Eliana, and Evan
and the memory of my dear wife, Nikki (1950–2015)

Contents

Preface ix

Lyndon B. Johnson, "Radio and Television Address to the American People from the Oval Office" xv

Chapter 1. The United States and Vietnam, 1945–67 1

Chapter 2. The Tet Offensive and After 31

Chapter 3. Designing the Speech 57

Chapter 4. The Bombing Halt 90

Chapter 5. The Troop Commitment 116

Chapter 6. Withdrawal from the Race. 148

Chapter 7. The Afterlife of March 31 174

Notes 191

Bibliography. 227

Index 231

Preface

A minute after 9:00 in the evening on Sunday, March 31, 1968, President Lyndon B. Johnson, seated at his desk in the Oval Office, began to read a much-awaited speech to the American people. Broadcast nationally on radio and television, the speech announced US policy regarding Vietnam in the wake of the Tet Offensive two months earlier. That operation had been a military disaster for the communist forces but a psychological blow to the United States because it made clear that a traditional military victory was not imminent and might not be possible. It flew in the face of optimistic expectations that had been articulated the previous fall. Public opinion was sharply divided between those favoring further escalation, in order to capitalize on the military success of Tet and bring the war to a speedier conclusion, and those favoring de-escalation because the war was no longer worth the cost, both human and financial. Very few, however, supported either all-out war or complete withdrawal. Threading the needle would be especially challenging for President Johnson.

Just over forty minutes into the speech, almost at the very end, Johnson stunned the nation with the announcement that he would not be a candidate for reelection. This statement did not go onto the Teleprompter with the rest of the speech text; nor was it in the advance copy distributed to White House reporters. Only a few family members and close aides knew it was coming, and Johnson himself said that he did not definitely decide to make the announcement until he began to deliver the speech. Some antiwar protesters claimed credit for forcing the president from the race, but it appears likely that Johnson's exit was presumptively decided the previous fall, prompted largely by concerns for his health. Nevertheless, his decision to announce his intentions on March 31 was shrewd.

If the speech is remembered today at all, it is remembered for the withdrawal announcement. In fact, it often is called "the withdrawal speech," "the renunciation speech," or (incorrectly) "the resignation speech." The Vietnam material is largely forgotten. Yet the parts of the speech were interrelated. The withdrawal announcement gave the Vietnam statements added credibility and positioned them as being above politics. This was so despite the fact that the Vietnam messages themselves were ambiguous and multivocal, as befit the troubled and divided state of public opinion. They could be read as continuity or change, as celebration of success or acknowledgment of failure. This was also not a situation in which policies were decided upon first, and then the speech was drafted to express them. Rather, in large measure, the exigence of an impending speech drove the formulation of the policies. The two key Vietnam announcements, a partial bombing halt over North Vietnam and a limited increase in the number of US troops, were shaped in part by how they could be harmonized in the speech.

With the passing of the Cold War, a veil of ignorance has fallen over many of the details of American diplomacy and military action in Vietnam, as far as the general public is concerned. The first task of this study therefore is to resituate these details in the Cold War context. While one could trace Vietnamese history back to ancient times, this study begins with the end of World War II and follows the growing US involvement, under four successive presidents, in the name of the greater national mission of containing communism. The second chapter then looks specifically at how the Tet Offensive reshaped the political and rhetorical situation during the months of February and March 1968.

Chapter 3 examines the preparation of the speech itself. Although there were earlier efforts to draft a post-Tet speech, concentrated attention to the task did not begin until March 20. Eleven drafts were composed in as many days. The drafting process revealed disagreement among the advisers and writers, many of whom were the same people. The differences involved matters of tone, nuance, order, and emphasis, but they gave rise to somewhat misleading appellations of a "war speech" and a "peace" speech. The first six drafts were more "hawkish" in tone, whereas the last five (labeled "Alternate Drafts") tilted in a more "dovish" direction. The chief writer for all the drafts was Harry McPherson, with the exception that the withdrawal announcement was drafted by Horace Busby. McPherson faithfully reflected the tone of the discussion in composing the earlier drafts; in the later drafts, he came closer to expressing his personal conviction.

Each of the three major decisions announced in the speech—the bombing halt, troop commitment, and withdrawal from the race—is the subject of a subsequent chapter. How the decisions evolved, how they were subject to varying interpretations and reflected strategic ambiguity, how policy and rhetorical choices evolved together, and how the composition of the speech proved consequential are among the topics considered. These analyses modify the conventional wisdom in certain respects. For example:

- Secretary of State Dean Rusk, who had a reputation as a "hawk," was the key figure within the administration advocating for a bombing halt and for undertaking it unilaterally rather than requiring a reciprocal commitment from North Vietnam.

- Although he adopted a stridently "hawkish" posture in public speeches during February and March, President Johnson never seriously considered an increased troop commitment on the scale requested by General William Westmoreland (and the sincerity of Westmoreland's request is itself open to question).

- The gold crisis of March 1968 and the threat to the dollar as an international reserve currency constrained Vietnam decision making to a greater degree than has generally been supposed.

- Even after President Johnson took himself out of the race, many found it far less than certain that he would not be a candidate.

These are some of the findings that emerge from a granular study of the development of the president's speech of March 31, 1968.

The final chapter considers the "afterlife" of this speech, which is somewhat paradoxical. It often is regarded as one of the most consequential speeches of the 1960s, a decade that featured many of them. Arguably, it reoriented the goals of American policy in Vietnam, put a cap on the number of American troops, initiated the policy that Richard

Nixon would call "Vietnamization," justified (albeit belatedly) higher taxes to pay for the war, and appealed (in different ways) for support from both hawks and doves. And, surprisingly, it elicited a positive response from North Vietnam to opening peace talks.

From the perspective of over fifty years, however, these consequences seem limited at best. The volume of bombing did not decrease; its location just changed. The months following the speech had the highest casualty rates of the war. The South Vietnamese army did not measure up to the standards required for Vietnamization to succeed. The negotiations focused only on how to achieve a complete bombing halt and even at that were bogged down in dispute over the shape of the negotiating table. Public opinion remained deeply divided until months into the Nixon administration, when it turned sharply against the war. The power of the speech, while great in the short run, did not outlast the immediacy of its context. But since the mindset of the Cold War, if not that conflict itself, can return, it is worthwhile to see how a speaker with the constraints Johnson faced skillfully navigated the situation and often made good choices under great pressure.

This book, then, has several objectives. One is to revise mistaken impressions and offer a more nuanced reading of the historical context. Another is to recover the Cold War worldview and show its influence on US foreign policy and rhetoric. A third is to capture the process of rhetorical invention—the discovery and selection of appeals and proofs—in the preparation of one of the most consequential presidential speeches of the 1960s, at a time before the White House speechwriting staff was separate from the policymakers. Still another purpose is to shed light on the complex beliefs, values, and motivations of the principal figures as they struggled toward making a set of key decisions. Yet another is to explore the state of public opinion in flux and the predicaments created by that situation. And finally, the book aims to show how the different Vietnam decisions worked together and how this speech became the kairotic moment, the ideal time for President Johnson to announce his decision not to run for reelection. These objectives will be pursued by unpacking the interwoven historical, political, and rhetorical forces reflected in the speech of March 31, 1968.

Primary-source materials for this study abound at the Lyndon Baines Johnson Library in Austin, Texas. I made use of several file series as described in the Bibliography at the end of this volume. As was true of previous visits there, the archivists were pleasant, knowledgeable, and uniformly helpful. For day-to-day developments, I followed a number of newspapers and newsmagazines that also are identified in the Bibliography. Although few of the principals remain alive, several have written memoirs that, along with secondary source materials, were valuable to the study as well.

I first examined this speech in a short essay for the Voices of Democracy Project, a website containing transcripts, critical essays, and teaching materials that was funded by the National Endowment for the Humanities. I am grateful to the Project Directors, J. Michael Hogan, then of Penn State University, and Shawn Parry-Giles of the University of Maryland, for the invitation to participate.

This book was written over a far lengthier time period than I would have desired. After completing much of the research but before beginning to organize my ideas or to write, I had to set the project aside for several years because of my wife's serious illness, leading to her death in 2015. I was then not in shape to resume any serious writing for some time. Fortunately, my interest in this study did not lag, and I was able to pick it up again in 2017. My ability to recover lost time was aided immensely by my appointment in the spring of 2018 as Visiting Senior Scholar in the Annenberg Public Policy Center at the University of Pennsylvania. I am deeply indebted to the Center's director, Kathleen Hall Jamieson, a friend of long standing, for providing a welcoming environment conducive to work on major projects, and to the several scholars and guests there, with whom I was able to discuss these ideas as they were taking shape.

Meanwhile, during the years I was working on this book, I had the very good fortune to become a grandfather four times over. My grandkids are an unmitigated source of joy in my life. I hope they may learn something of the forces convulsing the United States nearly fifty years before they were born, in the hope that they will not need to experience those forces again. It is to them and the memory of my beloved wife that I dedicate this book.

RADIO AND TELEVISION ADDRESS TO THE AMERICAN PEOPLE FROM THE OVAL OFFICE

President Lyndon B. Johnson
March 31, 1968

Good evening, my fellow Americans:

1. Tonight I want to speak to you of peace in Vietnam and Southeast Asia.

2. No other question so preoccupies our people. No other dream so absorbs the 250 million human beings who live in that part of the world. No other goal motivates American policy in Southeast Asia.

3. For years, representatives of our Government and others have traveled the world—seeking to find a basis for peace talks.

4. Since last September, they have carried the offer that I made public at San Antonio. And that offer was this:

5. That the United States would stop its bombardment of North Vietnam when that would lead promptly to productive discussions—and that we would assume that North Vietnam would not take military advantage of our restraint.

6. Hanoi denounced this offer, both privately and publicly. Even while the search for peace was going on, North Vietnam rushed their preparations for a savage assault on the people, the government, and the allies of South Vietnam.

7. Their attack—during the Tet holidays—failed to achieve its principal objectives.

8. It did not collapse the elected government of South Vietnam or shatter its army—as the Communists had hoped.

9. It did not produce a "general uprising" among the people of the cities as they had predicted.

10. The Communists were unable to maintain control of any of the more than 30 cities that they attacked. And they took very heavy casualties.

11. But they did compel the South Vietnamese and their allies to move certain forces from the countryside into the cities.

12. They caused widespread disruption and suffering. Their attacks, and the battles that followed, made refugees of half a million human beings.

13. The Communists may renew their attack any day.

14. They are, it appears, trying to make 1968 the year of decision in South Vietnam—the year that brings, if not final victory or defeat, at least a turning point in the struggle.

15. This much is clear:

16. If they do mount another round of heavy attacks, they will not succeed in destroying the fighting power of South Vietnam and its allies.

17. But tragically, this is also clear: Many men—on both sides of the struggle—will be lost. A nation that has already suffered 20 years of warfare will suffer once again. Armies on both sides will take new casualties. And the war will go on.

18. There is no need for this to be so.

19. There is no need to delay the talks that could bring an end to this long and this bloody war.

20. Tonight, I renew the offer I made last August—to stop the bombardment of North Vietnam. We ask that talks begin promptly, that they be serious talks on the substance of peace. We assume that during those talks Hanoi will not take advantage of our restraint.

21. We are prepared to move immediately toward peace through negotiations.

22. So, tonight, in the hope that this action will lead to early talks, I am taking the first step to deescalate the conflict. We are reducing—substantially reducing—the present level of hostilities.

23. And we are doing so unilaterally, and at once.

24. Tonight, I have ordered our aircraft and our naval vessels to make no attacks on North Vietnam, except in the area north of the demilitarized zone where the continuing enemy buildup threatens allied forward positions and where the movements of their troops and supplies are clearly related to that threat.

25. The area in which we are stopping our attack includes almost 90 percent of North Vietnam's population, and most of its territory. Thus there will be no attacks around the principal populated areas, or in the food-producing areas of North Vietnam.

26. Even this very limited bombing of the North could come to an early end—if our restraint is matched by restraint in Hanoi. But I cannot in good conscience stop all bombing so long as to do so would immediately and directly endanger the lives of our men and our allies. Whether a complete bombing halt becomes possible in the future will be determined by events.

27. Our purpose in this action is to bring about a reduction in the level of violence that now exists.

28. It is to save the lives of brave men—and to save the lives of innocent women and children. It is to permit the contending forces to move closer to a political settlement.

29. And tonight, I call upon the United Kingdom and I call upon the Soviet Union—as cochairmen of the Geneva Conferences, and as permanent members of the United Nations Security Council—to do all they can to move from the unilateral act of de-escalation that I have just announced toward genuine peace in Southeast Asia.

30. Now, as in the past, the United States is ready to send its representatives to any forum, at any time, to discuss the means of bringing this ugly war to an end.

31. I am designating one of our most distinguished Americans, Ambassador Averell Harriman, as my personal representative for such talks. In addition, I have asked Ambassador Llewellyn Thompson, who returned from Moscow for consultation, to be available to join Ambassador Harriman at Geneva or any other suitable place–just as soon as Hanoi agrees to a conference.

32. I call upon President Ho Chi Minh to respond positively, and favorably, to this new step toward peace.

33. But if peace does not come now through negotiations, it will come when Hanoi understands that our common resolve is unshakable, and our common strength is invincible.

34. Tonight, we and the other allied nations are contributing 600,000 fighting men to assist 700,000 South Vietnamese troops in defending their little country.

35. Our presence there has always rested on this basic belief: The main burden of preserving their freedom must be carried out by them—by the South Vietnamese themselves.

36. We and our allies can only help to provide a shield behind which the people of South Vietnam can survive and can grow and develop. On their efforts—on their determination and resourcefulness—the outcome will ultimately depend.

37. That small, beleaguered nation has suffered terrible punishment for more than 20 years.

38. I pay tribute once again to the great courage and the endurance of its people. South Vietnam supports armed forces tonight of almost 700,000 men—and I call your attention to the fact that that is the equivalent of more than 10 million in our own population. Its people maintain their firm determination to be free of domination by the North.

39. There has been substantial progress, I think, in building a durable government during these last 3 years. The South Vietnam of 1965 could not have survived the enemy's Tet offensive of 1968. The elected government of South Vietnam survived that attack—and is rapidly repairing the devastation that it wrought.

40. The South Vietnamese know that further efforts are going to be required:

- to expand their own armed forces,
- to move back into the countryside as quickly as possible,
- to increase their taxes,
- to select the very best men that they have for civil and military responsibility,
- to achieve a new unity within their constitutional government, and
- to include in the national effort all those groups who wish to preserve South Vietnam's control over its own destiny.

41. Last week President Thieu ordered the mobilization of 135,000 additional South Vietnamese. He plans to reach—as soon as possible—a total military strength of more than 800,000 men.

42. To achieve this, the Government of South Vietnam started the drafting of 19-year-olds on March 1st. On May 1st, the Government will begin the drafting of 18-year-olds.

43. Last month, 10,000 men volunteered for military service—that was two and a half times the number of volunteers during the same month last year. Since the middle of January, more than 48,000 South Vietnamese have joined the armed forces—and nearly half of them volunteered to do so.

44. All men in the South Vietnamese armed forces have had their tours of duty extended for the duration of the war, and reserves are now being called up for immediate active duty.

45. President Thieu told his people last week, I quote, "We must make greater efforts and accept more sacrifices because, as I have said many times, this is our country. The existence of our nation is at stake, and this is mainly a Vietnamese responsibility."

46. He warned his people that a major national effort is required to root out corruption and incompetence at all levels of government.

47. We applaud this evidence of determination on the part of South Vietnam. Our first priority will be to support their effort.

48. We shall accelerate the re-equipment of South Vietnam's armed forces—in order to meet the enemy's increased firepower. And this will enable them progressively to undertake a larger share of combat operations against the Communist invaders.

49. On many occasions I have told the American people that we would send to Vietnam those forces that are required to accomplish our mission there. So, with that as our guide, we have previously authorized a force level of approximately 525,000.

50. Some weeks ago—to help meet the enemy's new offensive—we sent to Vietnam about 11,000 additional Marine and airborne troops. They were deployed by air in 48 hours, on an emergency basis. But the artillery, tank, aircraft, medical, and other units that were needed to work with and to support these infantry troops in combat could not then accompany them by air on that short notice.

51. In order that these forces may reach maximum combat effectiveness, the Joint Chiefs of Staff have recommended to me that we should prepare to send—during the next 5 months—the support troops totaling approximately 13,500 men.

52. A portion of these men will be made available from our active forces. The balance will come from reserve component units which will be called up for service.

53.The actions that we have taken since the beginning of the year

- to reequip the South Vietnamese forces,

- to meet our responsibilities in Korea, as well as our responsibilities in Vietnam,

- to meet price increases and the cost of activating and deploying reserve forces,

- to replace helicopters and provide the other military supplies we need.

All of these actions are going to require additional expenditures.

54. The tentative estimate of those additional expenditures is $2.5 billion in this fiscal year, and $2.6 billion in the next fiscal year.

55. These projected increases in expenditures for our national security will bring into sharper focus the Nation's need for immediate action: action to protect the prosperity of the American people and to protect the strength and stability of our American dollar.

56. On many occasions I have pointed out that, without a tax bill or decreased expenditures, next year's deficit would again be around $20 billion. I have emphasized the need to set strict priorities in our spending. I have stressed that failure to act and act promptly and decisively would raise very strong doubts throughout the world about America's willingness to keep its financial house in order.

57. Yet Congress has not acted. And tonight we face the sharpest financial threat in the postwar era–a threat to the dollar's role as the keystone of international trade and finance in the world.

58. Last week, at the monetary conference in Stockholm, the major industrial countries decided to take a big step toward creating a new international monetary asset that will strengthen the international monetary system. I am very proud of the very able work done by Secretary Fowler and Chairman Martin of the Federal Reserve Board.

59. But to make this system work the United States just must bring its balance of payments to—or very close to—equilibrium. We must have a responsible fiscal policy in this country. The passage of a tax bill now, together with expenditure

control that the Congress may desire and dictate, is absolutely necessary to protect this Nation's security, to continue our prosperity, and to meet the needs of our people.

60. Now, what is at stake is 7 years of unparalleled prosperity. In those 7 years, the real income of the average American, after taxes, rose by almost 30 percent—a gain as large as that of the entire preceding 19 years.

61. So the steps that we must take to convince the world are exactly the steps we must take to sustain our own economic strength here at home. In the past 8 months, prices and interest rates have risen because of our inaction.

62. We must, therefore, now do everything we can to move from debate to action—from talking to voting. And there is, I believe—I hope there is—in both Houses of the Congress—a growing sense of urgency that this situation just must be acted upon and must be corrected.

63. My budget in January, we thought, was a tight one. It fully reflected our evaluation of most of the demanding needs of this Nation.

64. But in these budgetary matters, the President does not decide alone. The Congress has the power and the duty to determine appropriations and taxes.

65. And the Congress is now considering our proposals and they are considering reductions in the budget that we submitted.

66. As part of a program of fiscal restraint that includes the tax surcharge, I shall approve appropriate reductions in the January budget when and if Congress decides that that should be done.

67. One thing is unmistakably clear, however: Our deficit just must be reduced. Failure to act could bring on conditions that would strike hardest at those people that all of us are trying so hard to help.

68. So, these times call for prudence in this land of plenty. And I believe that we have the character to provide it, and tonight I plead with the Congress and with the people to act promptly to serve the national interest, and thereby serve all of our people.

69. Now let me give you my estimate of the chances for peace:

- the peace that will one day stop the bloodshed in South Vietnam,
- that will—all the Vietnamese people—be permitted to rebuild and develop their land,
- that will permit us to turn more fully to our own tasks here at home.

70. I cannot promise that the initiative I have announced tonight will be completely successful in achieving peace any more than the 30 others that we have undertaken and agreed to in recent years.

71. But it is our fervent hope that North Vietnam, after years of fighting that has left the issue unresolved, will now cease its efforts to achieve a military victory and will join with us in moving toward the peace table.

72. And there may come a time when South Vietnamese—on both sides—are able to work out a way to settle their own differences by free political choice rather than by war.

73. As Hanoi considers its course, it should be in no doubt of our intentions. It must not miscalculate the pressures within our democracy in this election year.

74. We have no intention of widening this war.

75. But the United States will never accept a fake solution to this long and arduous struggle and call it peace.

76. No one can foretell the precise terms of an eventual settlement.

77. Our objective in South Vietnam has never been the annihilation of the enemy. It has been to bring about a recognition in Hanoi that its objective—taking over the South by force—could not be achieved.

78. We think that peace can be based on the Geneva Accords of 1954—under political conditions that permit the South Vietnamese—all the South Vietnamese—to chart their course free of any outside domination or interference, from us or from anyone else.

79. So tonight I reaffirm the pledge that we made at Manila—that we are prepared to withdraw our forces from South Vietnam as the other side withdraws its forces to the north, stops the infiltration, and the level of violence thus subsides.

80. Our goal of peace and self-determination in Vietnam is directly related to the future of all of Southeast Asia—where much has happened to inspire confidence during the past 10 years. We have done all that we knew how to do to contribute and to help build that confidence.

81. A number of its nations have shown what can be accomplished under conditions of security. Since 1966, Indonesia, the fifth largest nation in the world, with a population of more than 100 million people, has had a government that is dedicated to peace with its neighbors and improved conditions for its own people. Political and economic cooperation between nations has grown rapidly.

82. And I think every American can take a great deal of pride in the role that we have played in bringing this about in Southeast Asia. We can rightly judge—as responsible Southeast Asians themselves do—that the progress of the past 3 years would have been far less likely—if not completely impossible—if America's sons and others had not made their stand in Vietnam.

83. At Johns Hopkins University, about 3 years ago, I announced that the United States would take part in the great work of developing Southeast Asia, including the Mekong Valley, for all the people of that region. Our determination to help build a better land—a better land for men on both sides of the present conflict—has not diminished in the least. Indeed, the ravages of war, I think, have made it more urgent than ever.

84. So, I repeat on behalf of the United States again tonight what I said at Johns Hopkins—that North Vietnam could take its place in this common effort just as soon as peace comes.

85. Over time, a wider framework of peace and security in Southeast Asia may become possible. The new cooperation of the nations of the area could be a foundation-stone. Certainly friendship with the nations of such a Southeast Asia is what the United States seeks—and that is all that the United States seeks.

86. One day, my fellow citizens, there will be peace in Southeast Asia.

87. It will come because the people of Southeast Asia want it—those whose armies are at war tonight. Those who, though threatened, have thus far been spared.

88. Peace will come because Asians were willing to work for it—and to sacrifice for it—and to die by the thousands for it.

89. But let it never be forgotten: Peace will come also because America sent her sons to help secure it.

90. It has not been easy—far from it. During the past 4-1/2 years, it has been my fate and my responsibility to be Commander in Chief. I have lived—daily and nightly—with the cost of this war. I know the pain that it has inflicted. I know, perhaps better than anyone, the misgivings that it has aroused.

91. Throughout this entire, long period, I have been sustained by a single principle: that what we are doing now, in Vietnam, is vital not only to the security of Southeast Asia, but it is vital to the security of every American.

92. Surely we have treaties which we must respect. Surely we have commitments that we are going to keep. Resolutions of the Congress testify to the need to resist aggression in the world and in Southeast Asia.

93. But the heart of our involvement in South Vietnam—under three different presidents, three separate administrations—has always been America's own security.

94. And the larger purpose of our involvement has always been to help the nations of Southeast Asia become independent and stand alone, self-sustaining, as members of a great world community—at peace with themselves, at peace with all others.

95. And with such an Asia, our country—and the world—will be far more secure than it is tonight.

96. I believe that a peaceful Asia is far nearer to reality because of what America has done in Vietnam. I believe that the men who endure the dangers of battle there—fighting there for us tonight—are helping the entire world avoid far greater conflicts, far wider wars, far more destruction, than this one.

97. The peace that will bring them home someday will come. Tonight I have offered the first in what I hope will be a series of mutual moves toward peace.

98. I pray that it will not be rejected by the leaders of North Vietnam. I pray that they will accept it as a means by which the sacrifices of their own people may be ended. And I ask your help and your support, my fellow citizens, for this effort to reach across the battlefield toward an early peace.

99. Finally, my fellow Americans, let me say this:

100. Of those to whom much is given, much is asked. I cannot say and no man could say that no more will be asked of us.

101. Yet, I believe that now, no less than when the decade began, this generation of Americans is willing to "pay any price, bear any burden, meet any hardship, support any friend, oppose any foe to assure the survival and the success of liberty."

102. Since those words were spoken by John F. Kennedy, the people of America have kept that compact with mankind's noblest cause.

103. And we shall continue to keep it.

104. Yet, I believe that we must always be mindful of this one thing, whatever the trials and tests ahead. The ultimate strength of our country and our cause will lie not in powerful weapons or infinite resources or boundless wealth, but will lie in the unity of our people.

105. This I believe very deeply.

106. Throughout my entire public career I have followed the personal philosophy that I am a free man, an American, a public servant, and a member of my party, in that order always and only.

107. For 37 years in the service of our Nation, first as a Congressman, as a Senator, and as Vice President, and now as your President, I have put the unity of the people first. I have put it ahead of any divisive partisanship.

108. And in these times as in times before, it is true that a house divided against itself by the spirit of faction, of party, of region, of religion, of race, is a house that cannot stand.

109. There is division in the American house now. There is divisiveness among us all tonight. And holding the trust that is mine, as President of all the people, I cannot disregard the peril to the progress of the American people and the hope and the prospects of peace for all peoples.

110. So, I would ask all Americans, whatever their personal interests or concern, to guard against divisiveness and all of its ugly consequences.

111. Fifty-two months and 10 days ago, in a moment of tragedy and trauma, the duties of this office fell upon me. I asked then for your help and God's, that we might continue America on its course, binding up our wounds, healing our history, moving forward in new unity, to clear the American agenda and to keep the American commitment for all of our people.

112. United we have kept that commitment. And united we have enlarged that commitment.

113. And through all time to come, I think America will be a stronger nation, a more just society, and a land of greater opportunity and fulfillment because of what we have all done together in these years of unparalleled achievement.

114. Our reward will come in the life of freedom, peace, and hope that our children will enjoy through ages ahead.

115. What we won when all our people united just must not now be lost in suspicion, and distrust, and selfishness, and politics among any of our people.

116. And believing this as I do, I have concluded that I should not permit the Presidency to become involved in the partisan divisions that are developing in this political year.

117. With America's sons in the fields far away, with America's future under challenge right here at home, with our hopes and the world's hopes for peace

in the balance every day, I do not believe that I should devote an hour or a day of my time to any personal partisan causes or to any duties other than the awesome duties of this office—the Presidency of your country.

118. Accordingly, I shall not seek, and I will not accept, the nomination of my party for another term as your President.

119. But let men everywhere know, however, that a strong, and a confident, and a vigilant America stands ready tonight to seek an honorable peace—and stands ready tonight to defend an honored cause—whatever the price, whatever the burden, whatever the sacrifice that duty may require.

120. Thank you for listening.

121. Good night and God bless all of you.

Lyndon Johnson,
Vietnam, and the Presidency

1

The United States and Vietnam, 1945–67

THE STORY OF US involvement in Vietnam is long and complicated. It goes back to the end of World War II in 1945 and is filtered through the prism of the Cold War.

Indochina, including Laos, Cambodia, and Vietnam, had been a French colony before the war but was captured and occupied by Japan during the early months of the war. During this time, an indigenous nationalist movement developed under the leadership of Ho Chi Minh. It was fighting against the Japanese but not for the purpose of being returned to the domination of the French. This was one of the anticolonial movements taking shape throughout the developing world.

President Franklin Roosevelt died in 1945 without declaring whether the United States would support nationalist efforts or restore colonies to the European nations that had been the United States' wartime allies. As might be expected of a person who had not made up his mind, Roosevelt issued statements and made gestures in both directions. After his death, with exceptions such as India and Pakistan, the United States tilted in the direction of supporting the former colonial powers, chiefly Britain and France. The reasons related largely to the emerging superpower competition known as the Cold War. The Cold War had a certain logic that may be hard to understand today when its premises seem faulty, but while it held sway, it yielded compelling arguments. In retrospect, it is tempting to dismiss the United States' growing involvement in Vietnam as a series of blunders, but at the time they were sensible moves in keeping with the Cold War's logic. As Schandler has summarized, "The United States did not stumble into Vietnam. Each step was a deliberate choice by a careful president who weighed the alternatives as he saw them, limited each response insofar as possible, and took into account the opinion of the public." In retrospect, what went wrong was a failure to consider "the revolutionary dynamics of the situation, the popular appeal of the Viet Cong [successors to the Viet Minh], the weakness of the half-formed, traditionalist military regimes in Saigon."[1] But these factors were obscured by the Cold War's logic.

This logic began with what might be called the paradox of nuclear weapons. After the destruction of Hiroshima and Nagasaki in August 1945, a widespread consensus developed that the sheer might of these weapons made it impossible for them to be used. There were attempts, ultimately abortive, to bring them under the control of the United Nations. The conviction that nuclear weapons must never be used gained strength after the Soviet Union ended the American nuclear monopoly and mutual destruction became assured. Superpowers developed nuclear arsenals of growing size and might so that political adversaries would be deterred from using their own nuclear weapons. Yet the logic of deterrence depended on convincing adversaries that the weapons just *might* be used. If one nation could be *assured* that the other would never attack it with nuclear weapons, then why should the first nation fear what the second might do in response to the first nation's military adventurism? Hence the paradox: how to convince a potential adversary that, in an extreme situation, you might use a weapon that any notion of reasonableness would dictate that you could not use. As much of the world divided into two power blocs, this question dominated the relationships between the "free world," led by the United States, and the communist world, led by the Soviet Union.

Before answering this paradox, it should be noted that many nations did not align themselves with either of these blocs. As former colonies of the Western powers became independent nations during the 1950s and early 1960s, they increasingly took this path. Occasionally, they did so out of genuine neutrality, but often they did so to play the blocs against each other as claimants for their loyalty. Even if that was not what was happening, it was what the superpowers often suspected. So it was important that the paradox of nuclear weapons be resolved not only for the superpowers themselves but also for the uncommitted nations presumably paying attention to the superpower competition.

As the answer to the paradox, the superpowers began to regard lower-level conflicts as surrogates for the ultimate conflict between them. If one nation committed itself (whether by declaratory policy, military assistance, a public show of force, or actual military intervention, as the case may be) to a local conflict and prevailed, that would be a symbol that the nation would do the same in an ultimate conflict, should the situation so require. This frame of reference sublimated superpower conflict, but it magnified local conflicts because of their symbolic nature. No conflict could be too small to be considered vital to the national interest, and no conflict was so isolated that it was not linked to something else. This perspective was demonstrated most clearly during the 1960 presidential campaign, when a major issue was whether the United States should respond with nuclear weapons if mainland China were to attack Quemoy and Matsu, two postage-stamp-sized islands just a few miles off the mainland but controlled by the nationalist Chinese government on Taiwan.

If everything is linked to something else, then the result is a zero-sum conflict. Any gain or loss for the communist side would be a loss or gain for the free world, and vice versa. For those in power, to "lose" any conflict carries serious political risks, as was evident in the intense and bitter conflict over who "lost" China in 1949 when the nationalists succumbed to the communist forces and retreated to Taiwan. While fierce controversies arose within this Cold War frame of reference, there was little challenge to the frame itself. On the contrary, it enjoyed widespread consensus, and it also benefited from the postwar norm that American foreign policy should be bipartisan, that, as the saying went, "politics stops at the water's edge." Moreover, this frame of reference remained largely intact until the Vietnam War strained it to the breaking point in the late 1960s. But until then, as Schandler summarizes, even in the mid-1960s "there were few voices raised to argue that Vietnam was not vital to our national security and that it could be allowed to fall into communist hands without damage to American interests."[2]

It was in this context that the United States became involved in Vietnam, first by aiding French efforts to restore colonial rule and overcome the nationalist insurgency. The nationalist war against the French began in December 1946. Ho Chi Minh appealed to the United States for recognition of the Democratic Republic of Vietnam, but the US president, Harry Truman (1945–53), never responded.[3] Instead, in early 1950, the Truman administration began providing aid to the French. The aid was used as leverage for French support for development of a common European defense, which was intended to deter threatened Soviet aggression against Western Europe. US aid also sought to preserve the strategic resources of Southeast Asia for the West and to deny them to communist nations. And in the immediate aftermath of the "loss" of China, for which Truman and the Democrats were being blamed, it enabled the administration to claim that it was holding the line against communism somewhere else.[4]

The Eisenhower administration (1953–61) quickly increased military aid to the point that, by January 1954, American assistance accounted for almost 80 percent of France's military spending in Southeast Asia.[5] But American assistance could not prevent the French defeat at Dienbienphu in May of that year. Eisenhower rebuffed a last-minute request for American intervention, but not because he was opposed in principle to American involvement. Rather, he concluded that France lacked the will to fight and that Britain was unwilling to join in. Ironically, it was at the urging of Texas Senator Lyndon B. Johnson that Eisenhower decided against getting involved. But Johnson also was not opposed to intervention per se but rather to acting without allied participation.[6] Under different circumstances, both would have been prepared to involve the United States. In fact, Prados lists a number of Eisenhower's actions that can be understood as preparation to intervene: strengthening a speech calling for "united action" in Indochina; convening an off-the-record meeting in the Oval Office; appealing to Winston Churchill to reconsider the British refusal to intervene; successfully opposing an attempt by Arizona Senator Barry Goldwater to make American intervention contingent on a French grant of independence to Vietnam; and his well-known April 7, 1954, press conference at which he defended the strategic importance of Vietnam by his analogy to a row of falling dominoes.[7] These were not the actions of someone working to keep the United States out of Vietnam but instead the actions of an interventionist for whom the time was not quite right. Eisenhower was motivated by the desire to keep Vietnam out of the clutches of communist China and its ally, the Soviet Union.

The French defeat at Dienbienphu prompted the Geneva Conference, called to negotiate the terms of France's withdrawal. The United States attended the conference as an observer but did not formally participate or sign the resulting agreement. The accords established the Kingdom of Laos and the Kingdom of Cambodia, and divided Vietnam at the 17th parallel into two zones. The French would remove their troops from the northern zone, which would be governed by the nationalist Viet Minh rebels. The southern zone would be headed by the pro-French emperor, Bao Dai. By not formally agreeing to this plan, Eisenhower avoided any charge that he had compromised with the communists as Franklin Roosevelt had at Yalta.[8]

Instead, immediately after the Geneva Conference, Eisenhower undertook to establish and support a multinational organization, the Southeast Asia Treaty Organization (SEATO), committed to the support of South Vietnam. It was apparent that Ho Chi Minh would have won a nationwide election in 1956, since the northern zone of Vietnam was far more populous. Committed to oppose the spread of communism and convinced that no election in North Vietnam would be fair, the United States interfered to prevent the election from taking place. By this time, Bao Dai had been ousted in a fraudulent referendum by Prime Minister Ngo Dinh Diem. Bao Dai fled to France, where he lived the remainder of his life in exile. The referendum that brought Diem to power established the southern zone as the Republic of Vietnam, which the United States recognized as the legitimate government of Vietnam and to which it contributed strong support, largely on the basis that Diem was a bulwark against communism.

Diem's anticommunist stance led the United States to overlook unsavory aspects of his regime, ranging from nepotism to financial irregularities and corruption. In fact, a strong argument can be made that American support for Diem became a case of the proverbial tail wagging the dog. No matter how corrupt or repressive Diem's regime, the United States could not sever ties with him because doing so would abandon the American commitment to an anticommunist South Vietnam. Instead of the United States being able to use its considerable aid to South Vietnam as leverage on Diem, the process of influence worked in reverse: Diem could defy American demands with impunity. Prados maintains that Saigon's leaders discovered this reality in the spring of 1955 when Washington's demands that Diem show greater tolerance toward dissenting religious sects (mostly Buddhists) were ignored, and yet American assistance not only was continued but was increased. Prados writes, "Diem learned the lesson well: at each higher level of commitment, the American stake [in South Vietnam] only grew, and unless Washington wished to abandon that investment, it had no choice but to acquiesce either to action or to the lack thereof."[9]

As the Diem regime became more repressive, resistance increased. Initially, the resistance to Diem was not sponsored by the North Vietnamese but it arose indigenously in the South. Communists and their supporters maintained that it stayed that way, while the United States and its supporters argued that it was organized and controlled by the North. In any case, the ties between northern and southern communists were close. In December of 1960, North Vietnam formally organized the National Liberation Front for Southern Vietnam (NLF, another name for the Viet Cong) to promote insurgency in the South. In response, American aid to the Diem regime increased, even though the repressive policies of the Diem government might be thought to have strengthened the Viet Cong. When Eisenhower left the White House in 1961, as Anderson has written, "the policy of wholehearted support of Diem remained in place not because it was achieving US objectives but because to waver even slightly could risk collapse of the administration's eight-year effort to keep the dominoes from falling."[10]

When he assumed office, John F. Kennedy was no stranger to Vietnam. Like the vast majority of Americans of his time, he was committed to South Vietnam because of its opposition to communism. Like most Americans, he also assumed that opposition to communism embodied the true aspirations of the Vietnamese people. As a senator, Kennedy had spoken at the first gala of the American Friends of Vietnam in June 1956. Explaining the importance of Vietnam to the United States, he said, "First, Vietnam represents the cornerstone of the Free World in Southeast Asia, the keystone to the arch, the finger in the dike. Burma, Thailand, India, Japan, the Philippines, and obviously Laos and Cambodia are among those whose security would be strengthened if the Red Tide of Communism overflowed into Vietnam." He went on to state that Vietnam was important as "a proving ground of democracy in Asia," a counterpoint to the "rising prestige and influence" of communist China. He added that the United States bore special responsibility, having assisted in the creation of the Republic of Vietnam. And finally, he noted that "America's stake in Vietnam . . . is a very selfish one," because the security of South Vietnam reduced the risk that the United States would need to intervene militarily.[11] These are the statements of someone thoroughly steeped, as Kennedy was, in the ideology of the Cold War. He was a charter member of American Friends of Vietnam and may well have been influenced as well by Diem's Catholicism. Diem's strongest supporters were Catholic refugees from the North, even though probably 75 percent or more of South Vietnam was Buddhist.[12] It is notable that Kennedy took for granted the legitimacy of the Diem government and its support among the people. Its importance stems from the fact that it was a domino in the Cold War, that it conveyed the message of democracy in the region, a test of American commitment, and a front line of American defense—all standard Cold War themes. Kennedy brought these beliefs with him to the White House.

Even if Kennedy had not been already convinced, however, events early in his term made it expedient for him to reaffirm and even to expand American commitment to South Vietnam. The foreign policy issue that would give him the greatest trouble, outgoing President Eisenhower predicted, was Laos; it might be necessary to intervene there. Kennedy instead relied on diplomacy and successfully developed a plan for a coalition government that was officially neutral. Although this was widely regarded as a diplomatic success, there was the danger of a right-wing reaction from those who equated neutralism with communism and who might condemn Kennedy for failing to protect against this loss. There was also the danger that the Soviet Union, in the person of Premier Nikita Khrushchev, would see Kennedy as weak for agreeing to neutralism rather than being willing to fight. This latter risk was even greater after the failure of the Bay of Pigs, an ill-conceived, disastrous plan launched just months into Kennedy's presidency to inspire an armed uprising against Fidel Castro in Cuba. Just as President Truman had used Vietnam to offset an area of potential political weakness, so did Kennedy. He reportedly told an aide, "There are just so many concessions one can make to the communists in one year and survive politically. . . . We just can't have another defeat in Vietnam."[13]

Kennedy took two actions in 1961 to reaffirm the nation's commitment to Vietnam. First, he sent Vice President Lyndon Johnson on tour to South Vietnam as a demonstration of US interest and loyalty. Engaging in unfortunate Texas hyperbole, Johnson hailed Diem as "the Winston Churchill of Southeast Asia."[14] Second, Kennedy introduced Americans on the ground in South Vietnam and continued the flow of military aid. The Americans were designated "military advisers" rather than combat troops, and their function was to provide training and assistance to the South Vietnamese, not to engage directly in combat themselves. It was sometimes hard to distinguish these functions. Kennedy dispatched 700 advisers in 1961; the number would grow to 16,000 by the time of his death in 1963. In theory, the increased number of advisers gave the United States more political and military influence over the South Vietnamese government. It could pressure the South to undertake new initiatives such as the Strategic Hamlet Program, and it allowed Americans to become more involved in South Vietnamese politics.[15] But it could not change the basic asymmetry of the relationship: the United States became dependent on Diem rather than the reverse.

As the Diem government grew more repressive, especially toward the Buddhist population, credible anticommunist alternatives to Diem identified themselves within the South Vietnamese military, and the possibility of a coup began to be considered. Although Diem was dependent on the military, he increasingly alienated them because of his personal rigidity and arbitrary exercise of power. Dissident generals made discreet inquiries of the American embassy about the US response to a possible coup. Although there were mixed signals and gaps in the chain of communication, the coup plotters got the signal that, if not an enthusiastic supporter, the United States would not interfere with a coup. A group of generals successfully launched a coup on November 1–2, 1963, capturing and killing Diem and his brother Ngo Dinh Nhu. When Kennedy learned of their deaths, he reportedly wept, having imagined that a coup would have sent the brothers into exile rather than to their deaths.

During the fall of 1963, as the situation in Vietnam continued to deteriorate, Kennedy began to reassess the American position. The United States was far more committed than Kennedy would have liked, but he was facing what Small called "two potentially failing policies: withdrawal from Vietnam without defeating the Communists, or continuing support for the government of South Vietnam with its embarrassing chaos in Saigon."[16] He told both Defense Secretary Robert McNamara and Senator Mike Mansfield that he planned to withdraw from Vietnam after the 1964 election, reasoning that it would be safe to do so after he was reelected. This is most likely what Mansfield and McNamara wanted to hear, but there is no document indicating that this was Kennedy's plan. And there are counterindications. On a television network news program that aired in September 1963, Kennedy was asked if he believed in the domino theory, and he replied in the affirmative. He was also escalating American involvement in Laos, which he would be unlikely to do while simultaneously planning to withdraw from Vietnam. The most likely conclusion is that, like Franklin Roosevelt, John F. Kennedy died without revealing his intentions for Vietnam and probably had not decided himself.

In any event, few Americans advocated withdrawal from Vietnam. George McGovern did so in 1963, on the basis that our position had so deteriorated that withdrawal was now in our interest. But as Hess writes, "such views were a distinct minority, for the preponderance of opinion in the press and Congress never questioned whether US interests necessitated involvement in Vietnam."[17] Throughout this period, however, there did not appear to be an overall strategy to achieve American objectives, but merely the overall goal of preventing the advance of communism and a commitment to do whatever was necessary to avoid the domestic political price of failure to meet that objective. Schandler points out that the consequence was that American strategic planning "assigned more rationality to the North Vietnamese decision-making process than it did to our own."[18]

After the coup in South Vietnam, Kennedy asked Ambassador Henry Cabot Lodge to return from Saigon for a top-to-bottom review of US policies regarding Vietnam. That review was scheduled for Monday, November 25, right after Kennedy would return from his trip to Texas. Lodge met instead with the new president, Lyndon Johnson, who reportedly told him, "I am not going to be the president who saw Southeast Asia go the way China went." Whether or not he actually uttered this statement, it captures Johnson's embrace of a Cold War perspective on Vietnam. The first premise of this policy was that a gain for communism anywhere was a threat to freedom everywhere. The contest between communism and freedom was zero-sum, and other countries or regions were potentially ours to "win" or "lose." The particular way in which communism posed a threat in Vietnam was through a "war of liberation." This term referred to a conflict that appeared to be a locally directed insurgency (like a civil war) but was in fact organized and directed, and often infiltrated, from outside. This formulation begs questions about the sovereignty of North and South Vietnam, but Johnson, like most Americans, rejected the view that the Vietnam War was a civil war. He saw the insurgency as just another face of overt aggression from the North,[19] which in turn was a proxy for China and the Soviet Union—notwithstanding a history of antagonism among these powers. This threat required a military defense. South Vietnam operating alone was not strong enough to provide such a defense; indeed, at several points during 1964 it appeared to be on the verge of collapse. But increasing American involvement would enable the South to stave off defeat and push back against the communists. Johnson's goal, however, was not a traditional military victory but a convincing argument that wars of liberation fail, an argument that would convince Ho Chi Minh to give up the effort. Johnson sought to make this argument both with sticks—escalation of the war—and with carrots—inducements to negotiate and offers of economic aid. Moreover, he appeared implicitly to believe that there was some "magic point" (through some level of troops, some negotiating formula) at which Ho would be convinced to give up the ghost. Johnson escalated the war in small increments at a time, "doing the minimum amount militarily to prevent a South Vietnamese defeat while convincing Hanoi that it could not succeed in its aggression," as Schandler explains it. Johnson could hope for the best, but he had no way to know when this "magic point" might be reached, so as a practical matter the decision to stop the fighting was always in the hands of the North Vietnamese and the United States was always in a reactive role.[20] Also consistent with the Cold War worldview, Johnson saw his military moves as devices to "signal" the North Vietnamese that America was resolute and would stay in the fight until the North got the message and abandoned the war of liberation. In one of his conversations with Doris Kearns, Johnson stated that he regarded bombing the North as "a means of bargaining without words." Prados also notes that the goal of the bombing campaign "from the beginning had been to influence [North Vietnam], not merely to hurt it."[21]

The president had other goals for his presidency as well, however, including an ambitious domestic agenda and the pursuit of détente with the Soviet Union. He had to calibrate his actions in Vietnam so that they did not impair these other goals. In particular, Johnson had to attract and maintain public support for his handling of the war, both to preserve his freedom of action and to depict the country as united in agreement with his message. In the beginning, Johnson simply had assumed that the public would support his actions in Vietnam. That had been the tradition in foreign affairs ever since bipartisanship had become the norm in the early months after the United States entered World War II. But another feature of public opinion is that Americans lose patience with long, inconclusive wars. This was a constant danger in Vietnam; avoiding it required convincing the public that things were going well and progress was being made. But Johnson did not want to arouse the public too much, for that would risk calls for an all-out military response. This would cause Johnson to lose control of the situation, sacrifice his beloved Great Society, and risk World War III by triggering secret treaties among North Vietnam, China, and the Soviet Union, which Johnson was convinced bound the communist nations together. (There was no evidence that such treaties existed.) So he must be both strong and restrained. As Anderson put it, Johnson's war leadership was defined by the fact that "he tried to proceed by measured steps that disguised the magnitude of the decision in order to avoid public debate."[22]

Initially, public opinion allowed Johnson considerable latitude. In May 1964, a poll by the American Institute for Public Opinion Research found that almost two-thirds of Americans had given no thought at all to Vietnam. The percentages favoring sending a United Nations peacekeeping force, maintaining the existing policy, "fighting or getting out," and "getting tougher and taking definite military action" were *all* in the single digits.[23] By March of 1966. a Stanford poll found 88 percent support for negotiations as the way to end the war. Even among those willing to send as many as 500,000 troops to Vietnam, there was 85 percent support for negotiations.[24] By mid-1967, the perception that the war had stalemated became widespread. Asked whether the United States and its allies were making progress, standing still, or losing ground, 46 percent of a sample—a plurality—responded, "standing still,"[25] a sign that continued public support could not be assured.

Probably because one could disagree with Johnson's policy from either a hawkish or a dovish direction, dissatisfaction did not necessarily imply a commitment to any particular alternative. In particular, distaste for the war did not imply support for protesters against the war, who often were seen as being outside the pale of legitimate disagreement. DeBenedetti reports that "poll data repeatedly indicated that if anything was more unpopular than the war, it was antiwar protesters." They were frequently identified in the public mind as either "discontented blacks" who were upset with everything or overprivileged and ungrateful "rowdy students" who bit the hand of the system that fed them. Either way, among many in the public, "antiwar protesters were viewed as troublemaking deviants who took to the streets either because they were Communist dupes or because they simply wanted to let off steam."[26] Illustrative of such a finding was a late 1967 poll showing that 68 percent agreed with the statement that antiwar demonstrations were "acts of disloyalty against the boys fighting in Vietnam," whereas only 22 percent disagreed.[27]

One repeatedly asked poll question was whether respondents thought that American involvement in the war had been a good idea or a mistake. Tracking responses to this question across time revealed a steady erosion of public support. At the high point of support, October–November 1965, 64 percent thought it had been a good idea and only 21 percent a mistake—a favorability margin of 43 percent. This margin shrank to 13 percent by February 1966, rose slightly to 20 percent in February 1967, then fell again to 13 percent in April 1967, and was down to 7 percent by July. By October 1967, for the first time, the margin was –2 percent: only 44 percent of the respondents thought American involvement had been a good idea, while 46 percent believed it to be a mistake.[28] A Gallup Poll in November 1967 showed that 57 percent disapproved of Johnson's handling of the war, whereas only 28 percent approved.[29] It was clear that Johnson had become a polarizing figure. Yet those who opposed his Vietnam policy were deeply divided among themselves. One survey in November 1967 found that 44 percent of them favored either a gradual or a complete withdrawal of American forces from Vietnam, but that 55 percent favored a more aggressive policy; some respondents in this latter group even advocated the use of nuclear weapons.[30] This erosion of support was not just sign of Johnson's political vulnerability. It also meant that he was losing control of the situation in Vietnam, his ability to keep to his foreign and domestic policy goals, and his ability to convince Ho Chi Minh that wars of liberation fail, for which he needed to hold the American people's support until he found the "magic point" that Ho would find convincing. If, on the other hand, North Vietnam could hold out until the American people lost patience and interest, then the best that Johnson could offer was the prospect of continued stalemate, and there was no future in that.

Musing to the president in March of 1968, former national security adviser McGeorge Bundy wrote, "I think it is a miracle, in a way, that our people have stayed with the war as long as they have, but I do not see how we can carry them with us very much longer if all we seem to offer is more of the same, with stalemate at a higher cost as the only prospect."[31] He had not been ready to make that claim in the fall of 1967, but the reality was already emerging. What was happening in the war to bring matters to this pass?

For much of 1964, as noted, the American public was not paying much attention to Vietnam, and that was just fine with Lyndon Johnson. It enabled him to maintain Kennedy's level of support without yet having to confront the fact that it was not enough to prevent the South Vietnamese from losing to the communist insurgency. Government officials made optimistic statements in public but privately expressed concern that the Saigon government appeared unable to reverse the trend without the infusion of significant numbers of American combat troops. Yet Johnson chose to campaign for the presidency in 1964 as the candidate of peace and restraint, in contrast to his opponent, Senator Barry Goldwater of Arizona, whom Johnson managed to portray as a loose cannon. Famously, the president told a cheering audience in Akron that he was not about "to send American boys nine or ten thousand miles away from home to do what Asian boys ought to do for themselves." Yet behind the scenes his administration was drawing up contingency plans for escalating the war.

The event that drew attention to Vietnam in 1964 was the reported attack by North Vietnamese patrol boats in the Gulf of Tonkin on August 2 and 4. It later developed that the first attack was in response to provocation by a vessel that was conducting spying operations off the coast of North Vietnam, and the second attack probably never occurred.

At the time, however, these incidents were understood as unjustified attacks against innocent vessels on the high seas. They gave Johnson the opportunity to respond, proving his determination, yet to keep his posture as a man of restraint by portraying his actions as limited and appropriate, called for by the unprovoked North Vietnamese actions. On his orders, planes from two carriers destroyed the fuel storage site at Vinh, not far inside North Vietnam, and sank or damaged thirty-three North Vietnamese naval vessels. Two days later, Congress passed the Gulf of Tonkin Resolution, a broad grant of authority to the president to take whatever measures he deemed necessary in retaliation for attacks on the United States in Southeast Asia, without a formal declaration of war. The resolution passed unanimously in the House and with only two dissenting votes in the Senate. At the time, many expected that the president would come back with specific requests for future escalations, but Johnson would claim that the Gulf of Tonkin Resolution gave him the prior authorization for virtually all the military actions he later undertook in Vietnam. As typically happens in moments of crisis, public opinion rallied in support of the president. One poll indicated 85 percent approval for his retaliatory measures and 72 percent approval for his policy in Vietnam[32] (even though that policy remained ill defined at the time). This sequence of events proved politically advantageous to Johnson, allowing him to campaign as a hawk and as a dove at the same time. He could take the steam out of Goldwater's calls for a more assertive response by pointing to his reprisal actions and his open-ended grant of authority should he need it, while pointing out that he was taking only those measures that were necessary and avoiding actions that might lead to a wider war. This combination effectively took Vietnam back off the front pages for the remainder of 1964.

The next American escalation was the introduction of sustained bombing of North Vietnam (as distinct from specific reprisals for particular aggressive acts), which was occasioned by the bombing of an American air base at Pleiku in early February 1965. First, the North Vietnamese attacked a US military installation, killing eight Americans and wounding over 100. A few days later, Viet Cong guerrillas blew up the US barracks about seventy-five miles east of Pleiku, killing twenty-three Americans and two Viet Cong and wounding twenty-one. Johnson responded by ordering Operation Flaming Dart—retaliatory raids on a barracks and staging areas at a guerrilla camp in North Vietnam. When this did not stop military actions against the United States, Johnson followed with Operation Rolling Thunder, a sustained program of bombing targets of military value in North Vietnam. This program would continue, with occasional pauses, for the rest of his presidency. There are different explanations of the goals of Rolling Thunder, but the principal ones included bolstering the morale of the South Vietnamese and hurting that of the North Vietnamese. Sending messages seemed to be a more important function than inflicting direct military damage. The sustained bombing had been proposed as a contingency plan; the Pleiku attacks created the reason to implement it.[33] Johnson approved the bombing campaign without much deliberation. The urgency of action was heightened by the fact that National Security Adviser McGeorge Bundy was in Vietnam at the time of the attacks on Qui Nhon and Pleiku. A strong warning from Vice President Hubert Humphrey against bombing the North was ignored, and Humphrey was punished for his apostasy by being excluded from meetings of the National Security Council for the next year.

The next escalatory moves seemed almost "natural." A sustained bombing campaign required secure air bases from which the bombers could launch. This was in doubt. Even before ordering Operation Rolling Thunder, therefore, Johnson approved the deployment of two Marine battalions to Danang. They arrived on March 8. Johnson understood the symbolic significance of "sending in the Marines" as a marker of an increased American combat role. But even that did not have much, if any, deterrent effect on the North Vietnamese, although it may have helped to bolster morale in the South. The Joint Chiefs of Staff recommended a combined effort, including naval patrols, covert operations, intelligence operations, continuing air strikes, and landing American combat troops in South Vietnam. Johnson approved a limited version of this plan, and the first American troops arrived in April. Although their mission originally was confined to protecting the bases, it evolved to include establishing secure enclaves surrounding the bases, and from there to more aggressive "search and destroy" missions to find and eliminate enemy forces. Since each of these steps seemed naturally to grow out of a previous one, Johnson could maintain that his policy remained consistent and he could repeat that he "sought no wider war." These decisions of early 1965 seemed to reflect no strategic judgment. Rather, they were responses to the frustration that earlier efforts had failed to make a difference. And there was a constant concern for bolstering the morale and confidence of the South Vietnamese, which seemed always to be on the verge of collapse.

Once combat troops were introduced, it was only natural to send more as the circumstances required, in order to achieve what the president described as unchanging goals. By late July, the number had risen to 75,000. That was when Johnson announced the next major escalation, bringing the total to 125,000. Arguably, it was this step that redefined the conflict as an American war, although Johnson denied that this was the case. Certainly he did not want the escalation to make news. The announcement was sandwiched inside a lengthy opening statement at a midday press conference, at which Johnson elaborated on the reasons we were in Vietnam, reaffirmed the commitments of Presidents Eisenhower and Kennedy, and also announced the appointment of newsman John Chancellor to head the Voice of America as well as his intention to nominate Abe Fortas to the Supreme Court. Fortas would fill the seat vacated by Arthur Goldberg who had announced his decision to leave the Court in order to become Ambassador to the United Nations. There, Johnson had assured him, Goldberg would play a major part in bringing about a diplomatic solution to the war. The understated announcement of a new troop commitment was consistent with Johnson's desire to expand the war without suggesting that anything was really changing, and certainly without putting the country on a war footing. In this way, as Small notes, the president could protect his investment in the Great Society, but "Americans did not rally around the flag in support of their president's foreign policies."[34] Expressions of support for Johnson's handling of the war were broad but not deep.

These decisions of early 1965 to escalate the war set a pattern that would be repeated until late 1967. By the end of 1965, there were over 184,000 American troops in Vietnam. At the end of the next year, the number had more than doubled, exceeding 385,000. Another 100,000 were added during 1967. (The maximum number of American troops, 536,100, were in Vietnam at the end of 1968. That was slightly below the authorized force level of 549,500.)[35] These numbers consisted mostly of draftees. Johnson consistently resisted pressure to call-up the reserves, which would have required congressional authorization. He feared that seeking Congress's approval would trigger a divisive debate resulting in a demand to cut domestic programs for the duration.[36]

Throughout this period, the Johnson administration sought to enlist American allies so that defending South Vietnam would be an international project. These efforts were largely unsuccessful. Britain was one of the co-chairs of the 1954 Geneva Conference and on that basis argued that it could not become a belligerent in the conflict. Neither France, Italy, Germany, nor Japan showed much interest either. (Ironically, perhaps, the United States had pledged to defend several of these countries through NATO. The credibility of that pledge was said to be on the line in Vietnam, where a similar commitment was being tested. This did not seem to bother the United States' principal allies, who increasingly distanced themselves from US Vietnam policy.) Prados concludes, "Possibly Washington's only ideological allies in the war were Australia and New Zealand."[37]

Furthermore, the successive American escalations did not make much difference to the shape of the war. Bombing did not seem to interfere with the warmaking ability of the North. For example, in 1966 the United States began bombing petroleum, oil, and lubricant (POL) facilities in North Vietnam. But as Dallek reports, "Two months after the POL strikes began, military planners described the bombing as having no significant impact on Hanoi's economy, will to fight, or capacity to move men and supplies to the South."[38] Increases in American troops were rapidly matched by increased infiltration from the North. The result, though not officially acknowledged, was to stalemate the war at progressively higher levels of activity, with growing American frustration that Ho Chi Minh was not getting the desired message.

Occasionally, the bombing would be interrupted in the hope that a bombing pause would lead to negotiations. The most prominent example occurred during the 1965 winter holidays, when a Christmas truce was extended by what turned out to be thirty-seven days, until the end of January 1966. Typically, these pauses were prompted by reports from third countries that stopping the bombing would indeed induce Hanoi to the negotiating table. These hopes were dashed repeatedly, and it is easy to see why. Although American ambassadors flew around the world in search of negotiating partners, they never resolved the basic impasse.

The North Vietnamese consistently demanded an unconditional, complete bombing halt (not just a pause) and a cessation of American combat activity as a precondition for talks, whereas Americans saw it, at best, as a possible outcome of talks. Moreover, Hanoi's goal in negotiations was to unify the country, whereas the American side wanted "an agreement that promised the survival of Saigon's freedom from Communist control," as Dallek put it.[39] The resumption of bombing after one of these pauses prompted expressions of disappointment and frustration, but Johnson held that to do otherwise would be to grant an unwarranted advantage to the enemy.

Johnson was ambivalent about negotiations. He welcomed any chance to bring the war to an end, but he thought that the communist demands would be flatly unacceptable. The Johnson Library contains historical files of the National Security Council. One memorandum concludes, "In any talks, Communist terms would involve the establishment of a new 'coalition' government, which would in fact if not in appearance be under the domination of the Communists. Secondly, they would insist on a guaranteed withdrawal of US forces within some precisely defined period."[40] Conversely, peace efforts undertaken by Hanoi moderates in 1966 through a diplomatic channel code-named "Marigold" and involving Poland, Italy, and the United States, ultimately were torpedoed by an American decision to order massive air strikes at the time that a sensitive and secret diplomatic meeting was to have taken place. The consequence, Prados claims, "lay in seeming to show that the Americans were not truly committed to talks, checking Hanoi's moderates, and opening the way to a military solution."[41] The motives of both sides may have been genuine, but each became convinced that the other professed to be committed to talks and yet imposed conditions that made talks impossible.

For most of the war, the American conditions for talks remained about the same. The United States would stop bombing North Vietnam if Hanoi would remove its troops from South Vietnam and pledge not to resume infiltration during the course of the talks. While this formula was seemingly evenhanded, it established the separate sovereignty of North and South Vietnam as a fact on the ground at the outset of the talks. Besides, for much of the war the North denied that it had any troops on the ground in the South, insisting that all the combatants were South Vietnamese insurgents.

In a speech in San Antonio in September 1967, although claiming merely to repeat the US negotiating position once again, in fact Johnson eased that position considerably. Now he pledged that the United States would stop the bombing if North Vietnam would agree to begin talks promptly and pledge not to take advantage of the talks as an opportunity to increase infiltration. What was missing was the requirement that the North remove its forces from the South before talks could begin. In other words, Johnson was accepting the possibility of a cease-fire-in-place, with the corollary that whatever government of South Vietnam emerged from successful negotiations would include communist elements. From the American perspective, this was not only a fair but a very generous set of terms, and it quickly became understood that the "San Antonio formula" was the "rock bottom" US negotiating position and that the ball was now in the other side's court. But from the perspective of the North Vietnamese, it was still unacceptable because it depended on a prior commitment to come to talks and not to take advantage of the bombing halt. These were conditions, and the North Vietnamese demanded a bombing halt that was complete and unconditional.

As the war continued, with occasional interludes for peace feelers, opposition to the war grew as well. Most dramatic were the protests and demonstrations organized by groups favoring withdrawal from Vietnam. These developed some novel rhetorical forms, such as staging sit-ins at draft board offices, massing bodies in public places, and blocking troop trains. They sought to counter the pro-administration predispositions of most media by violating norms of petitioning for redress of grievances, and instead engaging in outrageous behavior that was inherently attention-grabbing. The protests prompted intergenerational conflicts in many American families, even when both generations shared the same underlying values and ideology. But they ultimately had little effect on the president. Far more significant was dissent that emerged among opinion leaders and within the government.

In the former category, dissent grew as the president made the decision to escalate during the spring of 1965. Dissenters were largely liberals who saw Vietnam as a distraction from the twin goals of the

Great Society at home and economic development abroad. Partially in the hope of mollifying those critics, Walter Lippmann chief among them, Johnson spoke at Johns Hopkins University in April 1965. He laid out a vision of economic development for Southeast Asia that could be pursued if the communist insurgency in Vietnam were abandoned. His vision included developing electric power in the Mekong River delta on a scale that would surpass even that of the Tennessee Valley Authority. The United States pledged one billion dollars toward this economic development effort, and North Vietnam was invited to participate if it would abandon its quest for military domination. Reportedly, Johnson thought that Ho Chi Minh would take this bait and could not imagine his passing up one billion dollars, but Ho was not so easily bought off. Neither did Lippmann change from critic to eager supporter, and Johnson essentially wrote him off thereafter.

Within the government, Johnson frequently would tell aides that he wanted to hear whatever their views were, but the norms of discussion put pressure on others to agree with him. And once he made a decision, he expected everyone to fall into line. The fate of Vice President Humphrey for disagreeing with Johnson has already been described. Moreover, only limited aspects of an issue were considered; foundational premises were ignored. As Schandler explains, "the only alternative policies examined were alternate force levels or alternative bombing campaigns." Since the need for US intervention was stipulated, the cost of not intervening was by definition taken as greater than the cost of intervening. This meant that "the ultimate military cost of that intervention was not measured."[42]

Like Humphrey, most of those who objected to Johnson's decisions were frozen out of the decision-making circle. Under Secretary of State George Ball emerged as the "house dissenter," the persistent "devil's advocate." Running ideas by Ball and hearing his criticisms was regarded as a routine step on the path to getting ideas adopted. Ball wrote that Secretaries Rusk and McNamara shared Johnson's emphasis on "team play." Later, Ball said that McNamara regarded Ball's dissenting memos as "poisonous snakes." Ball said that the defense secretary was "absolutely horrified by them" and considered them "next to treason."[43] But Prados writes that Johnson worked much harder to draw Ball out than would be predicted by a devil's advocate role, "even baiting Ball to drag him out." Noting that Johnson was capable of taking on different personae and that the views he expressed for effect in a meeting were not always his true views, Prados notes, "Either LBJ was making a record or he truly hoped George Ball could convince others in the room."[44]

The first signs of significant dissent from Congress came in the spring of 1966, when the Senate Foreign Relations Committee held its first hearings on Vietnam. The chair, J. William Fulbright of Arkansas, had been a floor manager for the Gulf of Tonkin Resolution in 1964, but he later came to believe that Johnson had lied to him about its purpose, convincing the senator that it would not be used as a blank check to license military attack. Fulbright provided a platform for respected opponents of escalation. These included General James M. Gavin, a lieutenant general of the 82nd Airborne during World War II, who, after retiring from the Army, served as ambassador to France during the Kennedy administration. Another witness at the Fulbright hearings was George Kennan, who had been director of the State Department's Policy Planning Staff during the Truman administration. In that capacity, Kennan was the principal author of the "containment" doctrine setting out American goals in the emerging Cold War of the late 1940s. If figures with "such prominent credentials" as Gavin and Kennan, notes Prados, "publicly broke ranks with the uniformed services and foreign policy elite," their action "undermined "the pretension that professional opinion stood behind [Johnson's] Vietnam strategy."[45] Their dissent legitimized other critics from the left, even within the administration. Johnson speechwriter Harry McPherson wrote his boss in October 1967, in a properly deferential note, that he had grown concerned about the bombing of the North, fearing that it had no effect except to rally world opinion against the United States.[46] And on some occasions, dovish critics became a significant minority of the public. For example, in the spring of 1966, another Buddhist crisis in South Vietnam raised the percentage who opposed the war from 25 to 36 percent, and it stayed at that level or higher thereafter, signaling growing objection to "LBJ's staunch support for an ally that progressively seemed less worthy of it."[47]

Opposition from the right was slower to develop but was of more serious concern to Johnson because it had the potential to capture his control of the war, abandoning the practice of carefully limiting the conflict so as to prevent its eruption into general war. House Minority

Leader Gerald R. Ford was one of the more persistent critics. Originally opposed to Johnson's plan to use ground troops, in August 1967 Ford gave a major speech on the House floor, a rare occasion for him. It was a blistering indictment of the administration for "pulling our best punches" in Vietnam. Ford announced that he did not want to send any more troops or resources to Vietnam unless the administration was willing to go all the way.[48] This was an early expression of an approach to the war that has been dubbed "win or get out." In time, Richard Nixon, though professing his sympathy with President Johnson's efforts, would emerge as a harsh and persistent critic of the way the war was conducted.

In his early months in office, Johnson himself would entertain doubts about the war. In May of 1964, months before the Gulf of Tonkin incidents, he told McGeorge Bundy, "I just don't think it's worth fighting for, and I don't think we can get out. It's just the biggest damn mess."[49] He expressed similar thoughts in telephone conversations with his Senate mentor, Richard Russell. Yet as time went by, he did not charitably attribute that same sense of consternation to his critics. To be sure, sometimes in meetings he would ask his advisers if the effort was really worth it. The context, however, suggests that these were not genuine questions so much as requests for reassurance: he was looking for his advisers to tell him that yes, of course it was. But with critics he increasingly lost patience. Early on, he thought them misguided because of their youth; they had not witnessed, as he had, the dangerous appeasement before World War II that he took as his model of what to avoid in Vietnam. As their opposition persisted, he came to regard them not as people of goodwill who had a different view on the war "but as personal enemies who above all were out to get him." By late 1967, he regarded protesters against the war as "Communist-inspired if not directed," a view that was encouraged by the FBI as well as some of his Cabinet secretaries and personal aides.[50] This perspective was consistent with his tendency to see conspiracies and plots behind events, a reflection perhaps of his own shrewd and suspicious nature as a politician. DeBenedetti summarizes this view by noting Johnson's "belief that what happened in public life was the result of hidden scheming, elitist manipulation, or malevolent conspirators. . . . politics was the realm of shakers and movers, who operated through fronts, agents, and dupes."[51]

As he found himself increasingly under siege, at least he could take solace in the self-assurance that he knew what "really" was going on.

By the fall of 1967, the war was going at full strength. Hoopes summarizes that by October, "40 percent of our combat-ready divisions, half of our tactical airpower, and at least a third of our naval strength—the whole numbering some 480,000 men—were waging full-throated war on the Southeast Asian peninsula. The dollar cost of the effort was running at an annual rate in excess of $25 billion, and the number of Americans killed in action, which had totaled 6500 for the six-year period ending in 1966, was nearing the 9000 mark (plus 60,000 wounded) for 1967 alone."[52] Yet, by some measures things appeared to be going well. The preparation and military readiness of the South Vietnamese army were reassuring. Pacification of South Vietnamese villages appeared to be working. Johnson thought that there were enough US troops to do the job and, in an unusual memorandum for the file, wrote that he saw no basis for increasing forces above the recently authorized level.[53] Sixty percent of the population identified themselves as hawks, more than twice as many as those who self-identified as doves.[54] A secret memo by CIA Director Richard Helms even showed that the most senior analysts in the CIA believed that the United States could have withdrawn from Vietnam without permanent damage to the security of either the United States or the West, although the president, the military leaders, and most of the country disagreed with that view.[55]

But there were also notes of concern that fall. One, little noticed at the time, was the severity of Johnson's reaction to the March on the Pentagon in October. On its face, this was an act of street theater, marked by attempts to disarm Pentagon guards by placing flowers in the barrels of their rifles, or by efforts to levitate the Pentagon by having thousands of protesters chant "om" simultaneously. (The effort failed.) But this was the moment when Johnson decided that antiwar protesters were communist-directed dupes, if not communists themselves. Moreover, he also was convinced that they were out to attack him personally. He began more systematically to repress antiwar protesters, going after them as if they were enemies of the people. He also began to restrict his own movements and travel, going only where he could be assured of his personal safety—which limited him largely to military bases and venues that could be closed to the public. Prados describes Johnson's mindset by writing regarding the March on the Pentagon, "That became the moment that Lyndon Johnson built the big white jailhouse that trapped him and his successors. Ordering a war against the American people was not a formula for success."[56]

Another cause for concern, though not public at the time, was the emergence of Secretary McNamara's doubts about the war. If anything, McNamara had been the person most closely identified with the technocratic management of the war. Even as he began to harbor doubts, he steadfastly continued to defend the war in public. But at a regular Tuesday lunch on October 31, 1967, he passionately stated, "Continuation of our present course of action in Southeast Asia would be dangerous, costly in lives, and unsatisfactory to the American people."[57] The next day, McNamara delivered to the president a lengthy memo laying out his views; he proposed a "stabilization plan" that included capping the number of troops currently in South Vietnam and stopping the bombing of the North. In the memo, McNamara argued that progress toward US aims in Vietnam was so slow as to be invisible to the general public either in the United States or abroad. He also suggested that public support was not just a factor to be contended with but an absolute constraint on what the administration could do. In a short time it would force Johnson either to escalate or withdraw unless the United States acted immediately to stabilize the situation in Vietnam and move actively toward negotiations.[58] The memo was the first argument since Humphrey's in 1965 that the war could be won or lost based on the state of public opinion in America.[59]

This was the first indication that Johnson might even be considering major alterations in his war policy. The president had McNamara's memo retyped and circulated it to his aides without identifying McNamara's authorship. Virtually all his other advisers disagreed with McNamara's proposals, sometimes vehemently. For example, Dean Rusk (who himself would propose a bombing halt in March 1968) noted that Hanoi had not responded to the San Antonio formula and added, "They have never said that cessation will lead to talks. They resolutely resist any discussion of reciprocal military action or what we mean by 'taking no military advantage.'" Rusk urged, "I do not believe that we should cease the bombing before further probing on what the result would be."[60] Supreme Court Justice Abe Fortas, still acting as an informal adviser to the president, was even more insistent that decisions about Vietnam policy should not be made on the basis of domestic public opinion, even if McNamara's assessment of that public opinion was correct. Fortas noted, "The analysis and recommendations are based, *almost entirely*, upon an assessment of US public opinion and an *unspoken assumption* as to the effect that should be given to it," and emphatically informed Johnson, "I am in *total disagreement*" (emphasis in original).[61] A chart on file in the Johnson Library shows that of nine advisers to whom Johnson showed the anonymized McNamara recommendations, a decisive majority disagreed with the proposals both to halt the bombing of the North and to cap the number of troops in the South.[62] A few weeks later, the president took the unusual step of writing a memorandum for the file rejecting both of these recommendations but also noting that, at present, he saw no basis for increasing the number of troops beyond what already was authorized.[63] By that time, not coincidentally, Johnson had announced his decision to move McNamara, ostensibly at his request, from the Defense Department to the presidency of the World Bank, where he would remain until 1981. His successor at Defense would be Clark Clifford, a long-time Johnson (and earlier, Truman) adviser and a well-known hawk on Vietnam. One factor in his selection may have been the vigorous rebuttal he offered to the anonymized McNamara memorandum.

The day after McNamara's memo, on November 2, Johnson convened a group known as the Wise Men, composed of individuals regarded as elder statesmen on foreign policy. Many of them had held official positions in prior administrations. Clark Clifford, then still a private citizen, was among the group; so was McGeorge Bundy. The intellectual leader of the group was President Truman's secretary of state, Dean Acheson. If McNamara's memo had aroused any doubt or uncertainty on Johnson's part, the Wise Men provided reassurance. A lengthy memo from presidential aide Jim Jones provided a detailed summary of the meeting.[64] Prompted perhaps by Johnson's opening statement, the group quickly and generally agreed that US policy was sound and that the question was how to unify the country in its support. McGeorge Bundy, for example, opined that "public support is needed because people see dying with no picture of result in sight" and added, "If we can permeate to the public that we are seeing results at the end of the road, this will be helpful." Clark Clifford, embracing a position different from the one he would take just a few months later, objected to the idea of relying on public opinion. He flattered Johnson by saying that he and Kennedy "didn't wait for public opinion to catch up with them. They went ahead with what was right, and because of that the war is a success today." Acheson suggested that Johnson "not talk about negotiations anymore" because "this isn't the Communist method. If they can't win they just quit after a while." He described the Senate Foreign Relations Committee as "the cross you have to bear" and disparaged Senator Fulbright as a "dilettante fool." He urged that a range of government speakers talk along the same policy lines and that a public information campaign be developed, along the lines of the one that was used to mobilize support for the Marshall Plan during the late 1940s. The individual participants in the meeting endorsed these or similar ideas. Several of them alleged that, despite a vocal minority of protesters, public opinion was supportive of the war. Many expressed their personal convictions that the United States should not withdraw from Vietnam.

Of course, the views of the Wise Men were influenced by the information available to them. They were briefed by George Carver of the CIA, who identified various ways in which conditions in Vietnam had improved. But, as McNamara would note later in his memoirs, the group did not have access to a recent report by Rear Admiral Eugene La Rocque "that a military victory in Vietnam was highly unlikely." Nor did they see the analysis from Richard Helms of the CIA asserting that "the risks of US disengagement were limited and controllable." Nor, for that matter, did the Wise Men see or even know about the memo that McNamara had sent to the president the day before. "Unsurprisingly," McNamara notes, "in the absence of new information, their preconceived notions about the military and political situation in South Vietnam determined their answers."[65] But the meeting with the Wise Men was a great psychological boost for the president. With their support, he energetically made the case that the nation was making progress in Vietnam. Meanwhile, he castigated his critics with a ferocity previously underplayed. De Benedetti writes that he blasted them "for their 'storm trooper tactics' and for their craven willingness to 'surrender.'" While not providing any specifics, De Benedetti claims that as a result of these appeals, "public support for the president's position shot up impressively."[66]

These activities continued the efforts Johnson had begun earlier in the fall to increase his support and weaken his critics, as well as counter widespread talk of the war as a stalemate, by carefully orchestrating a campaign of optimistic statements. There had been earlier occasions for such statements, to be sure. At a press conference in July 1966, for instance, General William Westmoreland, commander of US forces in Vietnam (1964–68), said publicly for the first time that the United States was winning the war.[67] But statements such as this, and similar remarks by Johnson, were mere ad hoc posturing. In contrast, in mid-1967 "Westmoreland's superiors wanted him to report progress. Angering them by reporting a lack of progress would not put them in a mood to give him the extra troops he was requesting."[68] But the origins of the "optimism campaign" went all the way to the president. Berman reports that Johnson "took control of the campaign to dramatize progress to the American public but in ways that grossly exaggerated future military prospects. . . . [I]t was an active effort by the government to convince the American Congress and the American people that progress was being made in the war in Vietnam beyond what actually was the case."[69] Organizationally, this effort was centered in the Vietnam Information Group, under the leadership of National Security Adviser Walt Rostow. Prados went so far as to call the effort "psychological warfare against the American people."[70] They were to be convinced that the war was going well and that victory was in sight.

Moïse has described in detail several of the questionable interpretations, strange judgment calls, and possible outright deception that undergirded these efforts. One was to underestimate enemy strength, even though the rate at which the enemy was killing American troops was going up rather than down and even though the Viet Cong were claimed to be losing manpower at such a rapid rate that the guerrilla units should have been collapsing, which they were not.[71] Based on underestimates, American commanders claimed that they had reached the "crossover point." This was the point at which enemy forces were being captured faster than they could be replaced. This was regarded as a major turning point in the war and a sign of impending American victory, but there were no reliable indicators to tell whether or not this point had been reached.[72]

These were not innocent errors of judgment; rather, they were motivated responses to pressure to provide evidence of progress. For example, Rostow sent a confidential message to Ambassador Ellsworth Bunker in September "saying that press and television coverage of the war were being dominated by negative aspects of the situation and asking that Bunker, Westmoreland, and [Robert] Komer present evidence that progress was being made." One such item of evidence was the claim that enemy strength had declined, a conclusion reached by arbitrarily excluding "self-defense forces" and "secret self-defense forces" from the count of enemy strength, "even though the categories had been included in previous iterations of the exercise."[73] When MACV [Military Assistance Command, Vietnam] and the CIA disagreed in their estimates, the CIA was influenced to accept the lower MACV number, not because it was more likely to be accurate but because it was more likely to be useful.[74] (These and other examples of deliberately exaggerated success stories formed the basis for the CBS television documentary, *The Uncounted Enemy: A Vietnam Deception*, broadcast in 1982.[75])

The primary purpose of the "optimism campaign" was to buttress support for the war on the home front. It was an attempt to combat the antiwar movement, not by showing that it was communist-inspired (which, despite Johnson's occasional rants, it was not) but by convincing Americans, in Dallek's words, "that the war was going well and would be won if only they continued to back the boys in the field."[76] Johnson believed that, while the North Vietnamese and Viet Cong could not win militarily, they still might prevail if they could wait until Americans got tired of the war and demanded that their forces withdraw. The "optimism campaign," if successful, would nip that hope in the bud. In doing so, the administration hoped that it would force North Vietnam to enter into negotiations once the options of communist military victory, prolonged stalemate, and fatigue-induced American withdrawal were all off the table.

To be sure, Johnson did not ask anyone to develop or to use misleading statistics about enemy strength or to make exaggeratedly optimistic predictions. It is doubtful that he knew these things were happening, and it is likely that he would not have approved if he had. But he did create the environment in which such deceptive statements were made, by making clear that he wanted positive reports to counter talk of stalemate. Johnson not only wanted such reports from others; he produced them himself. In November 1967, he visited eight military bases on a 5100-mile tour to talk up the progress the United States was making in the war.[77] He held a press conference in mid-November at which, according to Herring, he "abandoned the stiff, formal style that had been his trademark and defended his policies in a conversational manner with great vigor and emotion,"[78] with a favorable response both to his presentational style and to the substance of his report. Most prominently, he called both Ambassador Ellsworth Bunker and General Westmoreland home from Saigon. He consulted with them both about next steps, which was the stated reason for their visit home, but the primary purpose of their visit was to reassure the American people that things were going well and that the end was in view.[79] Both men made appearances before congressional committees and on the television show *Meet the Press*. Westmoreland also gave a speech at the National Press Club, at which he famously stated that he saw light at the end of the tunnel. Taken together, Westmoreland's remarks that he had all the resources he needed took the steam out of the argument from the right that the war was not being prosecuted vigorously enough, while his optimistic judgments that things were going well took the steam out of the argument from the left that the war was a hopeless stalemate.[80] Prados points out that Westmoreland's *ethos* allowed him to claim that progress was being made "with an authority the White House and Pentagon civilians could not match."[81]

And it worked. Typical of Westmoreland's remarks were these claims from his congressional briefing: "We have got our opponent on the ropes. We are confident that we are winning this war. . . . We are grinding the enemy down. And at the same time, we are building up the South Vietnamese to the point where they will be able to progressively take over the greater part of the load."[82] Statements such as these elicited a favorable public reaction and led to an uptick in Johnson's approval ratings. In late 1967, his overall approval rating rose from 33 to 40 percent. The percentage agreeing with the statement that the United States was making progress in Vietnam rose from 34 percent in July 1967 to 50 percent in December. The percentage agreeing to the contrary, that the

United States was not making enough progress to win, declined from 56 percent to 41 percent during the same time period.[83] These upward movements were influenced by the growing feeling that the United States was winning the war, which was a product of the "optimism campaign."[84] The word "stalemate" appeared significantly less often. The Marine Corps commander in Vietnam told a visiting senator that the enemy forces were suffering unprecedented losses. "I think they are going to make one more try," General Robert Cushman stated. "It will be a great blood bath and we will murder or kill an awful lot of them and they will quit."[85] And a memo to National Security Adviser Walt Rostow from Robert G. Ginsburgh denied that things were at an impasse, because "the initiative is turning in favor of the government and the allies, and the enemy is suffering unprecedented casualties, indeed."[86] Cushman's memo was dated January 30, 1968.

It is not that no progress was being made, but judged against the expectations stimulated by the "optimism campaign," actual progress was illusory. In October 1967, McGeorge Bundy sent a memo gently chiding that officials "would be better able to influence public opinion in 1968 if they made fewer attempts in 1967 to prove how well the war is going."[87] With the benefit of hindsight, Zbigniew Brzezinski wrote in mid-March that public support "is waning because public expectations of peace or victory were stimulated by ill-considered statements and subsequently refuted by self-evident events."[88] The gap between the expectations raised by the "optimism campaign" and the reality of subsequent events was staggering. As Herring succinctly put it, "The administration itself was at least partially responsible for the shock of the North Vietnamese [Tet] offensive."[89]

Pride goeth before a fall.

2

The Tet Offensive and After

BEGINNING ON THE night of January 30–31, 1968, which marked the Vietnamese New Year holiday of Tet, Viet Cong guerrillas and North Vietnamese army regulars attacked population centers throughout South Vietnam. Previously confined mostly to rural areas, they brought their attack to the towns and cities, including 5 of the major cities, thirty-six
of forty-four provincial capitals, and sixty-six of the 242 district towns.[1] Approximately 80,000 North Vietnamese and Viet Cong were involved.[2] The most dramatic of the attacks were on Saigon itself, including nearby airfields and even the US embassy, whose walls were breached. It is less clear when the attack ended. Many accounts suggest that it was over in two or three days except for some areas of Saigon, Hue, and Khe Sanh, but Moïse, citing US death tolls, maintains that January 1968 began a period of heavy combat that lasted eighteen months.[3] In the first eight weeks, about 4000 American troops were killed, along with 5000 South Vietnamese troops and some 14,000 noncombatants.[4]

The Tet Offensive seemingly shattered illusions. The communist forces were supposed to be on their last legs, and the cities of South Vietnam were thought to be impregnable. The US embassy was thought to be especially well fortified. Yet, on the night of the offensive, only six Americans were on duty at the embassy. General Westmoreland, in charge of the US Military Assistance Command, had to move to a windowless command center, and US Ambassador Ellsworth Bunker was forced to move to a secret hideout.[5]

Except for the old imperial capital of Hue, which remained occupied for three weeks, US forces were able quickly to repulse the attacks and retake the cities. A planned general uprising among the South Vietnamese population, which was the principal goal of the attacks, did not materialize. Westmoreland soon telephoned to indicate that the US embassy had been retaken, Saigon was quiet, and while there was still fighting at the nearby Tan Son Nhut air base, it might be from Viet Cong who were trying to leave the area.[6] By all accounts, the offensive was a military disaster for the communists. President Johnson reported in his memoirs that "of the estimated 84,000 men the Communists sent into the attacks, about 45,000 were killed by the end of February, including some of their most experienced cadre. Thus, in one month," Johnson concluded, "the enemy sustained heavier losses than US forces had suffered in nine years in Vietnam."[7]

The president had thought about giving a speech to the country in early February to announce and celebrate the repulse of the Tet attacks, finding in the result further evidence of the success of US policies toward the troubled land of Vietnam. But he changed his plans and eventually postponed the speech until late March, probably for the same reasons he had said little about Vietnam in the State of the Union address on January 17. First, although he had intelligence predicting a major assault in South Vietnam, he did not know exactly what form it would take or when it would occur. Similarly, while the communists had been defeated militarily, they retained the capability to launch additional major attacks, and in fact did so. As George W. Bush would discover in Iraq in 2003, there are dangers in pronouncing "Mission Accomplished" before one is sure that the mission is over. Second, even if the cities had been retaken successfully, no one knew what the communists would try to do next. Although it did not turn out this way, a common interpretation of the attacks on the cities was that they were a diversion from a major attack on the American outpost at Khe Sanh, an isolated place in the far northwestern corner of South Vietnam which came under siege beginning in mid-January. That prospect was eerily reminiscent of Dienbienphu, a similarly isolated base whose capture had led to the French surrender in 1954.

The Tet attacks were indeed carefully planned but not in the way Americans generally assumed. American accounts attributed the attacks to an enemy failure in the war of attrition and the consequent need to change strategy.[8] The analogy frequently invoked was the Battle of the Bulge, a last-gasp effort by German troops in late 1944 to break through the lines behind which they were being encircled by the Allies. Like Tet, it was a simultaneous offensive at many points along the line. The comparison was invoked by General Earle Wheeler, chair of the Joint Chiefs of Staff, anticipating the offensive, even before it began. Ambassador Bunker used the same analogy, as did General Westmoreland, National Security Adviser Walt Rostow, and Secretary of State Dean Rusk.[9] Having made the comparison, Wheeler and Westmoreland recommended that the United States make a punishing response that might finish the war. The benefit of this view was that it interpreted the Tet Offensive in a manner consistent with the fall 1967 "optimism campaign." The problem was that, even if the most dramatic assaults on the provincial capitals were repulsed, the North Vietnamese and Viet Cong did not give up. The months following Tet saw a continuing high level of enemy activity.

Administration supporters attributed the Tet attacks to the communists' misjudgment of American strength. Probably overly influenced by the vigorous antiwar movement, the enemy was thought to have concluded that Americans were so divided that they would be easily overtaken by surprise.[10] It does not appear, however, that the decisions leading up to Tet were in fact influenced at all by either the state of the antiwar movement or the political situation in the United States. The political result that had been sought was a general uprising in South Vietnam, not instability in the United States.[11]

Similarly, Prados maintains that General Vo Nguyen Giap of North Vietnam was aware of American plans to build up force levels during 1968 to the mandated level of over 500,000.[12] But there is no evidence that the offensive was planned with an eye to the size of American forces or the speed with which they were built up. Like the other popular American interpretations, this one put American planning at the center of the Vietnamese decisions; it defined Tet as a last-gap strategy, and it viewed the gains produced as only short term. These interpretations deemphasized the ability of the communist forces to maintain a high level of activity after Tet, even if not the dramatic effect of simultaneous attacks seemingly everywhere.

What the Tet Offensive *did* aim to do was to capture several South

Vietnamese cities and to inspire a general revolt among the South Vietnamese. In a retrospective conference on the war, the North Vietnamese ambassador indicated that capture of several cities would force the United States to concentrate more on South Vietnam, reducing the pressure against the North.[13] And by driving a wedge between the Americans and the South Vietnamese, the communists may have hoped to undermine South Vietnam's support for the war. This could explain, for instance, the selection of the US embassy as a target, which, as Karnow noted, could "demonstrate to the South Vietnamese people that the United States was vulnerable despite its immense power." Similarly, the attacks on the cities and towns could be seen as an attempt to turn the urban elite against their American supporters.[14] Interviews with the communists sent south to fight in the Tet Offensive suggest that they were given misleading information, overstating the degree to which they could expect defections from the local population.[15] The offensive achieved neither of these desired results, yet, as will become clear, it had far more dramatic psychological and symbolic effects.

The Tet Offensive did not come as a complete surprise to the Americans, but its timing and breadth were not foreseen. Tet was the most important and sacred holiday in both North and South Vietnam, and it seemed unlikely that it would be desecrated by military action.[16] Nor did the reports and predictions available to the Americans indicate the scale of seemingly coordinated attacks.[17] Nine days before the attack, Westmoreland suggested that "the enemy is conducting a short-term surge effort," possibly designed to enhance its political position.[18] The president and Defense Secretary Robert McNamara speculated that the Tet Offensive might be coordinated with the almost simultaneous seizure of the USS *Pueblo* by North Korea, even though McNamara acknowledged that "I have no real evidence of the connection."[19] Perhaps the most common American interpretation was that Tet was either a prelude to or a diversion from a planned assault on the base at Khe Sanh, which had the potential to be an American Dienbienphu. Khe Sanh was where Westmoreland and Wheeler thought the major battle of the war would take place. The Americans deemed it important because it guarded the approach to the two northernmost provinces of South Vietnam.[20] In fact, however, the shelling of Khe Sanh began in mid-January. It was intended to attract American attention and resources to this remote location in order to reduce the opposition to the Tet Offensive, rather than the other way around.[21]

Although the Tet Offensive was a military failure for the North Vietnamese and Viet Cong, in other respects it proved a debacle for the United States. Several dimensions of its effect warrant review, after which speculation will be offered about why these effects were great enough to outweigh the military dimension. The most generalized way to describe the effect is to say that Tet created or awakened doubts that Americans previously had sublimated to their support for the war and brought these doubts into the open. Woods highlights some of the key questions: "Was there really a viable nation south of the seventeenth parallel? If so, why were the Vietnamese not willing to fight and die to defend it? How could the US military command have been caught so off-guard? Did Tet indicate that American strategic thinking was either fatally flawed or totally unrealistic?" William P. ("Bill") Bundy, Assistant Secretary of State for the Far East, produced a memorandum at the end of February, reporting that "the US public and the Congress have been shaken most seriously in their confidence that any course of action can now produce a useful result in Vietnam, worthy of its sacrifices." The *Chicago Tribune*, in its report on Westmoreland's troop request in mid-March, noted, "The scope and depth of the internal debate within the government reflect the uncertainty and doubt in Washington about every facet of the war left by the enemy's wave of attacks at Tet, the Asian new year holiday, six weeks ago."[22]

What were some of the effects of Tet summarized in general claims such as these? For one, a significant shift had taken place among government officials and other opinion leaders, who had supported the administration's policies up to this time, but who now took a different view. Some who already had expressed misgivings now became more fully convinced that the war was not worth the effort and cost. The Senate Foreign Relations Committee, which began hearings on the war on March 12, found its members moving more strongly toward opposition to the president's policy. It refused to consider Johnson's $2.9 billion request for foreign aid, its nominal business, until it could receive satisfactory answers about the future course of his policy in Vietnam. As Moïse notes, the people reassessing their views were not primarily the general public or long-standing critics, but those in the councils of government and those who had been moderates supporting the president.[23] For example, Clark Clifford, nominated on January 19 to be secretary of defense, said later, "Tet, to me, was the roof falling in." George Kennan, architect of the policy of containment in the 1940s, made his first public attack on Johnson's Vietnam policy to a group of Eugene McCarthy supporters, telling them that it was a "massive, unparalleled error . . . for which it is hard to find any parallels in our history."[24] The shock of Tet led some of these same opinion leaders to question the basic aims of the war or to suggest that the United States should lower its sights.

This shock, at least temporarily, seems to have overcome efforts to measure the progress of the war. Moïse offers one example. On most days in February, the Unites States produced statistics showing the number killed the previous day, since January 1, and since the Tet offensive began. Moïse points out that if the numbers were correct, all three sets would rise by the same amount, namely, those killed the previous day. But "instead," he wrote, "none of the three sets of figures even came close to being consistent with the other two. Nobody in the White House seems to have noticed." Meanwhile, administration spokesmen "were issuing regular claims for the number of casualties being inflicted on the Communist forces," although "it was obvious that nobody could really know how many enemy personnel had been killed at this point."[25]

Those who tracked media editorials noticed a decided shift as well. The *New York Times* reported in mid-February that seven major newspapers had shifted from general support of the president's policies to criticism of recent escalation. Reflecting the divisions emerging in the country, four other major newspapers had also moved away from the president, but in a more hawkish direction.[26] The only common thread was disagreement with the president.

To be sure, the Tet Offensive did not shake up the country in every respect. In a meeting in early February, President Johnson told the Democratic congressional leadership, "I am of the opinion that criticism is not worth much. I look at all these speeches that are in the [Congressional] Record. I look at all the people who are going around the country saying our policy is wrong. Where do they get us? Nowhere."[27] Johnson reportedly first reacted to the Tet Offensive by proposing "to counter the adverse press and television coverage and reassure the American

people." General Wheeler, chair of the Joint Chiefs of Staff, instructed Westmoreland to make a positive comment to the press every day.[28]
(Countering adverse press reaction was part of Johnson's original motivation for what became the March 31 speech.) President Eisenhower
also indicated his support for the course of the war.[29]

Perhaps revealing that they were somewhat out of touch with the situation, some of Johnson's advisers believed that the shock of Tet could
be dissipated, and trust and confidence restored, through a presidential
speech. Rostow advised Johnson that a single good presidential speech
would cure any credibility problem that might have been created by the
discrepancy between the optimistic projections of fall 1967 and the reality of Tet. Press Secretary George Christian advised Ambassador Bunker and General Westmoreland that they could convince the American
people that everything was under control "if they made frequent firm
statements, especially on television."[30]

Despite these counterindications, the weight of the evidence showed
that the Tet Offensive had a significant adverse effect on Americans,
notwithstanding that it was a military failure for the communist forces.
As will be seen, similar effects can be discerned in public opinion polls.
The question now is why, in the face of the military results, the Tet Offensive would have called support for Johnson's war policy so strongly
into question.

Probably the most obvious explanation is that, on the face of it,
the Tet Offensive undermined the claims of the "optimism campaign"
launched in fall 1967. Then, in coordinated fashion, administration
advocates had proclaimed that things were going well: the United
States had turned the corner, and victory was within grasp. But the Tet
Offensive—especially in its magnitude—was not the action of an enemy who had been all but vanquished. Granting that "the enemy had
not achieved his aims in South Vietnam," in his memoirs, McPherson
acknowledged that the enemy "had convinced the American public
that after all the bombing, after all our expenditure of lives and resources, he was still vitally alive, resourceful, and determined."[31] This
meant that reports of his imminent demise should be given no credence, and this in itself was deeply discouraging to Americans weary-
ing of a long war. Johnson adviser Joseph Califano explained how the
president's credibility was affected: "The administration had declared

that the Communists were losing the war. Victory or not, the sheer ability of the North Vietnamese and Vietcong to mount such a large-scale offensive had shattered the American people's confidence in the president's word." Califano went on to say, "For the first time, large numbers of Americans thought their country might lose the war."[32] That last claim may have been an overstatement. But if the prospect of American defeat went too far, the prospect of a stalemate seemed all too real. For increasing numbers of people, it did not justify the human and financial costs that the war continued to extract. Moreover, it suggested that Americans were not in control. Hoopes reports the view of Pentagon civilians that Tet "showed conclusively that the US did not control the situation, that it was not in fact winning, that the enemy retained enormous strength and vitality—certainly enough to extinguish the notion of a clear-cut allied victory in the minds of all objective men."[33]

It is easy to understand how this negative interpretation would support the seemingly contradictory position that the United States should "win or get out." Believers in the original American mission could conclude that its goals could not be accomplished by what were regarded as half-hearted means; as Tet demonstrated, they left the enemy in too strong a position. We should escalate without restraint, they believed. If we were not willing to do that, then we should abandon our efforts and at least avoid the further sacrifice of American lives and treasure. Meanwhile, others became convinced by Tet that the American effort was unworthy or that its costs were not worth the benefits that the administration was claiming. They did not believe that the prospect of a communist takeover of North Vietnam was fatal to American security or that the government of South Vietnam was worth defending.

One should not deemphasize the effect of visual images in catalyzing these doubts. Two in particular stand out. The visual of the storming of the US embassy, overpowering the small contingent on guard, conveyed the message that control had been lost. In addition, the photographed execution of a suspected Viet Cong turncoat by Colonel Nguyen Ngoc Loan of the South Vietnam Secret Police, who shot him in the head in public on a busy Saigon street, conveyed the message that South Vietnam was hardly a country valuing due process or rule of law, to say nothing of democracy or personal freedom. After identifying a series of images, including the execution, the battle for Hue, and the siege of Khe

Sanh, which one by one seemed to refute claims of American success, Prados reminds his readers that "all this happened on film, recorded by journalists throughout the land and played back every day on America's TV screens and in its print media."[34]

The "optimism campaign" had created perceptions and expectations that the Tet Offensive had undermined. But there were more fundamental reasons that Tet came as such a surprise, some of them quite mundane. For example, the United States was systematically underestimating enemy troop strength, then using these underestimates to support the misperception that the communists were losing, and the Americans winning, the war. After careful analysis, Moïse confirmed that the gap between American estimates and actual communist combat strength had developed by mid-1967 and that it had widened by the time of the Tet Offensive. The problem, he notes, was that North Vietnam was infiltrating large numbers of troops at the very time that US officials, in order to support the claims of the "optimism campaign," had an incentive to report low enemy strength.[35] Nor had President Johnson, in the wake of the "optimism campaign," given the public reason for concern. In his memoirs, the president wrote that it was a mistake to have shortchanged Vietnam in his January 17 State of the Union message. "In that address I underscored how intensely our will was being tested by the struggle in Vietnam," Johnson wrote, "but I did not go into details concerning the build-up of enemy forces or warn of the early major combat I believed was in the offing."[36] It is far from clear, however, whether a different messaging strategy by the president would have made much difference. If believed, it still would have undercut the optimistic projections of just a few weeks before and would have denied that the enemy was on its last legs. It is equally likely that it would have been dismissed as a ploy to win funding that could not be justified on its own merits, as an election-year scheme, or as a warning against impending danger once too often.

Media coverage of the Tet Offensive also became a target of criticism. The charge was that the media conveyed a false sense of the offensive, making it appear to be a greater disaster than it was. Blaming press coverage of unfavorable events for an adverse public reaction is an old staple in American politics. Johnson wrote in his memoirs, "There was a great deal of emotional and exaggerated reporting of the Tet offensive in our press and on television. The media seemed to be in competition as to who could provide the most lurid and depressing accounts. Columnists unsympathetic to American involvement in Southeast Asia jumped on the bandwagon."[37] General Westmoreland criticized "panicky and spiteful journalists" who "portrayed Tet as an enemy victory." General Wheeler said that the average newsman was immature, and in the same meeting General Creighton Abrams "said he was at wit's end on how to get people to report the war the way it is."[38] In particular, the attack on the Saigon embassy was thought to receive exaggerated media attention, perhaps because it was a familiar location and perhaps because it was such a spectacle. Moïse reports that the sappers who blew a hole in the wall were quickly killed without entering the building, but the attack was portrayed as a major breach of security. Besides, most of the regular communist troops that had been designated for the attack never arrived.[39]

In general, however, scholarship discredits the notion that the media were responsible for the widespread perception that the Tet Offensive was an American defeat. Although writing specifically about the Nixon administration, Melvin Small cites evidence that "during much of the Vietnam era the media were supportive of Washington's policies." Clifford also objected to the thesis that "inaccurate reporting by the press during the Tet offensive" was "a major reason for the turnaround in American public opinion." He answers that, while the press makes errors in reporting in every war, "the bulk of the reporting from the war zone reflected the official position." Small points out that, with exceptions such as the 1969 Moratorium, the press did not give favorable coverage to antiwar protests either. Clifford's conclusion is that what redirected public opinion was the magnitude of the Tet Offensive itself, not reporters and not the antiwar movement.[40]

From this discussion, several conclusions seem clear. First, Tet was a military defeat for the communist forces, who ultimately failed to achieve any of their objectives. They were driven back into the countryside and suffered over 40,000 casualties; the infrastructure of the Viet Cong was described as "shattered, never fully to recover."[41] There was no general uprising of the South Vietnamese population against their government. Second, however, the North Vietnamese communists remained a significant threat. Their force strength remained large despite the losses of Tet. They caused significant setbacks to South Vietnam,[42] and they continued to threaten Khe Sanh. But third, and ultimately most important, the Tet Offensive destabilized American support for the war. Large numbers of hawks and doves, in sharp disagreement as to the reasons, united in their opposition to Johnson's handling of the war. Clifford reflected years later, "the most serious American casualty at Tet was the loss of the public's confidence in its leaders." He added that Tet was harmful "not because of the reporting, but because of the event itself, and what it said about the credibility of America's leaders."[43] Many who were still not ready to break with Johnson were insisting that the government develop a strategic plan for victory as the price of their continued support. The Defense Department's Public Affairs Office, tasked with developing a public affairs plan, responded that it could not do so until more basic questions were settled. Its report noted, "If the people are to accept the war, the government must (1) prove that it is in our national interest, (2) Prove that we have a plan to win it, (3) Tell the people what resources are required to carry out that plan." These were basic questions. The office concluded, "In our opinion, we have not supplied effectively those three critical answers. Without them, the people cannot be rallied."[44]

The shifts noted in these elite or official sources also were reflected in public opinion polls, which, after an initial rally-round-the-flag reaction, turned markedly negative toward Johnson's handling of the war in the spring of 1968. In moments of crisis, it is customary for Americans to express support for the president's leadership, as long as the president appears to be showing leadership in responding to the crisis. This traditional pattern reasserted itself after Tet. For example, Moïse reports that the percentage of poll respondents who expected the war to end in victory was higher in February 1968 (immediately after Tet), at 20 percent, than it had ever been before. Similarly, Gallup asked whether people regarded themselves as hawks or doves. Before Tet, 56 percent called themselves hawks and 28 percent, doves. But in early February 1968, the hawks numbered 61 percent and the doves, 23 percent. Similarly, a Louis Harris Poll found that the percentage expressing general support for the war—not necessarily for Johnson's handling of it—rose from 61 percent in December 1967 to 74 percent in February 1968. Gallup Poll surveys asking whether the United States should continue or halt the bombing of North Vietnam found that, while 63 percent wanted to continue the bombing in October 1967, that number had risen to 70 percent by February 1968, whereas the percentage wanting to halt the bombing had fallen from 26 percent to 15 percent during the same period.[45] The hawkishness of public opinion in early 1968 was measured in a different way in a Harris Poll. Without making longitudinal comparisons, the poll found that 49 percent favored invading North Vietnam, with 29 percent opposed; 47 percent favored invading the Demilitarized Zone, with 21 percent opposed; 42 percent favored mining Haiphong harbor even if Soviet ships might be sunk, compared to 33 percent who opposed; and 25 percent were willing to go along with bombing China or using nuclear weapons if necessary (the percentage opposed was not indicated).[46] Whatever these figures indicate, they do not support the hypothesis that unfavorable media coverage of the Tet Offensive, which would have followed immediately upon the events, swayed people against the war.

But public opinion changed dramatically from early February to late March. DeBenedetti characterizes it as a shift from "a belligerent eagerness for further military action" to "a resigned mood of malleability, waiting for presidential management and direction."[47] It was not at all clear how the public would respond to such direction, however. Although Johnson was more actively attacking his critics during this time, as we shall see, the ratings for his handling of the war consistently were running lower than ratings for support of the war itself. Karnow summarized the trend: During the six weeks following the launch of the Tet Offensive, Johnson's overall approval rating fell from 48 to 36 percent. On the specific question of his handling of the war, his approval rating fell from 40 to just 26 percent. The ratings of 36 percent and 26 percent were below Johnson's previous lows (38 percent and 28 percent, respectively) in October of 1967. An early March Gallup Poll found that 49 percent of its respondents believed that Johnson made a mistake in sending combat troops to Vietnam in 1965—the first time that a plurality of poll respondents offered that retrospective assessment. Moreover, 61 percent of the respondents indicated that the United States and its allies were either losing the war or making no progress toward winning it. Finally, a Gallup Poll published on March 31—the day that President Johnson was to speak to the nation—found that nearly two-thirds of its respondents disapproved of Johnson's handling of the war.[48]

From the evidence presented, it seems safe to say that the Tet Offensive, despite its military results, significantly affected Americans' beliefs about the war and about the president's handling of it. At the very least, continued support for escalations such as Johnson had announced before, and for the official rationale for them, could not be assumed. In response to these developments, the administration spent much of February and March in a broad-based review of American policies, a review that would coincide with a transition in the Department of Defense. Robert McNamara, who had been secretary since 1961 but who had lost confidence in military escalation in Vietnam, was leaving on February 29 to head the World Bank, and Clark Clifford, a long-time Johnson adviser and widely known as a hawk on Vietnam, would take over on March 1.

As far as anyone could tell, Johnson's first response to reports of the Tet Offensive was belligerent. He viewed the war, at least in part, as a test of wills between himself and Ho Chi Minh. He continued to believe there was some level of escalation that would convince the North Vietnamese leader to back down and withdraw his forces from South Vietnam—an action that, together with the defeat of the Viet Cong inside South Vietnam, would constitute military victory. He first saw the policy review as being about how to corral the necessary resources for that objective. As for the possibility of a compromise political settlement, he had offered the San Antonio formula back in September (offering to stop the bombing of North Vietnam if Ho Chi Minh would agree to begin serious negotiations and not take advantage of the bombing halt to increase infiltration of troops and supplies into South Vietnam), and it had received no serious response. Instead, North Vietnam had launched the Tet Offensive, which seemed to close the door on further offers to negotiate, at least for now. Although probably overstating the case, Hoopes describes this situation as follows: "President Johnson and his close advisers had so defined our national purposes and so conducted the war that a compromise political settlement would be tantamount to a resounding defeat for US policy and prestige. Accordingly, it could not be faced."[49] Johnson, however, was not always as inflexible as he appeared.

The president's first instinct was to continue the bombing and to reinforce General Westmoreland so that he could take advantage of the success at Tet and protect against an intensified siege at Khe Sanh. As will be detailed in Chapter 5, however, Johnson had trouble figuring out what Westmoreland needed. At first, the general said that his currently available forces were adequate. Then he said that he wanted already authorized additional troops to be provided on a faster schedule. And soon after he submitted a request for additional troops of far greater magnitude than anyone had expected—a request that he later said was not a formal proposal but only a contingency plan. Before deciding what to do, the president determined that he needed a report on the situation on the ground in Vietnam. Previously, he had sent Robert McNamara on several such occasions to make inquiries and report his findings, but that made little sense this time since McNamara was about to leave the Defense Department. After considering other options, Johnson settled on General Earle Wheeler, chair of the Joint Chiefs of Staff. But McNamara needed Wheeler to accompany him to testify at the Senate Foreign Relations Committee hearings on the Gulf of Tonkin resolution, so he could not go to Vietnam until after February 21, when the hearings were expected to conclude. Meanwhile, Johnson emphasized that he wanted recommendations as quickly as possible from Wheeler, Secretary of State Dean Rusk, and incoming Secretary of Defense Clark Clifford on "a program for the most effective use of airpower against North Vietnam."[50]

Wheeler returned at the end of February with Westmoreland's recommendation for 206,000 additional troops. Johnson, without giving any indication that he was disposed toward granting this request, appointed a committee chaired by Clifford to review it and consider alternatives. At the same time, William P. Bundy of the State Department sent the Clifford team a memo noting, "Although there remain elements in the US and elsewhere who believe that an early move toward peace would be hopeful, this sentiment is not so strong that we need to give it overriding significance in our choice of options."[51] Johnson and his advisers would focus on that issue for the better part of the next three weeks.

Clifford took a somewhat different approach from Bundy's. Believing that he had been tasked to consider how and with what consequences Westmoreland's request could be met, Clifford soon asked broader questions, starting with how the administration could get support for tough measures that would need to be part of any escalation, in light of the steady stream of optimistic reports.[52] The task force also did not spend much effort on how to induce cooperation from Hanoi because it was assumed that the North Vietnamese would be intransigent. Bundy's memo predicted, "We cannot anticipate any change in this attitude unless and until Hanoi's offensive has run its course and been judged by them either to have failed or at least not to have achieved a degree of success balancing its costs."[53] Profound differences emerged among the group with regard to increased bombing of North Vietnam and the possible mining of Haiphong Harbor; this made it impossible for those topics to receive much consideration.[54]

The task force also did not consider strategies aimed at getting peace negotiations under way, The feeling among the group was that, in light of the Tet Offensive, any US push for negotiations would be seen as a sign of weakness. The task force maintained that the "rock bottom" position on that subject was still the San Antonio formula.[55] Johnson would write later that the absence of any peace proposal was what had disappointed him most about the task force report.[56] If true, this indicates that Johnson's thinking was further along at this early stage than any of his advisers realized.

In essence, the Clifford task force proposed immediately sending a modest number of additional troops (probably about 30,000) in order to meet what they understood to be Westmoreland's urgent needs and to defer a decision on sending a much larger number until later, recognizing that sending these would require calling up reserves. Despite its limited perspective, as Schandler notes, there were significant differences between the Clifford task force report and earlier studies following requests from military commanders for additional troops. First, it stated that new guidance was required about strategy, although it did not propose a new strategy itself. Second, it recognized that the US commitment could not be open-ended. Third, it stated that no number of American troops would be sufficient to achieve the US objectives without "significant improvement in the ability of the Vietnamese government to win popular support and to fight aggressively for its own security."[57] Clifford, meanwhile, concluded that the Joint Chiefs of Staff had no strategic plan to win the war at any level of manpower. He expressed his doubts to Johnson and determined that a wider review of the war's basic assumptions was necessary. It was also at the March 4 meeting that Dean Rusk floated his proposal for a bombing halt during the spring rainy season and President Johnson told him to "really get on your horses" on developing that idea.[58]

For his part, Johnson told his advisers on March 12 that "they had moderated my judgment" at the March 4 meeting to discuss the Clifford task force proposals. Previously, the president had been set on a hard-line military response; he described himself as "almost . . . ready to call up a large number of reserves; . . . to ask Congress for the authority to call additional selected reservists; and to continue to push hard for the tax bill on that basis." But, he said, "My opinion had changed as a result of what I had heard from my advisers and what I saw happening on the ground in Vietnam."[59]

Having learned that the Clifford task force was not going to recommend more aggressive military strategies, military leaders proposed on March 2 to expand the war into Laos in order to cut the Ho Chi Minh Trail, which North Vietnam used to infiltrate men and materials into the South.[60] But these proposals went against the grain of the task force's thinking. Indeed, there were doubts about approving the manpower increases that Westmoreland had recommended. If anything, the task force moved in the opposite direction, questioning what results would follow from any given increment of resources. Meanwhile, Clifford's own doubts were hardening. Invited to testify before the Senate Foreign Relations Committee to defend the administration's policy on the war, Clifford decided that he could not do it and instead met privately with the chair, J. William Fulbright of Arkansas, to discuss his concerns. Ironically, perhaps, he was moving closer to the reservations of his predecessor, Robert McNamara. Clifford's refutation of McNamara's November 1 memo probably contributed to his being named secretary of defense. But the more he examined the course the country was on, the closer he came to agreement with that document's reservations.[61] Although he was outspoken, Clifford was not alone. Barrett reports that Dean Rusk, Hubert Humphrey, McGeorge Bundy, and others were urging Johnson "to try a new approach." They were convinced, to varying degrees, that further escalation would not work.[62]

For his part, Johnson was sensitive to the shift of public opinion between early February and late March, although it is unclear exactly how it influenced his decisions. Schandler says that he "appears to have been influenced" by public opinion, especially on the bombing halt. Hoopes, not an impartial source, finds that Johnson grasped "the absolute political imperative" of yielding to a "seismic shift in public opinion." Johnson himself reported later that, while not as pessimistic as some of his advisers, he was "deeply conscious of the growing criticism" from the press and some opinion leaders.[63] But he revealed nothing of his concerns in public statements. *New York Times* reporter Max Frankel wrote in a story on March 31 that some of Johnson's comments had suggested that the real purpose of the policy review was "to regain the military initiative after the setbacks suffered in the enemy's attacks on cities and towns,"[64] not to reexamine the underlying assumptions of policy and strategy.

All the different forces weighing on President Johnson converged during the second week in March. On Sunday, March 10, the *New York Times* broke the story that Westmoreland had requested 206,000 new troops—the first the public knew of the size of the request.[65] This news intensified a run on the dollar beginning on Tuesday, March 12. (This episode will be discussed in Chapter 5, but its essentials can be mentioned here simply enough.) The escalating costs of the war worsened the US balance-of-payments deficit, which had been financed by European central banks' holding dollars as their reserve currency. They were willing to do so because of the United States' firm commitment at the 1944 Bretton Woods conference to convert dollars to gold at $35 per ounce. But the vast growth of foreign dollar reserves caused questioning about the ability of the United States to continue honoring its commitment, and fears that a devaluation of the dollar was pending led some of the European central banks to start converting significant dollar holdings into gold. During the second week in March, the run on the dollar intensified. Emergency confidence-building measures were undertaken and long-standing efforts to create a new international reserve asset gained greater urgency. By mid-March, there was no assurance that they would succeed.

Also on March 12, Fulbright began hearings of the Senate Foreign Relations Committee, with Dean Rusk as the opening witness. Ostensibly, the hearings were about the administration's foreign aid request for the coming fiscal year, but the committee had made clear that it was not going to approve any foreign aid bill until it received satisfactory answers to its questions about Vietnam. Not only Clifford declined to testify, so too did Deputy Secretary Paul Nitze, in Nitze's case because he had not been "privy to the reasons for limiting consideration to Option A in the chain from A to Z." In other words, he could not explain why increasing the troop commitment had been the only policy option seriously considered by the Clifford task force. "As a result," Nitze determined, "I do not feel myself to be in a position properly to defend the Executive Branch in a debate before the Foreign Relations Committee which would undoubtedly spread from [the Military Assistance Program] to the major policy issues before the country."[66] To say the least, this was highly embarrassing to the administration.

As if those developments were not enough, March 12 was also the date of the New Hampshire presidential primary election, then as now the first primary in the nation. The Democratic primary featured a challenge to President Johnson by Minnesota Senator Eugene McCarthy, who had entered the race on November 30, 1967, in order to contest Johnson's policy on the war. He was expected to be little more than a nuisance, with one state poll around New Year's showing Johnson ahead by 76 to 6 percent. Two weeks before the primary, a *Time* poll put McCarthy's support at 11 percent.[67] But in the actual event, McCarthy received 42 percent of the vote. When all the write-in votes were counted, the senator ran behind the president by only 230 votes. For anyone playing the expectations game, McCarthy was the big winner. McCarthy's result in New Hampshire was being understood, said *Wall Street Journal* writer Alan Otten, "as a protest vote against massive new escalation, and it also comes against a backdrop of widening press and Congressional criticism of the Administration's war policy."[68] That would be a misreading of the results, which showed that among McCarthy supporters in New Hampshire, those who believed that Johnson should use more force in Vietnam outnumbered those who favored using less force by a margin of 3 to 2.[69] Louis Harris analyzed the New Hampshire returns, finding that "if the Vietnamese issue had been the central basis of the McCarthy vote, he would have ended up with 22 instead of 42 percent"—still a significant protest vote, especially compared to the earlier polls, but hardly the shock that the new numbers represented. "The key finding," Harris concluded, "is that the vote was much more anti-LBJ than it was anti-Vietnam."[70] Johnson had become the unifying symbol of the otherwise highly fragmented opposition to American policy in Vietnam. Although he professed indifference to the primary results, Johnson must have been quite pained.

The New Hampshire results caused New York Senator Robert F. Kennedy to reconsider his refusal to enter the race. His stated reason for staying out had been that he did not want to be the cause of dividing the Democratic Party, particularly if doing so would throw the election to a Republican. But the New Hampshire results made clear that the party was already deeply divided, with or without him in the race. The last Gallup Poll before the New Hampshire primary found that in a hypothetical matchup, Johnson and Kennedy each would receive 41 percent of the votes of all adults, with Johnson ahead by one point among only Democrats.[71] Still, Kennedy did not decide immediately to enter the race. His main objective, he said, was to force a change in the US policy toward Vietnam. If that could be assured without his presidential candidacy, he would stay out of the race. On March 14 he presented his proposal to Clifford, who took it to President Johnson. Basically, Kennedy would stay out of the race if Johnson would agree to appoint a special commission to conduct a critical review of the war and recommend an alternate policy. Kennedy named the people who would serve as members of the proposed commission. He would be among them, although it would not be necessary that he serve as chair. The president would agree to follow the recommendations of the commission.

Johnson listened to Clifford's presentation but immediately, and unsurprisingly, turned the idea down. Accounts of the meeting are fairly consistent about his reasons. First, it would be recognized as a political deal, not a principled foreign policy review. Second, it would clearly imply, if not explicitly state, that the current US policy had been wrong. Third, the president would be surrendering his constitutional role in foreign policy to an unelected committee. Fourth, the names Kennedy proposed represented an unfair list—a stacked deck, as it were. Their views were already known; the review could not be impartial; and its conclusion was predetermined. Johnson also raised the question of McCarthy, who had just demonstrated that he could be a powerful vote getter; he was not included in the proposed deal.[72]

Also on March 14, Congress removed the "gold cover" requirement, which had designated a part of the gold reserve equal to 25 percent of the domestic currency in circulation to be kept to anchor that currency, even though the domestic convertibility of dollars to gold had been ended in the early years of the New Deal. This meant that the entire gold reserve, if necessary, could be used to defend against foreign banks threatening a run on the dollar. This action gave a short-term boost to the dollar and stopped the immediate speculation, but it did nothing either to solve the US balance-of-payments problem or to advance the work on a new international reserve asset that would be taking place in Stockholm.

On Friday, March 15, United Nations Ambassador Arthur Goldberg arrived from New York with a proposal that President Johnson order a complete halt to the bombing of North Vietnam. Following Rusk's mention of the idea on March 4, some of the president's advisers were talking about proposing a bombing halt as an appeal to doves, to go along with the proposed announcement of a troop increase, which would appeal to hawks. No decision had been made about a bombing halt, however. Discussions were considering whether a bombing halt, if announced, would be complete (covering all of North Vietnam) or partial (covering only the area north of the 20th parallel). Goldberg pointed out that only a complete bombing halt would fulfill the precondition of the North Vietnamese for opening negotiations. He also claimed that United Nations Secretary General U Thant and other UN diplomats had feelers indicating that North Vietnam would treat a complete bombing halt as a sufficient condition, not just a necessary one, for coming to the negotiating table. (This episode is discussed in detail in Chapter 4.) There are differences among commentators in their assessment of Johnson's response, but it is clear that Johnson rejected Goldberg's proposal. He was not yet ready to stop all bombing of the North.

Finally, on Saturday, March 16, Robert F. Kennedy announced his candidacy for president. He was running, he said, not to oppose any man but to propose new policies, both for the war in Vietnam and for the crisis in the cities. Johnson now confronted the challenge he had dreaded: facing a contest for the presidency with Robert Kennedy, who would try to reclaim the mantle of his slain brother. The result was far from certain, of course. There were only fifteen primaries in 1968, and Johnson had been planning to enter only those where state law required it—Wisconsin, Nebraska, and Oregon. The winner of the nomination would be determined not mainly by the primaries but by state party leaders in party meetings or conventions. Before the New Hampshire primary, McCarthy had been predicted to win about one-third of the vote in Wisconsin.[73] Afterward, he was expected to win handily. (Kennedy had entered the race too late to qualify for the Wisconsin ballot.) A Gallup Poll shortly after Kennedy's entry into the race found him leading Johnson by 44 to 41 percent among Democrats nationally. The California Poll by Mervin Field showed that Kennedy would win a three-way race with 42 percent of the vote to Johnson's 32 percent and McCarthy's 18 percent. If McCarthy were not still in the race, the poll predicted a decisive Kennedy win, 54 to 36 percent over the president.[74] Although it seemed unlikely, *Newsweek* reported that its Delegate Count survey showed that Johnson "may be in real danger of being dumped by his party" at the Democratic Convention, and in a preference poll for the general election, Nixon overtook him, 41 to 39 percent.[75] Surely, the political prospects seemed no more appealing than the decisions confronting Johnson and his advisers at the White House.

Occasionally during these difficult weeks, Johnson would leave the White House to speak to various groups and to honor military heroes. Although he usually mentioned that he was interested in seeking peace, the speeches were belligerent and shrill. If they were taken as windows into the president's thinking, they would show that he was set in his ways, doubling down on the goal of military victory and unwilling to consider alternatives. Many examples of Johnson's determination could be found. In a speech on Lincoln's birthday, he compared himself to the fallen Civil War leader: "Sad, but steady—always convinced of his cause—Lincoln stuck it out. Sad, but steady, so will we."[76] In a news conference on February 15, Johnson characterized the Tet Offensive as Hanoi's contemptuous response to the San Antonio formula and said that he thought every day about increasing the size of the American forces in Vietnam, never knowing for sure what the circumstances would require.[77] Referring to his critics in remarks at the El Toro Marine Air Station in California, he asked rhetorically, "When men cry 'Peace,' do they not know that Americans cannot give peace to the world by abandoning it to oppressors? When men cry, 'Peace,' do they not understand that we cannot keep peace for ourselves by withdrawing from the challenge that the enemies of peace present?"[78] On the flight deck of the USS *Constellation*, the president put in a nutshell what the war was about: "the foes of freedom are making ready to test America's will. Quite obviously, the enemy believes—he thinks—that our will is vulnerable. Quite clearly, the enemy hopes that he can break that will. And quite obviously, we know that the enemy is going to fail."[79]

In Dallas on February 27, the president spoke to the convention of the National Rural Electric Cooperative Association. In a speech that was described as designed to prepare the American people for major escalation, he said, "There must be no breaking of America's given word or America's commitments," and "I do not believe that we will ever buckle. I believe that every American will answer now for his future and the future of his children."[80] Johnson assured an audience in Beaumont, Texas, at a testimonial dinner for the local congressman, that until we find peace, "we are not going to be quislings, and we are not going to be appeasers, and we are not going to cut and run."[81]

Increasingly, on the stump Johnson was promising not only to maintain his course but to achieve victory. He usually was not specific about what counted as victory, but the context of his remarks suggested that he meant the term in the traditional military sense. At a meeting of the National Alliance of Businessmen on March 16, he said, "We must meet our commitments in the world and in Vietnam. We shall and we are going to win. To meet the needs of these fighting men, we shall do whatever is required." After saying that if the communists' position changes, we will meet them anywhere in a spirit of flexibility, he admonished his audience, "But make no mistake about it—I don't want a man in here to go back home thinking otherwise—we are going to win."[82] At the convention of the National Farmers Union on March 18, while his advisers were considering what should go into the forthcoming speech, Johnson proclaimed that "the time has come this morning when your President has come here to ask you people, and all the other people of this Nation, to join us in a total national effort to win the war, to win the peace, and to complete the job that must be done here at home." He repeated in that speech that "we will—make no mistake about it—win."[83] These grandiose boasts were sometimes linked to more modest statements of what we would "win," such as "the right of neighbors to be left alone," but not always. Johnson steeled the resolve of his audiences by telling them that he was not about to let the enemy win in Washington what he could not win on the battlefield. In a final example, speaking to a conference for leaders of nongovernmental organizations on March 19, the president raised the stakes. After invoking the precedents of Lincoln and Franklin Roosevelt, Johnson told the audience, "There is no cheap or easy way to find the road to freedom and the road to order. But danger and sacrifice built this land and today we are the number one nation. And we are going to stay the number one nation."[84]

Anyone examining these speeches for evidence that Johnson was reassessing anything about Vietnam would be sorely disappointed. But how is one to make sense of these remarks, given what we now know about simultaneous events—that Johnson had shown no sympathy toward Westmoreland's troop request, that he had told Dean Rusk to "get on your horses" about a bombing halt proposal, and that the gold crisis limited his options in the short run—not even to mention that the political world was in a state of great flux? Perhaps Johnson was giving voice to his frustration at having to make tough decisions with no easy outcomes. Perhaps he was trying deliberately to mislead the public that a major review of policy was underway. His penchant for secrecy was well known, and he might have reasoned that if word got out that he was considering options, public opinion would overwhelm him, pulling him at a faster rate or in a different direction than he wanted to go. Dallek has suggested that Johnson was looking for a way out but would not say anything publicly that would suggest that he had abandoned the goal of victory,[85] perhaps because he was fearful of being excoriated by the right wing, which is where he always thought his harshest critics could be found. Dallek also suggests that Johnson may have been playing a "double game" in these speeches, trying to encourage North Vietnam to believe that the United States remained committed to South Vietnam's independence. According to this view, Rusk's proposal for a limited bombing halt could succeed only if Hanoi saw a new peace overture coming not from weakness but from strength.[86] His belligerent rhetoric would provide that strength.

It is also possible that Lyndon Johnson truly was committed to the extreme positions he took on the stump in late February and March, and that his speeches were acts of stubbornness in the face of a more complex reality that was being discussed at the White House. But this is not likely, in light of other actions the president took. As Barrett mentioned, if Johnson really believed the sentiments he expressed in these speeches, then he "would not have sought Dean Acheson's lecture [explaining the change in views about the war that had come over many of Johnson's advisers] or Clark Clifford's elemental questions or spent time with innumerable other advisers. Nor would he have directed Rostow to have the State Department produce a massive compilation of current proposals on the war by a wide range of US leaders."[87]

Johnson also was receiving adverse reactions to some of his belligerent speeches on the stump. James Rowe, a long-time adviser, wrote that the Minneapolis speech to the National Farmers Union convention had 'hurt us badly'; they were dividing the party. By implying that all dissenters were unpatriotic, Johnson had caused much resentment and had even left war supporters disappointed."[88] (Reportedly, Johnson had this letter in hand when he called Clifford on March 20, asking him to develop a peace proposal for consideration.) In a luncheon meeting at the White House on March 22, McGeorge Bundy opined that "extreme care had to be taken in the president's statements. That a speech like the one last Saturday [to the National Alliance of Businessmen] will cost the President the election."[89] Although he gave no public indication of it, Johnson very likely was taking such warnings to heart.

What is probably more reflective of his unsettled mind was his agreement in mid-March to reconvene the "Wise Men," a group made up largely of former officeholders (many from previous administrations) and elder statesmen on whom he could call for advice. They had last met in November 1967, as noted above, and had strongly endorsed the president's Vietnam policies. Now Clifford had reason to believe that several of them had modified their views substantially. He convinced Johnson, who initially feared that the Wise Men would be confused with the Vietnam commission proposed by Robert Kennedy as an alternative to entering the presidential race. The Wise Men met on March 25 and 26. McGeorge Bundy reported for the majority of the group that "present policy had reached an impasse, could not achieve its objective without the application of virtually unlimited resources, was no longer supported by a majority of the American people, and therefore required significant change."[90] Several of the meeting participants reported that the change in their views was attributable to the briefings they had received the previous night about the unlikelihood of success following current policies. The briefers were younger staff members in the Defense Department. Johnson declared that the first thing he must do when the Wise Men disbanded was to meet with their briefers.

The Wise Men did not all agree that policy should shift to de-escalation. Bundy reports that three took a markedly different view: General Omar Bradley, General Maxwell Taylor, and Robert Murphy. As Bundy reported, "They all feel that we should not act to weaken our position and we should do what our military commanders suggest."[91] Moreover, the conclusions were not a complete surprise to Johnson, who already knew Ball's position and was aware of changes of mind by McGeorge Bundy, Cyrus Vance, Dean Acheson, and Henry Cabot Lodge; his potential receptiveness to their new views was probably implicit in his asking the Wise Men to meet.[92] It is unclear to what degree the Wise Men influenced Johnson's thinking and to what degree their meeting legitimized a shift Johnson already had decided to make.

The president wrote in his memoirs that he decided that the Wise Men had been less influenced by the briefers than they reported, and more by "the general mood of depression and frustration that had swept over so many people as a result of the Tet offensive."[93] He had known of Acheson's change of mind for about two weeks, even before the idea of convening the Wise Men had been raised. But Acheson had exceptional *ethos* as the dean of the foreign policy establishment when he summarized the belief of the majority that "we can no longer do the job we set out to do in the time we have left and we must begin to disengage."[94] Although Johnson professed to be "astonished" by the report of the Wise Men,[95] it is likely that he was working toward the same conclusion himself.

In short, at some point between the Tet Offensive and March 31, Johnson switched from a predisposition to escalate the war to a decision to approve only a small increment of troops and to partially halt bombing in an attempt to open negotiations. He was leaning against a major troop increase when he received Westmoreland's request on February 27 and was interested in a bombing halt by the time on March 4 when he told Rusk to "get on your horses" on that. He was not sure what the exact mix of his new proposals should be, and for a time he believed that "war" and "peace" measures should not be in the same speech. None of these decisions was final, and Johnson remained open on the policy matters even as work began on development of the speech in which he would announce them. Johnson had asked that a speech draft be ready for discussion on March 20. Harry McPherson, the chief writer of the speech, produced a draft with a distinctly hawkish tilt. It went through five rounds of revision, making six drafts in all, before McPherson and Clifford proposed that they create an "Alternative Draft" tilting in a dovish direction, so that the president would have two different versions from which to choose. The "Alternative Draft," which Johnson ultimately would select, was written very shortly after the meeting of the Wise Men was over.

3

Designing the Speech

THERE NEVER WAS any doubt that there would be a speech.

In recent years, a presidential speech to the nation from the Oval Office to discuss a major policy issue has become less customary than it used to be. Major addresses are more likely to be delivered on a college campus, to an audience assembled in a government auditorium, to a gathering of private citizens, or—if really important—to a joint session of Congress. Less substantial messages may come as announcements in the Rose Garden, at the daily press briefing, or, since their inception, posted on social media. Indeed, a body of scholarship has accumulated in recent years to suggest that presidential rhetoric has little tangible effect.[1] As the proliferation of media has created more objects for public attention, the president cannot be assumed to set the public agenda merely by sharing his views with a national television audience.

It was different in 1968. The Tet Offensive created an exigency that Lyndon Johnson would need to explain. The president, it was assumed, needed to clarify such a surprising event for the people: what had happened, what it meant, and what we were going to do about it.[2] What is more, the policy development and speech development processes were intertwined. Not only were the presidential policy advisers and speechwriters often the same people (the functions would not be separated until Richard Nixon created an Office of Speechwriting), but the needs of the writing process were as likely to drive the policy process as the other way around. As Clark Clifford explained it, "Sometimes the resolution of a controversial issue is deferred until a major speech is necessary, and the process of drafting the speech becomes the process by which policy is decided."[3] Clifford's judgment that this is what happened during February and March 1968 is borne out by an examination of how the March 31 speech was developed.

The State of the Union address of January 17 initially included a lengthy section on Vietnam. Johnson had read intelligence reports confirming a buildup of enemy forces and predicting a major attack (presumably at Khe Sanh), but warning of a new enemy initiative would seem inconsistent with the optimistic reports from the previous fall, so it was left out. Wanting to reserve the topic for a different occasion, Johnson instructed his aide Harry McPherson to prepare a draft. Immediately after the Tet Offensive, the president thought he might have made a mistake in omitting the discussion earlier. Now there was a clear need for a speech about Vietnam, but nobody was sure just what it would say.[4]

The Tet Offensive began barely a week after the seizure of the USS *Pueblo*, a Navy intelligence ship engaged in routine surveillance of the North Korean coast. The vessel was captured by North Korean forces who boarded the ship and took it to Wonson, transported the crew to Pyongyang, and held them in captivity for eleven months. At first, a speech was planned for early February dealing with both the *Pueblo* crisis and the Tet Offensive. National Security Adviser Walt Rostow envisioned as the theme that there was "a widespread, desperate, and dangerous Communist effort along the whole front in Asia to divert us from Vietnam, upset the progress made in Vietnam, and discourage and split the American people."[5] Rostow also urged that there be no discussion of a bombing pause since the communists in Vietnam had showed no inclination to comply with the San Antonio formula.

This was the first specific reference to a presidential speech. As the proposed content was discussed, there was disagreement about what should be said. Both Secretary of State Dean Rusk and General Earle Wheeler objected to a proposal to extend tours of duty in Vietnam because it would alarm the American people and seriously affect the morale of the troops. Rusk concluded, "Some parts of this speech are unnecessary. I do not think it should be given at this time."[6]

Thinking about a speech continued during February, as the administration tried to determine how to respond to Tet. A National Security

Council history file in the Johnson Library contains an agenda for a meeting with the president scheduled for February 12. There are three items: Westmoreland's request for more troops (which had not yet become public but was starting to percolate through the administration); instructions for Undersecretary Cyrus Vance in Saigon; and "A Speech."[7]

At least three drafts of a speech were prepared during February. The goal was to put the *Pueblo* affair and the Tet Offensive into perspective, defend the conduct of the war, and lay out a firm course for the rest of 1968. But this speech ultimately was put aside until General Wheeler returned from his mission to Saigon. In Clifford's view, it was "a tough speech supporting an aggressive response to the Tet offensive." Even while the advisers were waiting for Wheeler to return, however, Rostow advised the president on February 23 that he would brief McPherson "on the whole picture, at his request, this morning, to prepare him for drafting, if necessary.[8]

Wheeler returned from Vietnam on February 27, bringing Westmoreland's request for an additional 206,000 troops, which he endorsed. This is when Johnson asked Clifford, the incoming secretary of defense, to review the request and consider alternatives—an instruction that Clifford decided to expand to an "A to Z review" of American policy in Vietnam. Meanwhile, the advisers continued to discuss a speech as if the policy review were considering only alternative ways to meet Westmoreland's request. Johnson notes in his memoirs that the idea of a presidential statement was postponed once again when Wheeler returned, "but I knew that I would need one by the end of March."[9] The Clifford task force reported on March 4. As has been noted, it urged sending a much smaller number of troops than Westmoreland had requested, but it did not urge any change in the basic goals or policies underlying the war. At the same meeting on March 4, Rusk introduced the proposal for a bombing halt, which will be discussed in detail in the next chapter. But there was as yet no commitment to include either of these ideas in the speech, or even to share with the nation that a major review of Vietnam policy was underway. Barrett has written in retrospect that by March 4, "at what all administration figures agreed was a critical juncture in the war, it was becoming increasingly apparent that a presidential speech could not be given without confronting the most basic questions about the US commitment to Indochina."[10] Although this is a reasonable interpretation in retrospect, there is little evidence that the administration was considering such a radical reassessment at this time. It was not until March 12 that Johnson asked his advisers to consider specifically what the contents of his speech should be,[11] so it is hard to see how undetermined contents would have forced a major reappraisal of policy earlier in the month. As late as March 17, Clifford reports, Johnson "still thought of the March 31 speech primarily as a justification for the decision to send Westmoreland more troops and call up the Reserves." He adds that, even as McPherson began to produce drafts, "there was no mention of a bombing halt."[12]

Clifford's *post facto* recollection is somewhat of an overstatement. There is no evidence, other than speculation, that Johnson at any point considered calling up the reserves, although Wheeler and Westmoreland certainly were encouraging him to do so. In addition, McPherson was not yet producing speech drafts, although he would begin to do so by the following Monday. Still, Clifford accurately captured the decision makers' state of mind in mid-March. He reported that he was privately dissenting from the conclusions of his own task force because it did not question basic assumptions; for the most part the "A to Z" policy review could be characterized more accurately as "A to C." This is consistent with the mindset that Johnson displayed on those same days in mid-March when he traveled around the country delivering the hawkish speeches chronicled in the last chapter, when he left no opening for a basic change in policy but repeatedly called for victory by military means if it could not be achieved by negotiations, while holding out no hope for negotiations.

This state of affairs, however, would change markedly over the next ten days, and it would do so because of the interaction of external constraints and the demand for a speech. The external constraints were summarized by Ball: "a rapidly deteriorating situation in South Vietnam, other international crises diverting advisers, a gathering of challengers for the 1968 presidential election, rioting in American cities, and an American public that was increasingly disillusioned with its military and government.[13] On March 19, Johnson told his advisers that he wanted to have a draft ready for discussion in two days. Consideration of specific drafts began the next day, March 20.

The following sections of this chapter will examine a series of strategic considerations that emerged in the drafting process, after which the chronology of the drafts will be reviewed. Two points should be kept in mind. First, Johnson kept his cards close to the vest. He seldom revealed what he was thinking, but he asked many questions to probe his advisers. It is likely that he was far more open to changes than he let on, if only because it is highly unlikely that he would have undergone such a drastic and sudden conversion on about March 28 as it otherwise would be necessary to assume.[14] Second, the advisers were not perfectly consistent across this period of time but sometimes changed their views. Both Rusk and Clifford, in particular, became more open to the peace initiatives as the drafting process went on.

Johnson had been receiving a steady stream of hawkish advice during February, mostly in memos from Walt Rostow. That line of thinking influenced the early drafting process. But conflict among the staff quickly developed. McPherson's notes on the initial meeting on February 27 are instructive. He wrote, "General impression: prevailing uncertainty. Radically different proposals were offered and debated, none rejected out of hand." He added that Defense Secretary Robert McNamara, on his last days in office, had expressed "grave doubts over military, economic, political, diplomatic, and moral" consequences of further escalation. McPherson wondered whether "these profound doubts" will be presented to the president, not realizing that they already had been—in McNamara's memo of November 1, 1967.[15] Gardner described the situation in mid-March as fluid. Neither Rusk nor Clifford was rallying colleagues; rather, "as the drama unfolded, both principals and background players wandered back and forth, sometimes actually switching sides." Nor was Johnson "simply buffeted along" by this interplay, merely looking for a quick fix at any given moment. Rather, he was thinking about the cumulative effect of his decisions and was weighing in, usually with strident recommendations.[16] But later in the month the group settled into two factions. Rusk, Rostow, Ambassador Ellsworth Bunker, and the military thought that Tet had given the United States the upper hand and so they wanted to keep the pressure on; they were not disposed to make concessions. Clifford, Averell Harriman, Nicholas Katzenbach, Paul Warnke, and Paul Nitze had given up on military victory and sought mutual de-escalation through negotiations; McPherson would come to identify with this group.[17] Ball describes the speechwriting operation as "a fluid mosaic of conflicting personalities, word-wars, rivalries, and power plays."[18]

Several strategic decisions were made during this process. One was to stress perseverance. Despite some indications of growing public fatigue with the war, the staff emphasized the need to sustain the American effort. Changes in policy were characterized either as continuities or as the products of success, and drastic reversal of course, such as outright withdrawal, was not an option. This perspective was illustrated by language Rostow submitted, even though it did not make its way into the final speech: " . . . if the United States tires and withdraws at this stage when others have not yet achieved adequate strength, we can only turn the fate of these nations over to the Soviet Union and Communist China." He elaborated: "If we tire of the struggle—as they hope we will—I tell you that the whole of what this nation has built with others in the past 20 years would be endangered. The long, hard, slow demonstration that aggression does not work would be undone."[19] The unsupported assumption of a communist monolith went unchallenged. Although the final text did not include Rostow's suggestion and the speech deviated from his strictly hawkish position, it never deviated from the strategic emphasis on perseverance.

This theme was extended longitudinally by emphasizing the continuity of American commitment across successive presidential administrations. Johnson frequently emphasized that the American stake in Vietnam was articulated across three presidencies—Eisenhower's, Kennedy's, and his own. (It is unclear why he did not include President Truman in the list.) Even though the nature of the commitment had evolved—the *Wall Street Journal* editorialized that neither Eisenhower nor Kennedy imagined a conflict of the current scope[20]—still the speech discussed the American promise as if it were continuous.

A more complex strategic decision concerned how to treat the Tet Offensive. If it was a failure for the communists, then why did Wheeler request such a large increment of forces? Conversely, if the need for additional troops was so great, how could people be sure that Tet was such a disaster for the communist forces? Either horn of the dilemma seemed to challenge the belief in American invincibility and to suggest that there might be good reason for the growing war fatigue.

Early on, when it was thought that Johnson would be speaking shortly after Tet, McPherson emphasized that Tet was no surprise; we knew that it was coming, he said. It was a dramatic effort to raise the stakes of the war, and it had failed dramatically. It was an attempt to take advantage of the United States in an election year, and it had not destabilized us.[21] These early drafts were attempts to bolster American morale and to urge the country not to be discouraged by the seemingly surprise nature of the Tet attacks. They sought to counteract what Rusk would later describe as "the element of hope [that] has been taken away by Tet. People agree with the objectives but wonder what it will cost and don't see [an] end in sight."[22] Since Westmoreland's request for a major troop increase had not been received yet, it was not necessary to reconcile it explicitly with the claim that the Tet Offensive was a communist failure. Later, two different lines of argument would be used, sometimes singly and sometimes in combination. One emphasized threat: despite their losses in Tet, the communists had not lost the will to fight and would launch future initiatives (Khe Sanh was mentioned most often) for which we needed to be prepared. The other argument stressed opportunity: having weathered the Tet attacks, we were now in a position to take advantage of the enemy's weakness and exploit our victories by taking the offensive and bringing the war closer to a conclusion. These lines of argument offered the potential of avoiding inconsistency. Even after it became clear that Johnson was not going to approve Westmoreland's large troop request, though, Clifford in particular continued to stress the incongruity of emphasizing both that Tet was an unmitigated disaster for the communist forces and that we needed major increments of resources in order to prevail.

Another strategic question was how to account for the failure to get negotiations underway, especially in light of what had been portrayed as devastating defeats for the communists. This was an easy call: they were to blame. This, after all, had been a consistent theme in Johnson's defenses of his course going back to 1965. More recent scholars have pointed out that, while proclaiming his willingness to negotiate at any time, Johnson had established impossible preconditions, such as an end to North Vietnamese infiltration of the South, which would have required Hanoi to yield in advance the very thing Americans wanted to negotiate about. Meanwhile, the United States showed no inclination to meet Hanoi's requirement of an unconditional cessation of the bombing of North Vietnam as a prerequisite for negotiations. This was a reasonable demand if one accepted the premise that the Vietnamese struggle was a civil war in which the United States had intervened. Such retrospective analyses suggest that the United States may have been proclaiming its interest in negotiations while simultaneously acting to prevent them. But that was not the way it appeared to policymakers at the time. They instead told the story of successive American offers, each more generous than the last, culminating in the San Antonio formula of September 1967. Each offer, they maintained, was met with communist intransigence and perfidy, the same characteristics they had demonstrated by interrupting a truce on the sacred holiday of Tet in order to launch a new offensive.

Early drafters were consistent on this point. An unsigned draft, probably by Dean Rusk, called on Johnson to say, "On many occasions we have deliberately reduced the level of violence in one way or another in order to elicit some response from the other side." These moves were inducements to get talks started. But not only had there been no offer from the other side of talks, but "these steps have not met any response through reduction of violence by our opponents." Nevertheless, perhaps thinking of the bombing halt that he was proposing, Rusk added, "But we shall keep open such possibilities for the future."[23] Similarly, William P. Bundy suggested this language: "And we have tried unrelentingly to get talks or negotiations started that could consider these problems in the full spirit of negotiation. To date, these efforts have failed in the face of Hanoi's insistence on prior acceptance of unacceptable conditions that are not consistent with the conduct of negotiations in good faith." He added that Hanoi had "apparently rejected [the San Antonio formula] and . . . the experience of our discussions on it in recent months has been discouraging."[24] And McPherson, in one of his early drafts, wrote that those proposing that the United States change its terms for negotiations had the burden to demonstrate "whether their proposals [were] in fact consistent with a free and universal choice of government by all South Vietnamese, and whether their proposals, if thus consistent, would offer the slightest present hope that Hanoi would accept them." In the margin of his draft, someone had handwritten, "Bobby and all others," suggesting that domestic politics was not far from the drafters' minds.[25] Although they represented the spirit of the group at this time, it is clear in retrospect that these two conditions necessarily posed a "Catch-22" if a proposal could meet the first condition, it would fail the second, and vice versa. One can imagine why, holding these views, Johnson's advisers found Hanoi's acceptance of the invitation in the March 31 speech to begin talks such a surprise.

One particularly difficult strategic question was whether to combine the "war" and "peace" themes in a single speech. This question arose after the conferees began to look more favorably on the bombing halt proposal (shorthand for the "peace" theme) that Rusk had introduced on March 4. It had already been accepted that Westmoreland would receive some increment of troops (shorthand for the "war" theme), even though far short of the 206,000 he had requested. Should these themes go together? The argument in favor was that each theme would appeal to a different segment of the deeply divided American public, producing stronger acceptance of the overall speech as a package. The argument against it was that the resulting speech would be incoherent and that each proposal would undermine the credibility of the other.

This question was debated in the advisers' meeting of March 20, with the preponderance of the attendees arguing against combining the two themes. Asked by Johnson whether they should be combined, United Nations Ambassador Arthur Goldberg—who favored a bombing halt—said no: the peace proposal "won't be seen in good faith if you couple it with troops."[26] From the opposite side of the argument, Supreme Court Justice Abe Fortas, still serving as an informal adviser to the president, reached the same conclusion, He recommended that the speech focus only on the need for troops and on the economy, reasoning that peace moves would get lost in the speech and that, if noticed at all, they would be regarded as a sign of weakness.[27] After some discussion, the president resolved the question by saying, according to McPherson: "We are mixing two things when we include peace initiatives. Let's make it troops and war." According to Tom Johnson, the designated notetaker, the president said, "Let's get peace out of it except we're ready to talk."[28] It might seem that Johnson's final decision was that he was unwilling to consider

any moves to de-escalate the war. But it is clear from the context that
what he was ruling out was placing peace proposals *in the same speech*
as the announcement that he was sending more troops to Vietnam. In
fact, McPherson's notes on the March 20 meeting indicate that Johnson
immediately followed "Let's make it troops and war" with "Later we can
revive and extend our peace initiatives."[29] In his memoirs, Johnson explained his reasons for wanting to keep the two topics separate: he was
"deeply concerned" that a peace initiative would be misinterpreted, he
wanted more time to study the possibilities, and he wanted to minimize
leaks.[30] In any event, this decision did not survive into the final version
of the text: the March 31 speech included both the announcement of a
partial halt in the bombing of North Vietnam and the announcement
that additional troops would be going to South Vietnam, albeit far fewer than Westmoreland said he needed.

Once the inclusion of a bombing-halt proposal was agreed upon, another strategic question was whether to make the action reciprocal or
unilateral. A reciprocal proposal would have offered Hanoi a bombing
halt in return for some specific concessions on the communists' part. A
unilateral action would involve announcing what the United States was
going to do on its own, with or without any implicit understanding with
the other party. As he made clear in the introduction of his proposal,
Rusk had in mind a unilateral action. Unlike previous bombing halts,
it would not involve sending ambassadors around the world in search
of negotiating positions; it would not have to involve negotiations at
all. Rusk proposed only that the United States take an action and then
wait to see if or how the other side responded. It might be with a proposal for negotiations, but it might be through a unilateral move on
its own part to de-escalate. If the communist reaction was appropriate,
then the United States might take a further step to de-escalate, which
might in turn call forth another step from the communists, and so on,
illustrating the theory of graduated reduction in tensions. Accordingly,
in one of his later drafts, McPherson reiterated the call for negotiations
but then added a proposal to Hanoi to "pursue an alternative course to
peace—a course that would involve a reduction in the present level of
hostilities."[31]

The final strategic question to be discussed was how domestic political considerations should enter into discussions about the policy

and the speech. Ostensibly, the answer was "not at all." Horace Busby wrote in his memoir that, until March 30, politics had not been discussed in the Vietnam policy review; nor had the timing of the bombing halt announcement coming so soon before the Wisconsin primary been considered. When the decisions about the speech finally came together, Busby writes, "there was only characteristic haste to arrange television time, draft a speech, and get the president before a national audience."[32] Of course, the fact that the president had decided not to run for another term made it more credible to say that political considerations were absent in the preparation of the speech.

In another sense, however, political considerations were prominent. The country was witnessing a deepening divide between hawks and doves. Johnson wished to transcend this divide, offering something to each faction to pitch for its support, while ultimately identifying with neither. His speech gave something to each—the partial bombing halt to the doves, the additional troops to the hawks—but not enough to leave either element completely satisfied. The most avid doves were calling for a complete bombing halt, while the most fervent hawks wanted a substantially larger increase in manpower than Johnson was willing to provide. But if Johnson could peel away some support from each group and add it to the middle-of-the-road element that supported his policies or was at least deferential to the president, he could mobilize public opinion enough to sustain his course and tamp down the spirit of divisiveness against which he would warn in the speech. In listing the factors influencing his decisions of March 31, Johnson wrote in his memoirs that "the state of mind and morale on our domestic front was most important." A *New York Times* writer observed that while Hanoi might interpret military restraint as weakness, the fear was "that the divisive debate in the United States could be taken as a sign of even greater weakness." For that reason, the writer concluded, "an effort to appease his critics plainly lay behind tonight's order and address to the nation."[33]

What became the March 31 speech went through eleven drafts over about as many days. The president began the process by announcing at a Tuesday lunch meeting—his weekly meeting to discuss the war—that he wanted to see a draft by March 21.[34] It was expected that the draft would center on Westmoreland's troop request, although Clifford asked, "Do we have anything to offer except war?" to which there was no response.[35] The principal writer of all the drafts, not including the withdrawal announcement (on which work had not yet begun) was Harry McPherson. The procedure was that McPherson would produce a draft, send it out for comment to a group of White House staffers and Cabinet secretaries or undersecretaries (most of whom would not respond), then collate and evaluate the responses, produce the next draft taking the responses into account, and start the process again. The first six drafts were numbered #1 through #6. For reasons that will become clear, the remaining drafts were numbered Alternate Draft #1 through #5, the last being the copy from which the president read on March 31.[36]

McPherson had the first draft ready on March 20. It described multiple challenges facing the nation in Vietnam and recounts how previous generations met similar challenges, giving us confidence that we can persevere now. He proposed to "lay before you my understanding of the state of that struggle in Vietnam" and how we can meet and overcome it. He began by reviewing the Tet Offensive. Dispensing with possibilities for peace negotiations, Johnson would point out that the enemy not only rejected the San Antonio formula but "continued to plan and prepare for an unprecedented assault on the people, the government, and the allies of South Vietnam," plans that came to fruition in the Tet Offensive. The goals for the offensive were listed as reversing the tide of the struggle, collapsing the government of South Vietnam and destroying its army, stimulating a general uprising in the cities of South Vietnam, creating front groups to form a new government friendly to the communists, scoring a military victory on the battlefield, and destroying the will of the American people. (This list, it should be noted, was based on speculation by Johnson's staff, not on North Vietnamese statements or captured documents.) Following closely along the lines of earlier memos from Walt Rostow, the draft then examined enemy achievements and failures during the Tet Offensive.

The draft text then moved to the announcement of new actions to be taken. It proposed to call-up 48,000 reservists, with a later call-up of the ready reserves. The text confessed that "hard choices must be made" if the nation was to meet the budgetary requirements of Vietnam, and that "much that we hoped to do—to expand the social programs we have begun in these past few years—must be diminished or delayed."

The text reiterated that "we must reduce the part of our national budget that is controllable—the part that is not fixed by law," and without offering any specifics, Johnson would promise to propose such reductions. Meanwhile, he would repeat his request for the surtax (a temporary increase in income tax rates), which he predicted the American people will accept because, quoting Kennedy's Inaugural Address, "we shall pay any price, bear any burden. . . ."

The closing portion of the draft was Johnson's estimate of the chances for peace. Possibly as a trial balloon inserted by McPherson, the draft would announce that Johnson would avoid aerial bombardment within _____ miles of Hanoi and Haiphong (the blank is in the original draft). He could not give the precise terms of a settlement but reiterated American goals: "a return to the essential provisions of the Geneva Accords of 1954, and the establishment of political conditions that would permit the South Vietnamese—*all* the South Vietnamese— to chart their course under the rule of one man, one vote." The word "all" was thought to be highly significant, because it seemed to imply for the first time that there was a role for the Viet Cong to play in peace negotiations. Finally, on page 30 of the draft, as a placeholder, were the words, "Closing peroration." McPherson did not have time to write one.

Johnson called a meeting late in the afternoon on March 20 to discuss this draft. Clifford points out that nothing had yet been decided, and states, "With so many overlapping issues to resolve, it was a chaotic meeting," but that it was the first time that the policy of bombing was seriously discussed.[37] Johnson opened the meeting by saying that its purpose was "to help me prepare a well thought out, well balanced statement." He said that the speech should discuss military strength, economic strength, diplomatic strength, and peace, adding, "I want war like I want polio."[38] Tom Johnson's notes on the meeting indicate that the discussion was wide-ranging and free-wheeling. Secretary Rusk, early in the meeting, stated the conundrum: no peace proposals will be taken seriously unless we halt the bombing, but a bombing halt is incongruous with a call-up of reserves, which is thought to be necessary to protect American forces already in Vietnam. The pros and cons of different options were discussed at length and in no systematic order. At the end of the two-hour meeting, the president asked selected individuals to develop their ideas into specific proposals. He resolved the conundrum of mixing peace and war by saying, according to Tom Johnson's notes, "Let's get peace out of it except we're willing to talk," and according to McPherson's notes, "Let's make it troops and war."[39]

Although the meeting with the president did not focus specifically on McPherson's draft, the speechwriter did receive some feedback. William P. Bundy proposed to shorten a few sections of the speech but did not offer substantive suggestions. Clark Clifford apparently made oral remarks on which McPherson took handwritten notes. McPherson's annotations suggest that Clifford emphasized the American role in the future of Asia, the imperative of preventing the subjugation of South Vietnam, the prospect of a worse conflict if we faltered now, and the importance of our determination and will as the ways to achieve peace. Clifford strongly counseled against weakness. He was not at this point recommending any major reappraisal of policy.[40]

McPherson's first draft has been discussed in such detail because it was the basic template for drafts #2 through #6. The second draft was produced the same night through handwritten changes to Draft #1. McPherson reduced the list of enemy objectives from seven to five. He inserted a statement in the discussion of Tet, saying that the enemy power was greater militarily than we had imagined and that it remained to be seen what political effect that might have. He condensed several sections of the original text. He modified a question so far focused on the enemy's capabilities and instead emphasized the enemy's will to fight: "Shall we decide that because the enemy's *will* to conquer his neighbor has not been broken, we must yield to that will and retire from the field?" McPherson expanded the complimentary remarks about South Vietnam. As Johnson had instructed, McPherson dropped the reference to suspending aerial bombing around Hanoi and Haiphong. At the same time, he omitted the reference to having to "diminish" some of Johnson's social programs, saying only that they might need to be delayed. He fleshed out the closing section in which he harked back to the vision of peace sketched out in the president's 1965 speech at Johns Hopkins University, and he tried his hand at a peroration that urged the audience to make a new commitment to "the determination of free nations to assist the struggle against aggression—at its outset."

McPherson sent the second draft to be included in the president's night reading. It is not clear whether Johnson read this draft, but National

Security Adviser McGeorge Bundy did. He wrote a memo to the president the next day (March 21) in which he said, "Harry's present draft (second draft, 20 March) does just what was decided yesterday" in the meeting Johnson had convened. But, he went on, "as it stands it will be profoundly discouraging to the American people." He made this observation in the course of advancing a larger claim: the belief that "the sentiment in the country on the war has shifted very heavily since the Tet offensive. . . . What has happened is that a great many people—even very determined and loyal people—have begun to think that Vietnam really is a bottomless pit." Bundy thought it a miracle "that our people have stayed with the war as long as they have, but I do not see how we can carry them with us for very much longer if all we seem to offer is more of the same, with stalemate at a higher cost as the only prospect."[41] Bundy was offering the premises for putting some sort of peace proposal back into the speech draft, but, curiously, he did not advocate that in this memorandum. He suggested minor changes to the military part of the speech, but proposed expanding the section on the surtax and budget cuts. Then he made an interesting suggestion about venue: Johnson should consider giving the speech to a joint session of Congress in order to share the responsibility for making the difficult budgetary choices with the Congress rather than shouldering it alone.

The third draft was sent to the president on March 22. It was substantially the same as the second, with an expanded discussion of the surtax as Bundy had proposed. McPherson had Johnson express his preference for raising the funds needed for the war through taxes alone. His earlier budget requests had asked for only the funds that were really needed, so there were no targets for cuts. The country "would be better off as a people if we should keep these budget targets intact even at the price of higher taxes." But, Johnson would acknowledge, Congress strongly felt otherwise, and it had a right to its own judgment. So he recognized the political need for "some measure of reduction in present Federal programs," the needed measure being unspecified. This was a compromise in which nobody got exactly what he wanted, "but together we can do what needs doing most of all: we can keep our economy strong." McPherson's draft would acknowledge quite explicitly that Congress had taken the measure of the president and that, if he were to get the surtax, Johnson must yield to its wishes. Rusk and Clifford returned their copies of the draft with minor editing suggestions. Clifford sought to improve clarity in several places. Rusk noted in the closing section that we were fighting in Vietnam to fulfill a national commitment. Bill Bundy suggested a new closing section, referred to above, that sought to cast the responsibility for negotiations onto the North Vietnamese. He also suggested, contrary to Rusk, that the word "commitment" not be used. The files have no record of Johnson's opinion of this third draft.

A few days elapsed before the completion of Draft #4, which is dated March 26. This draft revised several portions of the earlier ones. Clifford redrafted the military section; Treasury Secretary Henry H. Fowler redrafted the economic section; and McGeorge Bundy redrafted the section on the prospects of peace.

Until this point, as Doris Kearns noted, the drafts "spelled out a tough and uncompromising stand: a refusal to consider a bombing halt without clear reciprocity, a call-up of 50,000 reserves, and a demand that Congress pass the surtax as a measure of patriotic support." Kearns goes on to assert, "These were bellicose speeches, suggesting from the outside that Johnson had abandoned his middle-of-the-road approach in favor of all-out war."[42] Surely an outside observer looking at these drafts would find no evidence that they reflected any sort of comprehensive "A to Z" review of American policy. But that was about to change.

Clifford's redraft of the military section included a proposal for a unilateral bombing halt north of the 20th parallel. This had been suggested in a memo to the president from McPherson dated March 23, while he was between writing the third and fourth drafts of the speech. Two points need mention here: the proposed halt was unilateral, and it was partial. It did not require prior negotiation or agreement by North Vietnam; it was an action the United States could take alone. Moreover, it did not cover all of North Vietnam, although it did cover most of the area and most of the population. But it allowed bombing to continue between the 17th and 20th parallel, where the bulk of the fighting was taking place. It could hold out the promise of a total bombing halt as a possibility for the future. Clifford argued that North Vietnam's reaction to the partial bombing halt would be a sign of how they would respond to a complete halt if one was offered during the course of negotiations. If the response was favorable, it could be construed as an *implicit* acceptance of the San Antonio formula requirement that North Vietnam not take advantage of any break in the fighting that might accompany the start of negotiations. The idea was that this might be a way to start negotiations without the face-threatening requirement for preliminary concessions involving the very objects of the negotiation.

Clifford had also broken down the troop requirements: 13,500 as support troops for an increment of 11,000 airborne and marine forces that already had been sent, plus 48,500 men to build up the ready reserve (not to be sent to Vietnam), for a total of 62,000. This did not sound as much like an expansion as had earlier versions of the speech. With all these modifications, McPherson acknowledged that the draft was long and complicated, but he said that was necessary.

Bill Bundy returned his copy of the draft with suggestions for deep cuts in the opening part of the speech, in order to reduce its total length. Phil Goulding, assistant secretary of defense for public affairs, made marginal comments on Clifford's copy of the draft. He mostly improved clarity and substituted words that a general audience might more easily understand, and he also made several cuts in order to reduce the length of the manuscript. Finally, he questioned several of the assertions and identified places where proof was needed.

Lady Bird Johnson also supplied a critique of Draft #4. Her comments were brief and to the point. First, the draft was "too long." Second, "last two pages *great*." Third. "Financial part especially must be simpler with more 'John Citizen' words"—echoing the concern of Phil Goulding. And finally, Mrs. Johnson wrote, "Strongly question the word '*assume*' on page 34—presumably a reference to the implicit assumption that North Vietnam would not take advantage of any bombing pause.[43]

Like the second draft, McPherson's fifth draft consisted mostly of handwritten changes on the copy of the fourth draft. He removed the numbering of the enemy's objectives to make that recitation less precise. He deleted paragraphs that were overly tentative, that speculated about the enemy's motivation, or that acknowledged enemy strengths. He strengthened references to the intervention of regular North Vietnamese army units in the South and stressed that our increased presence in the South since 1965 was a response to this intervention. He reduced the number of rhetorical questions in a series that asked repeatedly, "Shall we accept defeat?" He cut back the section on tax increases, spending cuts, and the balance of payments from what Secretary Fowler had proposed, deleted the admonishment of those members of Congress who had balked at the surtax, and emphasized not that higher taxes and budget cuts were unpopular but rather that they were necessary. He cut paragraphs that repeated our goals or repeated that we could not be sure what North Vietnam would do. He avoided overpromising results, changing predictions of what "will" happen to descriptions of what "may" happen. And instead of asking Americans, in the peroration, to "make" a new commitment, he asked them only to "support" it—the commitment presumably having been made by the president. Taken as a whole, McPherson's changes responded to the concern that his previous draft was too long and too defensive. In this draft, he was concerned not to take on a larger burden of proof than necessary, not to make assumptions about what others would do, and not to describe in overly complex terms the economic realities that the nation faced. It was clear that the speech was becoming more refined.

Still, there were opportunities to make minor changes. Rusk made the reference to the San Antonio formula simpler and pithier: "In both word and deed, Hanoi rejected this offer. In words, both privately and publicly, they denounced my San Antonio formula." He also deleted a reference to North Vietnam's receiving "massive assistance from Soviet Russia and China—two nations that are otherwise at violent odds with one another." Why, he might have wondered, invite additional antagonism that is not necessary to the argument?

Clifford took out the detailed explanation of the increased number of support troops and ready reserves that had been inserted into the previous draft. He also made some changes that inadvertently introduced grammatical errors, such as deleting one of two examples but leaving the word "both" in the text. Bill Bundy shortened the financial section by deleting references to the president's earlier efforts to obtain the surtax. He also raised some questions to double-check the accuracy of quantitative factual claims. All told, the proposed changes did not suggest to McPherson that much remained to be done. Indeed, comparing each draft to its predecessor, we see that the sixth draft probably reveals less change from the fifth than any pair of drafts so far.

McPherson transmitted the sixth draft with a cover note saying that it reflected the work "of Secretaries Rusk and Clifford, Bill Bundy, Walt

Rostow, and myself." Their efforts produced a significant condensation of the fifth draft, reducing it by 800 words to a new count of 4000, although "the number of pages have not been cut much but this is because the typing on this draft is less compact." The section on additional troops had been tightened, and the section on the surtax and economic impact had been edited and trimmed. Other changes were made for clarity, but there was little change in substance or tone.[44] McPherson also submitted the peroration he had written a month before, which he thought more humane than the one currently in the text. Bill Bundy suggested adding a statement to the effect that those who would say "it is not worth the effort" were risking "a far wider and more devastating conflict later, in order to get the respite of a year or two."[45] McPherson edited this language so that Johnson would join his critics in lamenting the cost of the war, but would pledge that he was determined to do all he could to prevent "a far more terrible war from engulfing Asia and the Pacific." Clifford and Bill Bundy each made a few minor adjustments on McPherson's draft, but nothing substantive.

But it was not that they all were satisfied with the speech. It was as though some of the advisers were resigned to it, whereas others had reached the judgment that the speech did a good job at what it set out to do, but that what it set out to do was all wrong. This concern had been raised, but not pursued, at various moments of the drafting process so far. What solidified this view now was not entirely clear, but the meeting of the Wise Men the day before—and their emerging concerns about Johnson's current course—probably played a large role. Vandiver describes Clifford's reaction to Draft #6: he "wallowed in gloom. Warlike phrases prickled through it, still. . . . Clifford had rummaged in vain for any mention of a bombing halt or pause and felt, instead, a blooming bellicosity, although troop numbers remained small. He thought the speech as drafted would hurt Johnson immensely and inflame the economy."[46] Clifford was hardly unaware of the development of the speech to this point; he had read each of the drafts. His newly raised consciousness was not the result of surprise but, more likely, of a contemporaneous development such as the conclusions reached by the Wise Men.

According to Johnson's memoirs, Clifford told a meeting of principal advisers on March 28 that Draft #6 was unsatisfactory "because it offered no de-escalation and no mention of negotiations." Clifford

reminded the others that the president had said on March 20 that he
wanted such proposals—even though he also had said that he did not
want them in *this* speech. But, Clifford went on, Draft #6 "held out no
hope for either military victory or for a negotiated settlement." Perhaps
hearing an echo of his own concern that the emerging draft did not
speak to the hopelessness of the country, Rusk agreed with Clifford and
dictated a statement embodying a bombing halt at the 20th parallel,
which he originally had presented at the meeting on March 4. As the
president recounted what he was told, "It was agreed that this proposal
would be incorporated in an alternate draft." In other words, the writing team would not withdraw Draft #6, but they would also propose an
alternative, so that Johnson would be able to consider two drafts at the
same time."[47] Importantly, the new draft was not labeled "Draft #7 but
"Alternate Draft #1." As Johnson concludes his account, "Rostow called
the White House to say that Rusk, Clifford, he, and the others were pro-
ceeding on an alternate draft."[48]

Clifford now insisted that merely inserting a bombing halt into an
otherwise warlike speech would not be good enough. Reprising arguments that had been made on March 20, he said that such a step
"would look like another public-relations gimmick."[49] In a meeting in
Rusk's office on March 28, he argued that the whole tone and emphasis of the speech needed to be changed. As Berman described it, Clifford told Rusk and Rostow "that the country could not accept a war
speech; the president as candidate and as Commander in Chief needed
a peace speech."[50] To be sure, this formulation overstates the difference
between the two approaches. But Clifford, who earlier in the month
had not called for drastic change, now spent "several hours, speaking
slowly, . . . [mustering] any available argument . . . why it was not in the
United States' interest to go on pouring military resources into South
Vietnam."[51] He assigned the primary writing responsibility to McPherson, whom he by now recognized as a kindred spirit.

Although Clifford's role in these events is widely recognized, Rusk's
is easily misunderstood. He did not simply agree to give Johnson a
choice because he thought the president would hold out for the hawkish text. Nor apparently was it the case that Rusk (and Rostow) were so
worn down "by the climactic encounter with the Wise Men," as Prados
claims, that they simply went along with Clifford and McPherson.[52]

Although Rusk's motives remain open to speculation, it must be remembered that he was one of the first to propose a bombing halt, on March 4, and had consistently, if quietly, advocated for that approach. In retrospective material prepared for the record after the president left office, Rostow refuted the claim made by Townsend Hoopes that Rusk only reluctantly agreed to preparation of an alternate draft. "I was at the March 28 meeting," Rostow wrote. "I remember no resistance to presenting the President with a choice. I do remember the drafting of the peace passage was by Sec. Rusk."[53] What seems most likely is that Clifford and Rusk were working on separate but parallel tracks, Clifford urging change in the tone of the speech and Rusk providing the specific language for the bombing halt proposal that was the centerpiece of that effort.

As was the case for Draft #1, Alternate Draft #1 would furnish the template for most of the remaining drafts. For this reason, a fairly comprehensive discussion of its contents is in order.

Whereas the earlier drafts had begun by expressing the president's desire to talk with his fellow citizens "about the war in Vietnam," Alternate Draft #1 began with the desire "to speak to you about the prospects for peace in Vietnam and Southeast Asia."[54] This change made the key difference, Clifford believed, distinguishing the speech from a "war speech." The treatment of Tet also differed in structure from that in the earlier drafts. McPherson began with and highlighted the enemy's failure to achieve its overriding objectives, and then he acknowledged that some of the enemy's goals *were* achieved. This was different from the emphasis of the earlier drafts, which focused on the continuing dangers in the aftermath of Tet. This challenge was presented in the Alternate Draft as the risk of *new* attacks, not of a continuing campaign. If there were new attacks, the draft confidently predicted, they would fail, but along the way many lives would be lost—presumably both North Vietnamese and allied lives—and this did not need to be. It was avoidable, and the way to avoid it was to enter on a path that would lead to peace negotiations. As the first step along that path, the draft would have Johnson announce that there would be no bombing attacks north of the 20th parallel, explaining that this was about 75 miles south of Hanoi and Haiphong. McPherson then inserted language suggesting that the North Vietnamese military response would determine whether the

United States could keep the bombing confined, and also would be taken as a sign of whether it could reasonably be assumed that the North would not take advantage of a complete bombing halt. Then Johnson was to hold out an even more optimistic possibility: "If there is a response to the action I am announcing tonight, other actions can follow"—including, presumably, the complete stoppage of the bombing that the North had insisted was its precondition for substantive talks.

This section of the speech represented the truly new material. That it would be called a "peace" speech only emphasizes that virtually no one in the political mainstream was yet calling for complete American withdrawal. But what about the problem first noticed back on March 20? How could this partial bombing halt be combined with the dispatch of more troops without the bombing halt seeming like a gimmick or the speech seeming incoherent?

McPherson addressed that problem by employing the language and logic of conditionality. Simply put, these two themes of the speech were not on the same plane. The bombing halt was what we were going to do, unconditionally. That it might lead to negotiations and to further de-escalatory moves was our genuine hope. That was the way to avoid further deaths that the president had proclaimed to be unnecessary. But McPherson then introduced a conditional alternative: Perhaps, he reasoned, Hanoi would not want to enter into negotiations, especially having launched a major military offensive. *If* that happens, McPherson reasoned, then the Americans must demonstrate that Hanoi could not destroy the United States' will and fighting power. Therefore, the United States must send more troops to South Vietnam to be prepared to make that demonstration if it should prove necessary. This line of reasoning placed the onus for any further military effort squarely on Hanoi and offered a starkly different rationale for the additional troops from that originally provided by General Westmoreland. It is not that we needed them to launch a major new offensive on our part, or to plan for a long siege at Khe Sanh (which by the end of March seemed unlikely), but rather to be prepared to frustrate the ambitions of the North Vietnamese if they unwisely opted for the battlefield rather than the United States' clear preference, the path to the negotiating table.

But there was a problem of proportionality. How could the United States achieve that goal, or any military objective, with such a relatively small number of additional troops? (In the context of more recent high-technology, low-manpower wars in Iraq and Afghanistan, 13,500 seems like a very large number of additional troops, but in the context of the Vietnam War and especially the public expectation that 206,000 troops might be sent, it was a very small number. And the proposed increase of 48,500 in the ready reserve did not seem to count because they would be remaining in the States, not going to Vietnam.) Here McPherson made a strategic move. He did not say that 13,500 was all the United States could send without calling up the reserves, nor did he say that it was as high as we could go without exacerbating the balance-of-payments deficit and threatening the dollar—although both of these statements probably were true. Rather, he made a positive argument: We could achieve major results with only a small increment of forces because of the dramatic improvement in the training and preparedness of our allies, the South Vietnamese. The speech draft reviewed the history of US military involvement but made clear that that involvement always rested on the belief that the burden of preserving the freedom of South Vietnam must be borne mainly by the South Vietnamese themselves. And they were stepping up their efforts: McPherson devoted four pages to detailing improvements in the size of the South Vietnamese army, the level of training and military preparedness, and the results that had been achieved in battle. The draft text then announced the specific increments needed: 13,500 support troops and 48,500 troops for the ready reserve. Most of those who had anticipated that they would be among the 206,000 could breathe a long sigh of relief.[55]

The material about the need for the surtax and the president's willingness to accept spending cuts was left largely as it was from the earlier drafts. Then McPherson brought the speech to a close by cautioning, "It is too soon to make confident predictions, for the experience of recent years has shown us that we face in Hanoi men whose simple objective is to take over South Vietnam. And it is only Hanoi that can decide the issue of aggression that has brought us into this war." Although McPherson considerably oversimplified the story of how the war began, he was right that after this speech the next move would have to be Hanoi's.

Although it largely escaped notice, McPherson reintroduced the word
"all" in the reference to the South Vietnamese who were to exercise
self-determination. The implication was that the United States recognized that there would be a role for the Viet Cong in a future South
Vietnamese government.

Rather than leading directly into the peroration, McPherson incorporated the earlier language that those who would advocate a different
course of action must shoulder the burden of proof that these alternatives would work and that they would be acceptable to North Vietnam.
This language had been inserted earlier in an attempt to marginalize the
positions being advocated by Robert Kennedy. But now, instead of placing the burden on Johnson's critics, McPherson wrote that if *we* advocate these alternatives, *we* must carry the burden of proof. The language
was more conciliatory.

Although it was repetitive, McPherson again commended Asians
who, he said, were mostly responsible for the improved position of
Southeast Asia. And yet he noted that responsible Southeast Asians
themselves recognized "that the progress of the past three years would
have been far less likely—if not impossible—if America and others had
not made the stand in Vietnam."

McPherson's time and, probably, his energy were running out, and
he did not have time to do much with the peroration. He picked up his
earlier musings about why war was sometimes necessary and added that
"the hope of human freedom must ultimately be defended by human
beings." The final sentences asked Americans to strengthen the arms of
the South Vietnamese and to "let them know that all America stands
with them. Divided we are in danger. Together we cannot and will not
fail." When he delivered Alternate Draft #1 to the president, McPherson
noted that the peroration did not quite fit and apologized for not having had time to work much on it. Don't worry about it, Johnson reportedly told him, I may have one of my own.

There is little record in the Johnson Library of comments received
on Alternate Draft #1. There would have been little time for comments
since the president had convened a meeting at 6:30 p.m. with Rusk, Clifford, Rostow, and others to discuss the alternate drafts.[56] Warnke and
Goulding did suggest revisions of some sentences, making narrower
claims in order to avoid introducing proof requirements that could not

be met. They also proposed that, in the speech, Johnson should name his negotiators in case Hanoi responded positively. Their reasoning was that this would generate additional press commentary and keep the focus on Johnson's search for peace.

There also does not appear to be a record of the evening meeting with the president. Immediately afterward, McPherson went back to work, producing Alternate Draft #2 at 9:00 p.m. He also did some minor cleanup work on Draft #6 in case Johnson wanted to pursue that course. But he did not give the draft a new number, instead calling it "Sixth Draft Alternative," presumably because the changes were minor. Clifford objected to this option for several reasons: (1) there was no suggestion that the additional troops were anything other than the first increment; (2) the tone made it seem that the president was still pursuing the same course as earlier (so that the "A" to "Z" review had achieved nothing); and (3) there was no move toward de-escalation or negotiation. Clifford summarized that this proposed text offered "neither hope nor plan for either military victory or negotiated settlement.[57]

It seems, however, that McPherson focused more on developing Alternate Draft #2. He made four major changes. First, he elaborated the idea of gradual reduction in tensions by explaining where the partial bombing halt could lead: "[I]f there is restraint on their part, this could give us the reasonable basis we have been seeking for assuming that they would not take advantage of a complete bombing halt." In other words, it might not be necessary for North Vietnam to make any specific commitments in order for the United States to halt all bombing, which North Vietnam had insisted must be done unconditionally. The San Antonio formula could be implemented *de facto* without loss of face by either side.

Second, as mentioned, the draft named the proposed US negotiators, Averell Harriman and Llewellyn Thompson. Third, McPherson hedged his bets on the success of the proposed initiative: "I cannot promise that the initiative I am announcing tonight will be any more successful in achieving peace than the others we have taken in recent years," but he had the president express "our hope that North Vietnam, after years of fighting that has left the issue unresolved, will cease its efforts to achieve a military victory." Interestingly, McPherson implicitly accepted the popular view that the war was a stalemate, but he expressed that view in terms of the inability of North Vietnam, rather than the United States, to achieve its goals. This matched the discussion of the troop increase, which was explained as a means to keep the North from reaching its goals, not to achieve a military victory for the United States.

Finally, McPherson rewrote the peroration to reflect the new tone of the speech. In this version, he had the president "ask for your support, my fellow Americans, for the efforts I have described this evening—to reach across the battlefield for an early peace, and to strengthen the arms of those who are fighting for us in South Vietnam," and he ended with a call for national unity.

According to Hoopes's account, McPherson worked late into the night and then sent both Alternative Draft #2 and Sixth Draft Alternative to the president early in the morning on Friday, March 29. Later in the day he received a call from Johnson asking about a passage "on page 3." McPherson had to compare the different speech drafts in order to discover that the president was working from Alternate Draft #2, or "the peace speech.[58] The only comments on this draft in the files are from Rostow, who expanded the discussion of the failures of Tet and the strengths of the South Vietnamese government, and deleted several pages of the text that looked toward a peaceful future for Vietnam.

Alternate Draft #3, dated 2:30 p.m. on March 29, reflected comments made by Rusk, Rostow, and Bill Bundy. It revised the paragraphs on Hanoi's response to the San Antonio formula, making it seem as though the Tet Offensive was its response. (In fact, there was nothing to indicate that Hanoi had considered the San Antonio formula in any way when planning the offensive.) Rusk inserted a call to the United Kingdom and the Soviet Union, in particular, "as Co-Chairmen of the Geneva Conferences and as permanent members of the United Nations Security Council, to do their utmost to move from this step of de-escalation toward a genuine peace in Southeast Asia," in effect expanding the responsibility for seeking peace and doing so by a specific charge to the named nations rather than by a vague expression of hope.

There is no specific indication in the files of Rostow or Bundy's suggestions regarding this specific draft. Clifford, however, deleted the reference to the call-up of the 48,500 ready reserve troops who would not be sent to Vietnam. They did not count as additional troops to Vietnam.

This limited the discussion of additional troops to the 13,500 support troops and, on the face of it, made the increment sound much smaller. Clifford also updated the proposed increase in defense spending and explained what it was for. He also attached changes recommended by Warnke, Nitze, and Goulding, including deletions of references to corruption in North Vietnam—the fifth time, they said, that they had tried to remove this passage. Their reasons are not stated, but it can be inferred that it would not have helped the cause of a favorable response to the bombing halt to have accused the North of corruption while overlooking the equally endemic corruption in South Vietnam while praising the South for its military achievement. Nitze also recommended deleting the entire section near the end in which Johnson was going to "give you my best estimate" of the chances of peace and then would prophesy what peace in Southeast Asia would be like.

The time remaining before the speech was getting short, but McPherson was still hard at work. He produced Alternate Draft #4 on Saturday, March 30, at 4:00 p.m. Several changes tightened the argument as it had evolved across the Alternate Drafts. To begin with, McPherson removed the reference to reducing the level of hostilities through the unilateral bombing halt as a possible *alternative* to negotiations as a path to peace. This change recognized that *either* a reciprocal de-escalation by Hanoi *or* acceptance of an offer to negotiate would be an acceptable response to the bombing halt. In the draft, McPherson fuzzed the difference between the two, announcing, "We are prepared to move immediately toward peace through negotiations" and then following with "Tonight, I am taking the first step to de-escalate the conflict by substantially reducing the present level of hostilities."

Second, McPherson took out the specific reference to the 20th parallel as the northern limit of bombing, and replaced it with the vaguer statement that no attacks would be made on North Vietnam "except in the area north of the DeMilitarized Zone where the continuing enemy build-up directly threatens allied forward positions and where movements of troops and supplies are clearly related to that threat." This gave the United States some degree of flexibility about where to bomb, and it also removed disputes about whether some pilot inadvertently had crossed a particular line. McPherson emphasized, however, that attacks would stop on 90 percent of the population of North Vietnam and much of the territory, including the major populated areas and the food-producing areas.

Third, McPherson slightly revised the hint that the partial bombing halt could lead to a total one. He still said that restraint on Hanoi's part "could, of course, be an important factor in our decisions," but he omitted a reference to meeting the terms of the San Antonio formula.

Fourth, in discussing the budget and surtax, McPherson deleted the statement that the president would have preferred to raise the necessary revenue through taxes alone. Johnson was still conceding that some budget cuts would be politically necessary, but he was not explicitly marking it as a concession. Furthermore, this draft placed the onus for deciding on the specific cuts on Congress, having Johnson say, "As part of a program of fiscal restraint that includes the tax surcharge, I shall approve appropriate reductions in the January budget where and if Congress so decides." In other words, he would not be recommending specific cuts in advance. This may have been a shrewd move by McPherson, anticipating that Congress would have great difficulty identifying specific reductions because any particular cut would jeopardize the standing of some members in their own districts. Moreover, if Congress did come to agreement on specific cuts, Johnson would retain the prerogative to determine whether or not these cuts were "appropriate."

Finally, McPherson deleted from the text the quotation from President Kennedy's Inaugural Address committing the country to "pay any price, bear any burden . . ." No reason was given.

This draft did not include a peroration, although McPherson sent one over later on March 30. Similar to Alternate Draft #3, this one summarized the speech and prayed that North Vietnam would not reject the peace initiative, which Americans were asked to support. There was still no mention of Johnson not running for reelection. This is the other possible time at which Johnson may have told McPherson not to worry about a conclusion to the speech. This was about the time that Johnson called Horace Busby to the White House to work on what became the withdrawal statement, which would serve as the peroration.

McPherson was getting close. Clark Clifford returned his copy of the draft without comments. There still were suggestions from others, however. Mrs. Johnson proposed two small but significant changes (she may have been responding to Alternate Draft #3 rather than #4.) She changed "I profoundly hope that North Vietnam will respond favorably . . ." to "I call upon President Ho Chi Minh . . .," both converting a hope into a demand and making a particular person its object. On the sur-tax, she changed the passive "yet that action has not been taken" to "Up to now, Congress has taken no action," thereby naming an agent and fixing responsibility. Otherwise, Mrs. Johnson wrote "good" by paragraphs stressing the importance of the struggle in South Vietnam, the fear that American withdrawal could lead to a wider war later, and the statement that the president lamented the cost of the war but would do all he could to prevent an even more terrible war from spreading across Asia and the Pacific.[59]

Arthur Okun, chair of the Council of Economic Advisers, who had not commented on earlier drafts, suggested changes intended to emphasize the urgency of action on the surtax. After saying that the budget deficit jeopardized the post–World War II trade and payments system, he inserted a reference to the just-completed negotiations in Stockholm to create a new reserve asset so that the international monetary system would not depend solely on the US dollar. He then pointedly noted, "It is our special responsibility to insure the success of this historic agreement by correcting our deficit."[60] Prompt passage of the surtax would be the means to that end.

The other set of comments in the file was from Horace Busby, who recommended reinserting the Kennedy quotation—which was done—and substituting the "Busby close," on which he had been called in to the White House to work. Presumably McPherson and the others did not yet know what it was.

McPherson incorporated these various suggestions and produced Alternate Draft #5, the final copy of the speech. The Johnson Library includes both the teleprompter text (without the peroration, although the president put it on the teleprompter separately) and the reading copy that was in a binder on the president's desk. The Johnson Library also has a videotape of the speech as delivered. The authoritative text is in *Public Papers of the Presidents.*[61]

The structure of the final speech follows closely from the last of the Alternate Drafts. It opened with the statement, "Tonight I want to speak to you of peace in Vietnam and Southeast Asia," and then came a reminder of the San Antonio formula. Johnson said that "Hanoi denounced this offer, both privately and publicly," and he portrayed the Tet Offensive as their response. This attack "failed to achieve its principal objectives," but it did cause "widespread disruption and suffering." They might renew their attack at any time; if they did, they would not succeed. But they would cause further death and suffering—needlessly, because "we are prepared to move immediately toward peace through negotiations." As the first step toward de-escalation, he said, the United States would unilaterally halt the bombing of North Vietnam except in the area north of the Demilitarized Zone. If our restraint were matched by Hanoi, even this limited bombing could be brought to an end. Johnson called on the United Kingdom and the Soviet Union to help to move from unilateral de-escalation to genuine peace, repeated American willingness to send negotiators anywhere, identified Harriman and Thompson, and called on Ho Chi Minh to respond.

But, he went on, if peace did not come through negotiations, it would come when Hanoi realized that it could not prevail militarily. The president mentioned that 600,000 American and allied troops were assisting 700,000 South Vietnamese, reaffirmed that the South Vietnamese appropriately bore most of the burden of the fighting, and praised recent improvements in their military performance and in their efforts to build a durable government. He also said that the South Vietnamese realized that even more efforts would be necessary and that the United States would assist them with accelerated deliveries of equipment and with 13,500 support troops.

These actions, the president observed, would cost over $5 billion in the next two years and that, absent a tax bill or spending cuts, would produce a $20 billion deficit, which would jeopardize the international monetary system and the efforts just completed to reform it, as well as threatening prosperity at home. For these reasons, prompt action on the surtax was essential, along with expenditure reductions if Congress so chose. Then the president went into his "estimate of the chances of peace"—a section of the speech that more than once had been omitted and then reinserted. He included a warning that Hanoi "must not miscalculate the pressures within our democracy in this election year." He reaffirmed the pledge made at Manila for a reciprocal withdrawal of troops, related the goal of peace in Vietnam to the broader development of Southeast Asia, praised what had been achieved, and reiterated the pledge he had made at Johns Hopkins University in 1965 that the United States would contribute financially to the development of Southeast Asia, including North Vietnam.

Eventually, he said, peace would come to Vietnam, and a peaceful Asia was far nearer because of what the United States had done in Vietnam, helping to avoid a wider war. "Tonight," he said, he had offered "the first in what I hope will be a series of mutual moves toward peace." He prayed that it would not be rejected by the leaders of North Vietnam, and he asked Americans for their support.

Throughout an intense ten days of drafting and discussion, Johnson and his advisers had woven somewhat discordant elements into a coherent narrative, And then, noting the importance of national unity and the dangers of divisiveness, he moved into his peroration, which is considered in detail in Chapter 6.

While these efforts to design the speech were underway privately, Johnson said little publicly. When he did speak, his rhetoric was hawkish, and his remarks did not suggest that any major change was being considered. On March 30 he announced that he would reveal his Vietnam plan the next night in a television address. By coincidence, Republican candidate Richard Nixon was scheduled to speak about Vietnam on March 31; he promptly canceled his speech so as not to preempt the president.[62] During the day on March 31, Johnson spent most of his time with family and friends. He and Mrs. Johnson began the day by welcoming their daughter Lynda, who had returned from seeing her husband off to Vietnam. He met intermittently with Horace Busby, who—unbeknownst to most others—was working on the peroration. He went to church with his other daughter, Luci, her husband Pat Nugent, and Johnson aide Jim Jones. He also visited Vice President Humphrey at his apartment. Humphrey would be leaving for Mexico City that night and probably would be unable to see the speech on live television, so Johnson let him see the text, including the peroration that might be used.[63] Late in the afternoon, Johnson met with Rostow, Harriman, and Soviet ambassador Anatoly Dobrynin to preview the speech. From Rostow's notes, it appears that Johnson wanted to make clear to Ambassador Dobrynin that the United States was not going to withdraw from Vietnam. Only 5 percent of the people wanted that, he said.

Another 15 percent wanted de-escalation, but at least 40 percent wanted more aggressive American action. Balancing these competing pressures and protecting the doves from the hawks was the problem with which he must deal. He told the Soviet ambassador that, as president, he had gone 90 percent of the way to peace negotiations and he needed the Geneva Conference co-chairs (of which the Soviet Union was one) to go the last 10 percent of the way.[64] The president spent the early evening with friends, interspersed with brief periods with Horace Busby.

The speech began at 9:00 p.m. Eastern time and lasted forty minutes. Based on samples of viewership in twenty cities, NBC estimated that Johnson's live audience may have included as many as seventy-seven million people, quite possibly a record.[65] Among the military, it was the most watched address of the war.[66] State Department officials said they presumed that the Soviets would relay a copy of the speech to North Vietnam,[67] but there was no formal delivery from the Americans to the North Vietnamese, since there were no formal diplomatic channels.

New York Times commentator Jack Gould judged that Johnson's performance "will undoubtedly stand as one of his more successful tilts with the electronic camera." Gould noted that the president relied on the Teleprompter but also turned his manuscript pages "as a precaution. When he looked away from the camera," Gould reported, "it was to catch a glimpse of Mrs. Johnson, their daughter, and Secretary of Defense Clark Clifford," who were in the Oval Office with him. Gould referred to unnamed "long-time LBJ observers" who thought "the President's determination to get across what he believed transcended the nervousness that he had frequently displayed in the past."[68]

After the speech, the Johnsons and Clifford returned to the White House residence. An hour later, Assistant Press Secretary Tom Johnson escorted thirty-five reporters to the second floor of the White House for a press conference. They left forty-five minutes later; Secretary and Mrs. Clifford departed shortly after midnight; and the president retired at 1:00 a.m.[69]

Almost immediately, commentators noted aporias and ambiguities in the speech. *New York Times* reporter Hedrick Smith wrote in a story appearing the next day, "the President announced that he would try de-escalation. But he did not commit himself to pursue that strategy if rebuffed by North Vietnam, nor did he alter his terms for a political set-tlement." Johnson used "the conciliatory language of civilian advisers" but he "stopped short of adopting any new strategy at this time."[70] All that would remain to be seen.

4

The Bombing Halt

ALTHOUGH THE SPEECH structure was complex and several subjects were mentioned briefly, there were three major announcements: a partial bombing halt over most of North Vietnam, a limited increment of troops to be sent to South Vietnam, and the president's withdrawal from the 1968 election contest. Each merits consideration in some detail. Of the three, the bombing halt received the most sustained attention as Johnson's advisers reviewed the situation after Tet and tried to decide what to do next.

To understand why this was so, one must consider how bombing related to American war objectives. The primary goal of the war was not military conquest or self-defense against attack, but to prove a point: that wars of liberation fail. Although official discourse spoke of "aggression" being committed against the sovereign nation of South Vietnam, with analogies to the Korean War, the circumstances were different. South Vietnam was a provisional entity that was not supposed to last beyond Vietnamese elections in 1956—elections that the United States acted to prevent when it became clear that Ho Chi Minh would win. So strictly speaking, there was no outside aggression to be resisted. Rather, there was an indigenous uprising led by the Viet Cong against the South Vietnamese government, with the Viet Cong supported and encouraged by aid from North Vietnam and other communist governments. This was referred to as a war of liberation, conducted through subversion rather than outright aggression.

As Chapter 1 details, the United States took the major role in helping South Vietnam to defeat this insurgency following the fall of the

French at Dienbienphu in 1954. This assistance took the form of military aid and then the introduction of American "advisers" who seemed increasingly indistinguishable from combat troops. They aimed to resist subversion in the South. Although specific targets in North Vietnam were bombed in reprisal for the alleged attacks in the Gulf of Tonkin, in August of 1964, sustained bombing of North Vietnam (code-named Rolling Thunder) did not begin until the American barracks at Pleiku was attacked in February 1965.

For Johnson, bombing the North was a way to inflict additional pain in the hope that Ho Chi Minh would finally decide that continuing the war was not worth it. He would do so not primarily because of the damage the bombing caused—though that sometimes was considerable—but because of what the bombing symbolized: the depth of American intentions and resolve, and the fact that the United States keeps its word and honors its commitments. Doris Kearns wrote that, to Johnson, bombing was "a means of bargaining without words." This was consistent with the belief that limited war—the only kind that was feasible in the face of nuclear deterrence—was "essentially a means of tacit bargaining with the enemy," sending messages that we would be willing to go the distance if threatened and thereby to deter the threat.[1] Bombing was intended to increase the morale of the South Vietnamese, showing them that the United States would stand by them; to discourage the North Vietnamese from holding out against the United States, showing them the futility of such an effort; and to convince US allies that America kept its word.

Since bombing was valued primarily for the messages it symbolically conveyed, it stood to reason that decisions about halting or resuming the bombing also were taken primarily for the messages they would convey. While the North might take bombing halts as signs of weakness and lack of American persistence, the United States took them as signs of magnanimity and genuine commitment to peace, as well as a foretaste of what life might be like when the war came to an end. They were also able to convey to US allies and supporters that, if negotiations were not forthcoming, the onus was on the communists rather than on the Americans. In no meaningful sense were the American people an audience for all these messages. Rather, it was assumed that they agreed with and supported the president because it was essential that the country

speak with one voice, lest our message be misunderstood or our determination underestimated.

The most significant halt in the bombing lasted thirty-seven days, beginning with the Christmas season in 1965 and extending through the
end of January 1966. During this pause, Johnson sent envoys around
the world, responding to peace feelers and hoping to start negotiations.
The pause would also appeal to US allies who, in fact, had become increasingly disenchanted with the war. On the other hand, if the pause
failed to prompt negotiations—as one might reasonably have predicted—it would justify escalating the war. The United States would have
proved that it was not inherently warlike, but the "carrot" would not
have worked. Thus, the thing to do was to return to the "stick" and increase the pain. In his history of the war, Prados concludes that "the
diplomatic effort was the ploy and the deployment plan the president's
real business." He cites the Army's official historian of the Military Assistance Command, Vietnam, to the effect that Johnson fully expected
that the intense diplomatic effort would fail and that he intended the
pause mainly to prepare American public opinion for escalation.[2] That
way, the nation would continue to speak with one voice.

Ever since the Christmas 1965 bombing halt, Johnson had been skeptical of proposals for future halts, although there had been short pauses occasionally—to mark the Christmas and Tet holidays, for example.
But Bornet maintains that almost all of the seventy-two possible peace
overtures brought to the president's attention were perceived by their
initiators as having been met with "a chilly Johnsonian reception that
left them permanently estranged."[3] In part, his refusal to consider a new
pause was based on the fact that the communist forces had exploited
previous pauses to resupply the troops and improve their military position. In his memoirs, Johnson relates that he received memos in the
spring of 1967 from Walt Rostow, Robert McNamara, and Cyrus Vance,
and from the State Department, all recommending that he halt the
bombing of North Vietnam north of the 20th parallel. But, he says, he
was persuaded by quite different advice he received from General Westmoreland and the Joint Chiefs of Staff, and he reached the conclusion
that such a cutback in 1967 would have been "misunderstood in Hanoi
as a sign of weakness."[4]

In a speech in San Antonio, in September of 1967, the president offered a new proposal, mentioned earlier, which came to be known as the San Antonio formula: the United States would stop the bombing of North Vietnam if that would lead to peace negotiations and if the United States could be assured that Hanoi would not take advantage of the suspension to improve its military position. Hanoi rejected this formula, insisting on an unconditional American cessation of all bombing as a precondition for talks. It seemed that each side had stated its rock-bottom position and that there was no room for maneuver.

In light of his later position, it is worth noting that in November of 1967 Clark Clifford responded quite negatively when he was asked whether a bombing halt without a quid pro quo would be helpful. He said that North Vietnam would regard it as evidence of American fatigue and frustration, a confession of error, and a prelude to withdrawal.[5]

Even as late as February 1968, Dean Rusk sought to dampen what he regarded as false hope for peace talks, and a CIA analysis found it "most doubtful that Hanoi will be prepared for a serious move toward peace, except on its own terms, for the immediate future. . . . While Hanoi may continue to play public and diplomatic games to give the impression of a peace posture, it seems most unlikely that they would give us anything convincing on the 'no advantage' assumption in the San Antonio formula."[6]

Nevertheless, during the fall of 1967 references to the possibility of a bombing halt intensified. To many, it had become clear that bombing of the North had not stopped infiltration of the South; that is, it had not taught Hanoi the intended lesson. Meanwhile, it had become the focal point of opposition to Johnson's war policy, both in America and abroad. The reason for a pause, then, was less that it would lead to talks than that it would stop an activity that seemed to be hurting the United States more than North Vietnam. But Johnson was not yet convinced of this.[7]

On October 27, 1967, Johnson aide Harry McPherson submitted a memo to the president that floated the idea, gently, of a partial bombing halt. Noting that "a lot of Harry McPhersons out in private life—middle-road Democrats who've supported American foreign policy decisions since 1948 and who believe we have to stay in Vietnam for one reason or another" had serious qualms about the bombing program. "Indeed," McPherson wrote, "I think it is one of the main causes of disaffection with our Vietnam policy." He then identified nine specific criticisms, ranging from "It doesn't look as if it will get the North to the conference table or otherwise out of the South" to "It *may be* the greatest obstacle to talks" to "Obviously it rallies world opinion against us."[8] By attributing these criticisms to unnamed "a lot of Harry McPhersons," he softened their force, but it is fairly clear that they were his views, even though he began the memo by saying that he never would oppose the bombing openly because he did not know enough about it. He also gently admonished Johnson, "You are the Commander in Chief. If you think a policy is wrong, you should not follow it just to quiet the generals and admirals." Then he ended his memo with the suggestion that "we should give new consideration to bombing the area fifty or a hundred miles north of South Vietnam, and indefinitely postponing further bombing around Hanoi and Haphong [*sic*]." He did not think that would meet the North's demands for a total bombing halt, but he did believe that "we could recapture a good deal of the moderate support that we are now losing."[9] This appears to be the first document proposing a partial bombing halt as a way to split the difference between complete stoppage and continuation of the present policy. At this point, however, the president appeared to be more impressed with the contrary views of Westmoreland and the Joint Chiefs than was McPherson, who noted that "Generals and admirals like to bomb," and thought that they should not be trusted on matters of policy, as opposed to questions of tactics.

Little more than a week later, Johnson received a proposal from Defense Secretary Robert McNamara recommending a bombing halt and arguing against continuation of current policies. This was a write-up of views that McNamara had expressed the previous day at lunch. McNamara's cover note acknowledged that the memo expressed his personal views and that "these may be incompatible with your own."[10] McNamara recommended a total bombing halt, even though he could not be sure that it would elicit a response from Hanoi. At the very least, the defense secretary wrote, stopping the bombing would demonstrate that bombing was not an obstacle to peace, as the North Vietnamese maintained. The president indeed was not happy with this proposal.

Where McNamara had written that it was probable that Hanoi would respond by moving to talks, Johnson circled the word "probable" and wrote on the document, "How do we get this conclusion?" Where McNamara thought it a strong possibility that a bombing halt would be met by a stoppage of the enemy's military activity across the Demilitarized Zone, Johnson circled "strong possibility" and wrote, "Chapter & Verse—Why believe this." The only statement eliciting the comment, "I agree," from Johnson was McNamara's concession that, at least initially, Hanoi would be likely to use any talks for propaganda purposes rather than for serious negotiations.[11]

Nevertheless, President Johnson asked Walt Rostow to circulate the memo, without identifying its author, among a group of advisers including Secretary Rusk, Ambassador Ellsworth Bunker, General Westmoreland, Under Secretary of State Nicholas Katzenbach, Clark Clifford (then still a private citizen), Justice Abe Fortas, General Maxwell Taylor, McGeorge Bundy, and Rostow himself. While several of these men agreed with other parts of McNamara's memo, all objected to the bombing halt except for Rusk and Katzenbach. Rusk thought that bombing should be used as a bargaining card but that perhaps the United States should reduce attacks around Hanoi and Haiphong; Katzenbach favored "a qualified but indefinite halt in bombing."[12] Fortas and, interestingly, Clifford wrote especially sharp dissents, arguing that stopping the bombing would have the opposite effect from what McNamara had predicted.

Not coincidentally, shortly after receiving McNamara's memo, President Johnson announced that McNamara would be resigning as secretary of defense and moving to head up the World Bank. He was concerned that the secretary had "burned out" at the Pentagon and could not be trusted any longer to support the basic premises underlying the American presence in Vietnam. But the president continued to mull over the idea of a bombing halt. On December 16 he took the highly unusual step of writing a memorandum for the file outlining his views on McNamara's proposal. Johnson concluded that "under present circumstances, a unilateral and unrequited bombing stand-down would be read in both Hanoi and the United States as a sign of weakening will." He elaborated that it would "encourage the extreme doves; increase the pressure for withdrawal from those who argue 'bomb or get out'; decrease support from our most steady friends; and pick up support from only a small group of moderate doves." Importantly, he "would not, of course, rule out playing our bombing card under circumstances where there is reason for confidence that it would move us toward peace," but we should continue "our present policy unless hard evidence suggests such a change would be profitable."[13] When Johnson met with the Pope in December, he again said that a bombing pause would not be effective then, but that he "would not exclude the possibility that it may again appear wise at some point."[14]

That stopped discussion of a possible bombing halt but not for long. In anticipating a favorable military response to the anticipated winter–spring offensive, a group of advisers chaired by Katzenbach thought about the idea of a bombing pause once the offensive had been defeated. When Johnson sent General Wheeler to Vietnam in February to assess the situation after Tet, discussion of a bombing halt was put on hiatus. But it naturally reemerged when Wheeler returned, in the course of discussion of the Wheeler–Westmoreland recommendation to send 206,000 more troops to Vietnam. At a meeting on February 27, according to McPherson's notes, Rusk proposed that "we will stop bombing North of 20th parallel if NVN [North Vietnam] withdraws from Quang Tri province; or stop altogether in that event; or other specific proposal."[15] Here Rusk was still considering reciprocal actions. There was no pickup on Rusk's suggestion, and the meeting ended in what McPherson described as "prevailing uncertainty," with no proposals having been rejected out of hand.

Rusk tried again six days later, at a meeting to discuss the Clifford task force review of Westmoreland's manpower request. Well into that meeting, Paul Nitze urged that "we have to look at what we can do to get into negotiations. We must choose our own time" and should choose no later than May or June. Implicit in his remarks was the notion that, whenever the United States chose to enter into negotiations, it must stop the bombing, since that was the precondition consistently imposed by the North Vietnamese. In response to Nitze, Rusk said, "We could stop the bombing during the rainy period in the North." Immediately and probably instinctively, the president responded, telling Rusk, "Really 'get on your horses' on that."[16] Again, there was no further pickup in the meeting on this suggestion, but the interchange is significant. Both earlier and later, the president expressed his opposition to a unilateral bombing halt. In this brief exchange, however, he made clear that he was not as inflexible as he might have seemed. If not right at the moment, the upcoming spring rains might change the calculus so that a bombing halt would be worth the risk.

Meanwhile, in his summary of the group's ideas, Clifford made clear his skepticism about Westmoreland's troop request, But he was equally clear that "this is not the time to negotiate."[17] Interestingly, in early March Rusk's and Clifford's positions were just the opposite of what we often imagine them to be. Clifford, though highly dubious about sending large numbers of additional troops, was not yet ready to support stopping the bombing of North Vietnam. Rusk, often imagined to be a hard-liner, was the person showing the earliest flexibility on the topic of bombing of the North.

The next day (March 5), at the regular meeting of the Tuesday Lunch Group (Johnson's principal advisers on Vietnam), the president turned to Rusk and asked, "What about the suggestion of last night?" Rusk answered, "There is one idea which would throw additional responsibility on Hanoi," and then he read a proposal "that US bombing attacks on North Vietnam be limited to those areas which are integrally related with the battlefield. . . . Whether this stage can be a step toward peace is for Hanoi to determine. We shall watch the situation carefully."[18] Here was the idea McPherson had introduced the previous fall: a middle ground between the status quo and a complete bombing halt. What Rusk added, however, was the idea that the next step would be determined by how Hanoi responded to this one, so that the partial bombing halt had the effect of shifting the burden of proof to the North Vietnamese.

The next proposal for a bombing halt arrived on March 15 in a cable from United Nations Ambassador Arthur Goldberg, who proposed a complete halt of the bombing. Goldberg took at face value the North Vietnamese insistence that only a complete halt would satisfy them as a precondition for negotiations. He urged Johnson not to submit anything less and then say that North Vietnam had rejected the offer; no one would find such a stance credible.[19] Rostow passed along Goldberg's cable to the president, noting his own view that the time to consider a bombing halt would be in a few months, assuming that Westmoreland's

forces weathered the anticipated winter–spring offensive at Khe Sanh
"in tolerably good shape."[20] Hoopes contends that Johnson met with
Goldberg on March 16 and told him that he had heard every possible
argument and was not going to stop the bombing. Barrett also reports
that Johnson shouted in a rage that he would not stop the bombing.
There is no record of such an exchange in the files in the Johnson Library, however, and Barrett notes that "its anonymous and dubious
lineage is contradicted by some who talked to Johnson and, more importantly, by the rapidity with which the Goldberg plan became a focus
of analysis in subsequent days."[21]

Indeed, both the March 15 Goldberg proposal and the March 5 Rusk
proposal were discussed at the March 20 meeting of the president and
his principal advisers. The meeting notes show that McGeorge Bundy
supported Goldberg's plan, but it is unclear whether this meant that
Bundy supported the plan on the merits or was indicating only that
if there were to be a bombing halt, it should be complete rather than
partial. Clifford still demurred, however, believing that no overture to
Hanoi would be accepted at the time. Rusk also did not support the
Goldberg plan, preferring his own idea of a limited bombing halt.[22]
Johnson's own reaction, as recorded in his memoirs, was that "Goldberg
made a strong case for a total bombing halt, but not strong enough. I
could not take the risk of such a move at that time." He continued to
believe "that the North Vietnamese would interpret it as a clear sign of
weakness."[23]

March 20 was the point at which discussion of the bombing halt as a
policy became intertwined with drafting of the speech, as discussed in
the last chapter. Distilled, the first question was whether to announce
a bombing halt and a troop increase in the same speech. The original
decision was no, and an early attempt to insert a "peace" reference was
withdrawn. As successive drafts of the "war" version proved unsatisfactory, the decision was made to put the bombing halt back in. The version that went in was Rusk's March 5 proposal, which he reintroduced
on March 20. McPherson had become a convert to this approach, which
was similar to his own suggestion from the previous fall. By this time,
Clifford had also favored this proposal. Rusk remained where he had
been since early in the month.

The next issue was whether to specify the 20th parallel as the northern limit for bombing North Vietnam or to use more general and vague language; in the end, they opted for vagueness. Finally, some differences arose about how specifically to state that a favorable response by North Vietnam could lead to further concessions by the United States and South Vietnamese forces. Each of these key strategic decisions will be discussed in turn.

When Johnson concluded the March 20 meeting by saying, "Let's make it troops and war," he was not rejecting peace proposals. As we have seen, two weeks earlier he had instructed Rusk to "get on your horses" on a proposal to stop bombing during the rainy season. The president had traveled around the country delivering hawkish speeches on the war because he did not want to tip his hand that he was considering a change until he was ready to announce it. His comment on March 20 meant that he did not want to combine "war" and "peace" proposals in a single speech. Advisors who took that position thought that such a speech would be incoherent. But the contrary proposal was also advanced, and it was defended on political grounds: with the country divided between "hawks" and "doves," and with support for the "doves" growing in the aftermath of Tet, there must be something in the speech to appeal to them. Otherwise, in their disillusionment, they would abandon the administration altogether and call instead for a hasty withdrawal. Seeing that happen, Ho Chi Minh would conclude that he could wait out the growing American impatience until it led to American withdrawal. Far from Johnson finding the magic spot at which Ho's willingness to carry on would waver, Ho could make it impossible for Johnson to prevail either at the negotiating table or on the battlefield.

So a bombing halt proposal was added to the speech. But the advisers who urged against it were right: it made the speech incoherent. Nestled in the midst of an appeal for "troops and war," the bombing halt proposal would be dismissed as insincere. Johnson would be no better off, either with the doves or the North Vietnamese, than if he had left it out. This realization led Clifford to the view that the whole speech needed to be recast. It needed to be mainly a "peace" speech, not a "war" speech, he advised—although this distinction applied more to the overall framing of the speech than to its specific policy recommendations. This shift was embodied in the distinction between Alternate Draft #1 and the six drafts that preceded it.

Once the decision was made to feature a proposed bombing halt, two questions presented themselves: Should the bombing halt be complete, stopping *all* American bombing, or should it be partial, stopping only bombing in selected areas? And should the offer be conditioned on some sort of response or understanding by the North Vietnamese, or should it be made without preconditions?

Previous bombing halts had been unproductive, and if anything had been exploited by communist forces to build up their military strength. In turn, many Americans concluded that the communists viewed bombing halts as signs of US weakness. In retrospect, they were unsuccessful, in part because they were encumbered by conditions that the North had made clear it would not accept. Only a complete and unconditional halt of the bombing of the North could possibly lead to talks, but the Johnson administration vacillated about whether such a stoppage would be a sufficient condition for starting peace talks or only a necessary one. Ambassador Goldberg proposed a complete halt in order to test the hypothesis that such a move would lead to talks, and he reported several feelers to the effect that it would. But as Johnson noted in his memoirs, Goldberg's case was not strong enough. Goldberg had said that "the only thing that offers the possibility of talks is cessation of bombing." A month earlier, he had participated in a meeting in which United Nations Secretary General U Thant discussed a report from the French UN delegate that if the United States stopped the bombing, Hanoi would agree to open talks shortly thereafter.[24] But the president remained concerned that the North would view a halt as a sign of weakness and use it to intensify the fighting, putting American troops in danger. The troops were concentrated in the area immediately north of the Demilitarized Zone. Rusk had proposed on March 5 that this area, south of the 20th parallel, be excluded from a proposed bombing halt. He reiterated this idea on March 20 and endorsed Harry McPherson's proposal when it was developed on March 22.[25] While there was no way to be sure, Rusk had received feelers that continued bombing near the Demilitarized Zone, to protect American forces there and at Khe Sanh, would be tolerated if bombing on northern North Vietnam were ended.[26]

Rusk advanced his proposal out of concern "that this tumult in Congress and in the press continued to deprive Hanoi of any incentive to negotiate. The home front collapse would give them politically what they could not get militarily," and Rusk wanted to preempt that scenario by advancing a serious but practical effort to get to negotiations.[27] Limiting the halt to the area north of the 20th parallel, he thought, could achieve his goal. Schandler reports that Johnson, soured as he was by the failure of earlier bombing pauses and diplomatic initiatives, did not find the Rusk proposal attractive but that he went along with it because it was the only serious peace proposal on the table and because it came from Rusk, for whom the president had high regard. Johnson wrote in his memoirs that by March 23 he had decided in principle to "go ahead with the plan" proposed by Rusk.[28] But he did not tell anybody.[29]

In the process of drafting the speech, however, Johnson's advisers considered just how clear they should be about the geographic area encompassed by the bombing halt. For example, Alternate Draft #1 clearly identified the 20th parallel as the limit to which bombing would extend, and it explained that this was about 75 miles south of Hanoi and Haiphong, so that the major population centers of the North would be spared.[30] In Alternate Draft #3, McPherson retained the reference to the 20th parallel and added that 80 percent of the North Vietnamese population lived north of that line. He described where air attacks would continue: "They will be aimed at North Vietnamese artillery, supply lines, and forces which directly threaten the security of allied forces in the area south of the de-militarized zone."[31] By Alternate Draft #4, however, the specific reference to the 20th parallel had been deleted and replaced with a more general reference to "the area north of the DeMilitarized Zone where the continuing enemy build-up directly threatens allied forward positions and where movements of troops and supplies are clearly related to that threat."[32]

Why the change? Restricting the bombing to the region "just north of the demilitarized zone" was proposed by Kentucky Senator John Sherman Cooper, a Republican, in a speech in May 1967, and by Paul Warnke, assistant secretary of defense, in a memo to Deputy Secretary Paul Nitze in early March of 1968.[33] Perhaps engaging in wishful thinking, Warnke supposed that a bombing halt so described might be deemed to meet North Vietnam's demand for a complete bombing halt because the North had not previously included the Demilitarized Zone within the scope of its statements. But most observers, including President Johnson, credited the change in language to Under Secretary of State Nicholas Katzenbach, sitting in for Rusk at a meeting on March 30 to review the speech draft. Reportedly, Katzenbach believed that "the 20th parallel" would not mean anything to most people, and also that the specific reference would decrease American flexibility.[34] It also would create credibility problems in the event that an American plane inadvertently bombed slightly north of the 20th parallel. When, in conversations shortly after the speech, the president asked Katzenbach directly what the theory was in taking out the reference to the 20th parallel, the under secretary replied that he wanted to relate the pause "functionally rather than geographically."[35] In other words, he wanted to explain why certain areas were excluded from the bombing halt rather than simply to designate a seemingly arbitrary geographic line. This change was made largely with the domestic audience in mind, for, as Katzenbach indicated, foreign governments knew that the 20th parallel was the dividing line. Secretary Clifford made clear that Senator Fulbright (and hence, presumably, other members of the Foreign Relations Committee) knew that fact as well.[36]

Along with the question of the area to which the halt applied was the question of whether it should be conditional on any reciprocal action by the North Vietnamese. As noted above, the imposition of conditions had been the deal-breaker of previous efforts, up to and including the San Antonio formula. Rusk argued strongly against imposing any conditions and in favor of stopping the bombing unilaterally. As he put it, "It would be very important for us not to embroider the statement with all sorts of 'conditions' or 'assumptions.' Just take the action and see whether anybody is able to make anything out of it." He elaborated, "We would not send Ambassadors rushing all over the world to convert bombing action into negotiations but would just sit back and wait for Hanoi to respond."[37] Since Rusk had prepared a written document, Johnson realized that this was a serious proposal and that Rusk was not just "thinking out loud."[38]

In fact, Rusk was not particularly eager to push for negotiations right away. He thought that North Vietnam had no incentive to negotiate seriously, bolstered as it was by the psychological, if not military, damage it had inflicted on the United States. And if it *did* agree to start negotiations immediately, that could prove harmful to the efforts of the South Vietnamese government to rally the support of its own people.[39] Rather, in proposing a unilateral halt, Rusk was in effect changing the theory underlying the bombing halt proposals. Previously, they had been seen primarily as an inducement to get talks underway; the relief offered by a stoppage of bombing would entice the enemy to agree to negotiations that they might otherwise prefer to avoid. Rusk's approach regarded it as an *alternative* to negotiations as a means to de-escalate the war. His reasoning was that a unilateral American act of de-escalation would change the military context, presenting a new scene. This change would call forth a corresponding unilateral action by the North Vietnamese, since their previous stance would no longer be appropriate to the new scene. The two parties would engage in a series of reciprocal unilateral moves that might, in time, produce the same result as formal negotiations.

What Rusk was proposing, whether he knew it or not, was an application of the theory of graduated and reciprocated initiatives in tension reduction (GRIT) developed by the conflict theorist Charles Osgood.[40] His idea, developed in the context of the Cold War, was based on the norm of reciprocity, such that, when one side makes a concession, the other side should feel responsible for making one in return. The pattern of reciprocal concessions builds confidence between the disputants and can result in starting or restarting stalled negotiations. But it could also serve to promote peace even in the absence of negotiations. What Osgood theorized in 1962 was quite similar to ideas advanced in the 1940s by the literary and rhetorical critic Kenneth Burke. Burke discussed five key terms of analysis—scene, act, agent, agency, and purpose—and the various ratios that can be constructed from them. The scene-act ratio holds that "the scene contains the act,"[41] implying that a change in the scene brings forward a corresponding change in the acts deemed appropriate within the scene. According to this theory, the halt in American bombing would create a new scene, which should bring forward a new act on the part of the North Vietnamese.

Some of the commentary at the time reflects the application of these theories. *New York Times* reporter Hedrick Smith quoted "one well-placed Administration official" as saying, "I think there's going to be tremendous world pressure on Hanoi now to respond favorably in kind." And reporter John Hughes of the *Christian Science Monitor* wrote, "Confronted by President Johnson's dramatic new initiative to end the Vietnam war, the North Vietnamese leader must either turn back and away from his policy of adamancy and obduracy, or he must continue with his hard line and face consequences which might be awesome."[42]

From this standpoint, the bombing that was *not* halted on March 31 represented a potential "carrot" the United States could offer as a subsequent move, if a favorable response to the initial American move were forthcoming from Hanoi. In the Alternative Drafts, McPherson acknowledged that the remaining bombing could be eliminated if there were a favorable response to the partial bombing halt, and Johnson made such an offer explicit in his speech. Conversely, if Hanoi did *not* respond in a manner appropriate to the new scene—or, even worse, if it took advantage of the bombing halt by escalating the level of hostilities at Khe Sanh or elsewhere—then the United States justifiably could re-new the bombing.

The question of whether the unilateral bombing halt was a path to negotiations or an alternative to negotiations was left somewhat fuzzy in the speech, which mentioned the virtues of negotiations and then an-nounced that, "in the hope that this action will lead to early talks,. . . . I am taking the first step to de-escalate the conflict." Then, after announc-ing the bombing halt, he stated, "Our purpose in this action is to bring about a reduction in the level of violence that now exists." However, he did not make explicit whether the success of the bombing halt depend-ed on whether it led directly to negotiations.

This account of the evolution of the bombing halt gives great-er weight to Secretary Rusk's efforts than is generally conceded and, correspondingly, less weight to Secretary Clifford's influence. Clifford emerged at the end as a very strong influence on the content and tone of the March 31 speech. As Schandler summarizes, Clifford "was able to change the tone of the speech in order to make it conciliatory in nature, de-escalatory in emphasis, and easier for North Vietnam to ac-cept as a basis for talks," whereas for Rusk and Rostow, "the language in which [the bombing halt] was couched seemed to be less import-ant."[43] But a postpresidency memo from Rostow to Johnson, review-ing the history of the bombing halt proposal, concluded that Clifford opposed the peace initiative on March 4, that he insisted on reciprocity such as North Vietnamese stoppage of firing artillery and rockets from the DMZ at the meeting on March 20, and that only on March 28 had he moved to the position that Rusk had occupied four weeks earlier.[44] Similarly, Schandler quotes McPherson, who at the time was strongly influenced by Clifford, as having said later that "Clifford spoke in a way that didn't seem to set us on a clear course, but at the same time doubted the course we were on."[45]

But Clifford's role was more subtle. He was engaged in an "A to Z" review of Vietnam policy in his first weeks as secretary of defense, and he had come to the conclusion that a major reorientation was needed. Although he had testified in January at his confirmation hearing that he "would not favor cessation of the bombing under present circumstances,"[46] as a result of his review, he had changed his mind and now believed that a complete halt was necessary. But he was not ready to say so. He initially opposed the Rusk plan not because he opposed a bombing halt but because the Rusk plan did not go far enough. Schandler suggests that Clifford thought the Rusk proposal "was not conciliatory and would not lead to negotiations." He thought it would be used instead to justify new escalation of the war when, as expected, North Vietnam would reject the offer. He finally was persuaded to accept Rusk's approach, according to this view, "because he was convinced that it was as far as the president would go."[47] In his memoirs, Clifford accounts for his shifting views by saying that, while he favored a complete bombing halt, "it was clear that the President was not ready to approve a position that was opposed by Rusk, Bunker, Rostow, and the entire military leadership." Under these circumstances, there was no gain for Clifford in revealing his true convictions. So, instead, he "decided to 'lock' Dean Rusk into support for a limited bombing halt for the time being" and then work on the tone of the speech, while also encouraging Goldberg and others to advocate a complete bombing halt as a counterweight to Rostow and the hard-liners.[48] Like any memoirist, Clifford wrote with the advantage of 20–20 hindsight. But regardless of Clifford's role, the significance of Rusk's advocacy should not be underemphasized. His stature and his past record as a "hawk," no less than Clifford's, led President Johnson to take his views very seriously.

There were practical problems with the Rusk proposal for a limited bombing halt; chief among them was that it was not expected to work. The advisers present for the March 20 meeting all recognized that it did not meet the North Vietnamese demand for total cessation of bombing as a precondition for talks.[49] Like President Johnson, however, most believed that a complete halt would endanger American troops in the vicinity of the Demilitarized Zone and at Khe Sanh. So they decided to give a partial halt a try. Besides, even if the offer did not lead anywhere, the act of making it would produce benefits for the United States. For one thing, it would prove American bona fides. Writing in his memoirs, McPherson said of the proposal, "I did not expect it to produce negotiations, but I thought it would show the American people, and people in other nations, that we were truly seeking them."[50] Placating domestic opposition to the war was especially prominent in the thinking of Johnson's advisers. Rusk's March 5 proposal "explicitly stated that the purpose of a limited bombing cutback was to offset growing public opposition to the war," while acknowledging the possibility of a favorable North Vietnamese response. William P. Bundy recalled that quieting domestic dissent was the primary focus of discussion of a bombing halt.[51] Similarly, a partial halt could influence world opinion in a positive way. In the March 20 discussion, Rostow noted that a bombing halt would have a more positive impact on world opinion than troop increases in South Vietnam, which affected opinion adversely. (Not completely convinced, the president retorted, "Standing down bombing gets the hawks furious.") *Christian Science Monitor* correspondent Joseph C. Harsch noted that the bombing of North Vietnam was "the one tactic used in the Vietnam war which has most alienated outside opinion."[52]

Some participants in the discussions, as well as some later writers, saw the prospect of appealing to domestic public opinion more cynically. In the Defense Department, Paul Warnke favored a complete bombing halt and believed that the terms of the San Antonio formula had been fulfilled, thereby justifying it. But the Rusk proposal, in contrast, "was merely a gesture designed to rally American and world opinion." His fear was that it might indeed regain domestic political support for the president but fail to bring North Vietnam to negotiations. Such a result would "spoil the opportunity for other peace initiatives for a long time in the future" and also "increase hawkish pressure on the president to resume the bombing."[53] What Warnke saw as a fear, others viewed as an opportunity. The *Jackson Citizen Patriot* (quoted approvingly in the *Chicago Tribune*) noted, "If the gamble fails, as it probably will, the war situation should be clarified in the public mind. The doves will have been proved wrong." Similarly, *New York Times* reporter Hedrick Smith wrote, "if North Vietnam were to spurn the President's concilia-tory gesture . . . the President would then be free to appeal for popular support for stepping up attacks against North Vietnam."[54] Even Ambas-sador Ellsworth Bunker was "informed that most likely Hanoi would denounce the project and, then, free our hand after a short period." This prediction was suggested as an inducement for Johnson to offer Thieu and Ky of South Vietnam in order to obtain their quick concurrence with the bombing halt proposal.[55]

Compounding the cynicism some saw in the bombing halt propos-al, while bolstering others who saw its symbolic value in responding to domestic public opinion, was the widely held judgment that bombing over the next four weeks or so—the anticipated length of an unrequited pause—could not take place anyway to any significant degree because of the weather. When Rusk introduced his proposal in early March, he argued, as Herring notes, "that it would cost nothing militarily since the weather would prevent heavy bombing anyway." When Johnson inter-rupted the discussion and told Rusk to "really 'get on your horses' on that," he was responding to Rusk's suggestion that "we could stop the bombing during the rainy period in the North."[56] In fact, when the State Department cabled American diplomats in Asia with portions of the March 31 speech, the cable explained that weather conditions over the next four weeks were likely to curtail opportunities for bombing north of the 20th parallel in any event, and concluded, "Hence, we are not giv-ing up anything really serious in this time frame."[57]

But there was another way to look at the question of whether stop-ping the bombing really was giving anything up. It could be argued that the bombing itself was not accomplishing anything militarily, so stop-ping it would not harm the military position of the United States. Such an argument would follow naturally from the observation at the outset of this chapter, that bombing was undertaken in the first place not so much for military as for rhetorical reasons. A paper in the Defense De-partment concluded, "It has become abundantly clear that no level of

bombing can prevent the North Vietnamese from supplying the necessary forces and materiel necessary to maintain their military operations
in the South." The paper cited forecasts from the Central Intelligence
Agency that even an intensified bombing campaign, "even . . . a protracted bombing campaign directed at population centers . . ." would
fail "to break the will of the North Vietnamese leaders."[58] In the March
20 meeting, McGeorge Bundy noted that bombing around Hanoi and
Haiphong did not do much, prompting Johnson to interject that "it sure
enrages the world."[59] If bombing had produced insignificant military
results, then giving it up would sacrifice little of military value. After the
March 31 speech, reporters for the *Christian Science Monitor* observed
that bombing the North "has worked so badly that few here think its
ending will bring a substantial quid pro quo from the Communists."[60]
Of course, the absence of such a quid pro quo could reinforce the belief
of American hawks that the president's gesture toward peace was futile
and that escalation therefore was in order.

To be sure, not everyone agreed that the bombing halt had been in-
effectual. Among those who doubted this premise would be the opponents of a bombing halt, especially within the military and the South
Vietnamese government. Reports in the *Chicago Tribune* indicated that
most of the military commanders in the war zone as well as the Joint
Chiefs of Staff had been opposed to a halt; the Joint Chiefs subsequently
announced their support for Johnson's decision, but this is not unlike
an employee "saying yes when the boss has spoken."[61] *New York Times*
reporter Hedrick Smith indicated that, asked to comment on the president's bombing halt, his source replied, "Yes, I have a comment. It's no
comment."[62] And a *Wall Street Journal* writer supposed that Johnson's
decision to continue the bombing in the area north of the Demilitarized Zone was made in deference to his military advisers, who were
even more strongly opposed to a complete bombing halt.[63] One could
cite Hanoi's seizing of the offensive at Tet as evidence that the North
Vietnamese, not the Americans, were in a position to negotiate from
strength. On this view, the Americans should not be offering bombing
halts but should be building military strength.

In the March 20 meeting, Supreme Court Justice Abe Fortas indicated his opposition to a bombing halt, saying that it would be seen
as a sign of weakness and that the McCarthy and Kennedy campaigns

would view it as an admission of error on Johnson's part. Ambassador Bunker was also opposed.[64] There was concern that a bombing halt could destabilize the South Vietnamese government. Thieu and Ky were informed of the halt only shortly before the delivery of the March 31 speech, and Rusk's cable to Bunker suggested talking points to use with Thieu in order to reduce the significance of the president's announcement. Bunker should tell Thieu, Rusk advised, that (1) a troop increase was being announced in the same speech, so it was not unabashedly a "peace" speech, (2) Hanoi was likely to denounce the offer of a bombing halt, thereby freeing our hand, (3) Hanoi might feel constrained from offensive acts in the northern areas anyway, (4) the weather would limit bombing north of the 20th parallel anyway, and (5) a full bombing halt was unlikely.[65] Moreover, if and when the war moved to the conference table, South Vietnam would have a major role to play in the talks.[66] These were face-saving arguments designed to bring along a reluctant but necessary ally; they hardly represented full-throated defenses of the bombing halt.

Weighing all the various considerations, President Johnson decided to implement a unilateral, but partial, bombing halt. He probably reached that decision within a few days of the March 20 meeting. The meeting of the Wise Men on March 26 must have convinced him that a move in the direction of peace was necessary; this conviction probably resolved any lingering doubts. Barrett believes that the accumulation of antibombing sentiment from a variety of sources, rather than any one adviser's views, changed Johnson's mind. He discussed the bombing halt proposal with Senate Majority Leader Mike Mansfield on March 27, received Alternate Draft #1 on March 28, and without announcing a change in his stance, called McPherson to discuss changes he wanted to make "on page 3."[67]

But Johnson's decision to halt the bombing was not meant to be seen as a major change in policy. As Schandler observes, "bombing pauses had been used before to test Hanoi's willingness to negotiate." It had been anticipated that the president would undertake a new initiative after the winter–spring offensive was over, but the improvement in the military situation in Vietnam and the deterioration of the political situation at home made it necessary to accelerate the timetable. In Herring's view, the bombing halt proposal "would neutralize the doves without inciting the hawks. It was the sort of compromise, halfway measure that had appealed to him from the start of the war, the 'lesser of evils.'"[68] And yet, Johnson undertook this initiative "apparently in the expectation that Hanoi would reject" the overture for negotiations. In reflecting on the proposal two days after offering it, Johnson thought, "This pause is only going to aggravate the hawks and won't please the doves."[69]

Yet the bombing halt proposal had significant consequences. President Johnson met with Soviet Ambassador Anatoly Dobrynin to emphasize his seriousness. His selection of Averell Harriman and Llewellyn Thompson (the latter the US ambassador to the USSR) indicated his seriousness and his hope that the Soviet Union, as one of the co-chairs of the 1954 Geneva negotiations, would play an active role in getting talks underway. But the immediate Soviet response was not encouraging, repeating that Johnson's offer failed to fulfill the conditions Hanoi had established for beginning negotiations and therefore could not be taken seriously. For good measure, a Radio Moscow broadcast added the view that the president's alleged withdrawal from the race for reelection appeared to be a "pre-election maneuver."[70]

A writer for the *Christian Science Monitor* speculated that, when he made the March 31 speech, Johnson must have known that there was a good chance for a favorable response by Hanoi.[71] The record, however, does not bear out this speculation. It is not even clear that the government in Hanoi even had a copy of the speech in advance. In the text, Johnson specifically stated, "I cannot promise that the initiative that I have announced tonight will be completely successful in achieving peace any more than the 30 others that we have undertaken and agreed to in recent years," and there is no reason to think that the president was dissembling here. David K. Willis, in the *Christian Science Monitor*, reported that unnamed sources "say they 'would not bet' on Hanoi responding affirmatively. Government officials had no advance word of a favorable response. In fact, just what Hanoi's response would be remained something of a guessing game. Eastern European diplomats predicted that North Vietnam would not peremptorily reject the president's proposal "but would seek a clarification of the United States' position on the bombing halt." Ambassador Bunker hypothesized that the North Vietnamese would take the unilateral bombing reduction "as an indication of the success of the Tet offensive and of their diplomatic and propaganda campaign around the world" and would think that South Vietnam had been shaken and the American resolve weakened, even more than they had imagined. Bunker went on to predict that "Hanoi would not take any real step toward peace, but their leaders would seek to give a world-wide impression that they were doing precisely this."[72]

Contrary to most expectations, however, North Vietnam on April 3 did respond favorably—or at least its response could have been interpreted as favorable—to the president's proposal. As Vandiver describes it, that morning the president was playing with his grandson and entertaining Democratic Senator Henry Jackson and his wife when Assistant Press Secretary Tom Johnson burst into the Oval Office with a piece of ticker tape: "A bulletin from Singapore said, in effect, that Hanoi was ready to talk." Vandiver added that a long statement followed, "filled with expected rhetoric but stating its willingness to meet."[73] The response from Hanoi did not mention the March 31 speech specifically but seemed clearly to have been influenced by it. Senator Fulbright, who initially had deemed the bombing halt of "no consequence" because it was not complete, now apologized and said that Johnson's move on March 31 was the "significant development" leading to Hanoi's favorable response, and he offered the president "full credit" for the resulting surprise.[74]

Clifford pointed out that this was "the first time Hanoi had offered to meet with us on any basis at all," and used that fact to justify the "enormous worldwide excitement" the North Vietnamese response received.[75] But just what was the "expected rhetoric" to which Vandiver referred? North Vietnam did not accept the "assumption" of the San Antonio formula and never mentioned President Johnson's March 31 speech. It agreed to discuss only how to end the bombing completely so that its long-standing preconditions would be met. Secretary Rusk, not willing to regard Hanoi's overture as a move toward peace, took a wait-and-see attitude toward that matter.[76] The long delays in determining a site for the talks and deciding on the shape of the table provided additional reasons for doubt. Analysis in the *Wall Street Journal* was similarly pessimistic, noting that Hanoi's statement "is of no large significance . . . it means precisely what it says and nothing more. . . . Even if Hanoi is willing to meet, it may not be willing to bargain." And Frank Giles of the *Times* (London) pointed out that "for all the bright hopes and talk about lights at the end of tunnels, there is at the moment nothing approaching a firm promise that a peace settlement is close at hand."[77]

While warnings against overoptimism are always wise, in fact the statement from Hanoi *was* significant. As Katzenbach explained at a meeting on April 3, "This is further than Hanoi has ever gone. Treat it as a willingness to get together." Clifford added, "The offer of Sunday night was a first step. It seems clear this is their first step."[78] Clifford was on to something, Just as the United States had found in the partial bombing halt a middle ground between sustained bombing and a complete halt, North Vietnam had found a middle ground between demanding a complete cessation of bombing as a prerequisite for *any* talks and abandoning that requirement altogether. If they were willing to talk about how to get a complete cessation, that meant that they were willing to talk about *something* without preconditions. In the small spaces that each side opened up, there was the opportunity for talks to begin. And once they got underway, who knew where they might lead?

Such was the enthusiasm that suffused both domestic and international reaction to the Hanoi message of April 3. Washington's Senator Henry Jackson, who, as noted, was at the White House when the president learned the news, understated significantly when he told reporters that Johnson was "very interested." Senators Mike Mansfield, George Smathers, George Aiken (a moderate Republican who the previous year had said we should "declare victory and get out),'" and House Speaker John McCormack all responded very positively. Even House Minority Leader Gerald R. Ford said that "all Americans should unite behind President Johnson . . . the peace initiative currently under way is a bipartisan peace initiative." Ford added, however, that it was based on a plan for gradual de-escalation put forward the previous year by Republican Representative F. Bradford Morse of Massachusetts.[79] Peace movement leaders were described as "guardedly pleased by President Johnson's peace offer, but generally skeptical that it would lead to a settlement in Vietnam,[80] especially when combined with the commitment of additional troops, which also was announced in the March 31 speech (see Chapter 5). The governments of Great Britain and Australia issued statements supporting de-escalation of the war, while the foreign ministers of the seven allied nations fighting in Vietnam released a statement saying that any peace settlement must guarantee democracy and security for South Vietnam. This statement was probably in response to fears among Asian allies that American determination to persevere in the fight was weakening.[81] Interestingly, this concern presupposed, just as did some of the enthusiastic domestic statements, that a peace breakthrough was a reasonable expectation.

Any judgment about the bombing halt must take note of its ambiguity. As Schandler notes, "No conditions were placed upon the bombing pause, and indeed, it was not designated as a pause but rather as a "stopping." Neither was any specific duration mentioned, and the speech contained no threat and listed no conditions under which "bombing would be resumed. The president did not discuss what would happen if negotiations failed. . . ."[82] Johnson had not avoided these topics because he wanted to keep them secret; rather, it appeared that he had not thought the matters through. He seized on the bombing halt as a way to placate the doves so as not to ignore a growing and vocal segment of public opinion. Where it might lead, he was not sure. He saw his move as tactical and did not rule out the possibility that he would resume the bombing, although he did not say so in the speech. What converted Johnson's tentative statement into a firmer one was the reframing efforts undertaken by Clifford, who "interpreted the bombing halt as permanent, even though LBJ did not" and later reminded colleagues that it was the American bombing halt that brought Hanoi to the table, implying that a resumption of bombing would irreparably damage the negotiations.[83]

But yet, after all, the bombing continued. It was halted in the area the president mentioned in his speech. Some were surprised to discover that the area where the bombing continued extended quite a bit north of the Demilitarized Zone—as much as 200 miles north, all the way to the 20th parallel, just as Johnson intended but did not say explicitly in the speech. North of that line the bombing did stop, but south of it— and in South Vietnam and Laos—it continued and indeed intensified. The bombing, as Hoopes put it, "was not really curtailed, but only geographically rearranged."[84] Moïse accuses the president of having "falsely stated in his speech that he was 'reducing—substantially reducing— the present levels of hostilities'" when, in fact, he simply refocused the American bombing campaign—an *expanding* bombing campaign" that hit other areas more heavily than before.[85] When one remembers that the coming rainy season probably would have forced a reduction of the bombing in northern North Vietnam anyway, one would be forgiven for marveling at how limited was the opening to North Vietnam or the overture to the doves in the United States.

Yet, except for the occasional comment about the rainy season or the opinion that a halt above the 20th parallel would pose no military risk, there is no evidence that anyone involved in this decision treated it disingenuously. The president did not do so when he retreated from his instructions to make the speech all about "troops and war." Rusk did not do so when he put forward a proposal that he doubted that North Vietnam would accept but thought just might break through the impasse blocking negotiations. Certainly, Clifford and McPherson did not do so when they moved to make the bid for talks to end the war the central feature of the speech. Fortas did not do so when he argued vigorously against a bombing halt, sure that it would be seen as a sign of weakness. The Joint Chiefs, who came aboard probably with some reluctance, did not believe they were yielding to an empty gesture. In fact, Gardner writes, by yielding to the bombing halt the hawks "gained ground in setting the terms for negotiations, which were designed to prevent the fall of the South Vietnamese government during the short term" and the Joint Chiefs proposed terms "that could be imposed only as a victor's peace."[86]

The bombing halt was a response to real factors in the situation, which Schandler summarizes as "the apparent military effectiveness of the bombing," "the growing public disillusionment with the bombing," which seemed to symbolize the ineffectiveness of the American war effort, and "the desire to seek a negotiated end to the war" as an alternative to what increasingly seemed to be a stalemate.[87] The response to these factors was largely symbolic, just as the bombing itself had been largely symbolic—a way to convey a message. If the message of the bombing was to convince North Vietnam that wars of liberation fail while reassuring South Vietnam and other allies of the fidelity of American commitments, the message of the bombing halt was that the United States was genuinely committed to pursue peaceful alternatives as well. If this message found an audience on this occasion, when it had not done so in the past, that is probably because of the psychological effect of the Tet Offensive on the American people, combined with the sincerity bestowed on the proposals by President Johnson's simultaneous announcement that he would not run for reelection.

Yet President Johnson was characteristically reluctant to reveal his hand. In an article in the *New York Times* on March 31, anticipating that night's speech, reporter Max Frankel noted that the president "would not comment on speculation that he might order another halt in the bombing of North Vietnam. He said his offer to halt the bombing if Hanoi pledged not to take advantage of the halt [the San Antonio formula] still stood. But he had seen no indication of Hanoi's interest, he added."[88]

5

The Troop Commitment

IF ANYTHING SEEMED perfectly clear in the March 31 speech, it was that President Johnson was escalating the war by sending an additional 13,500 troops to Vietnam, adding to monthly draft calls and worsening the nation's balance-of-payments problem. To those whose frame of reference is the high-technology, low-manpower conflicts since the 1991 Gulf War, it strains credulity to imagine the 1968 action as anything other than a major escalation. In fact, however, many at the time regarded it as an act of de-escalation rather than escalation; as significant because the number was so small rather than so large; as capping rather than expanding the number of troops; as complementary to rather than inconsistent with the bombing halt. To unravel this curious paradox, it is necessary to pursue the "back story" behind the troop commitment as well as the process by which it was incorporated into the March 31 speech.

The story begins with President Johnson himself. In December of 1967, he had written a memorandum for the file stating that he was unconvinced of the value of a bombing halt at that time, but also that he saw no need for an increase in the number of US troops beyond the 525,000 that had already been authorized.[1] That number had not yet been reached, but additional troops were being phased in and the authorized number would be reached later in 1968 or 1969. But in the aftermath of Tet, the president questioned his own judgment. Anticipating the need for a major commitment of troops to Khe Sanh and the possibility of other enemy offensives, Johnson rather than Generals Westmoreland and Wheeler was the first to raise the question of whether more troops were needed. In a press conference on February 2, asked whether the Tet Offensive would lead to a major new commitment of troops, Johnson replied that the phase-up would continue until the previously authorized level of 525,000 was reached, but that he saw no need for "any great new overall moves." Privately, however, he was asking a different question. In a meeting with his senior foreign policy advisers on February 11, he asked departing Defense Secretary Robert McNamara about the possible need for more troops. McNamara felt secure with the current number and added the observation that General Westmoreland had not asked for any more, suggesting that there was no cause for alarm. The president then asked, "But when they [ARVN, Army of the Republic of Vietnam] are unable to do the job and when we are in a fight to the finish, then don't you think we should give the troops as they are necessary?" Despite the tone of his question, Johnson was not necessarily advocating more troops. He often asked probing questions in order to elicit the views of his advisers. In this case, McNamara stuck to his position that no additional troops were required and added that, if necessary, troops operating elsewhere in Vietnam could be redeployed.[2]

It was deemed advisable to ask Westmoreland whether he needed more troops. The specific context of the request was possible action at Khe Sanh, not the formulation of a new general strategy after Tet. General Wheeler, chair of the Joint Chiefs of Staff, raised the issue with Westmoreland and mentioned that he would be coming out to Saigon to discuss it further.[3] Westmoreland's first response to Wheeler generally has been interpreted, perhaps mistakenly, as saying that while he could use additional troops, he really did not need them and had no fear of imminent defeat if they were not forthcoming. Assistant Press Secretary Tom Johnson's notes from February 11 report that the general consensus was that Westmoreland did not need more troops and was not asking for them.[4] Wheeler wrote back to Westmoreland that he could not promise that reinforcements would be provided even if Westmoreland asked for them, a response that Moïse regards as a strong signal that Johnson was not disposed to send them.[5]

Wheeler's visit to Saigon resulted in a significantly different message from Westmoreland. First, even before Wheeler arrived, Westmoreland asked to accelerate the schedule for deploying the already promised troops to reach the authorized level of 525,000. Noting that they would not be scheduled to arrive until 1969, he wrote, "I need these 525,000 troops now. . . . Time is of the essence." Moïse believes that Westmoreland thought that Wheeler's message was inviting, even urging, him to seek reinforcements.[6]

During the conversation with Wheeler, Westmoreland described a proposal for 40,000 additional troops. Wheeler reportedly said that, in light of depleted military reserves at home and tensions with North Korea over its capture of the *Pueblo*, he did not believe that the president could spare that many additional troops without a general call-up of the reserves. If that Rubicon were crossed, he added, the country would experience the same political fallout over 40,000 reserves as over a much larger number. So he and Westmoreland might as well think in larger terms and request a substantially larger troop increment.[7] After all, both generals thought that the Tet Offensive was only the beginning of a year-long offensive and that the United States, despite its military success at Tet, needed a substantially augmented force level in order to be ready for any contingency.

On February 12, the senior foreign policy advisers met again. By this time, Westmoreland's second cable—coached by Wheeler—urgently requesting more troops had arrived. There was some discussion about why he had "changed his mind" from the earlier cable. Clark Clifford, nominated to be defense secretary but not yet in office, persistently questioned Wheeler. Among his questions, Clifford asked, "General Westmoreland's telegram has a much greater sense of urgency in it. Why is that?" and Wheeler replied, "General Westmoreland realized that his earlier low-key approach was not proper based on a full assessment of the situation." Wheeler attributed to Westmoreland the altered perspective that he himself had urged on the commanding general when he visited him in Saigon. He said, "General Westmoreland has been conservative in his troop requests in the past. Now he finds that his campain [*sic*] plan has been pre-empted by enemy action."[8] The change Wheeler attributed to the North Vietnamese, prompting the need for a major increase in US troops, was that "the enemy has been on a protracted fighting basis. Now he seeks to 'grab' for immediate success." He amplified, "There is a new determination for major attacks coupled with the

TET actions. Prior to now, the enemy the enemy [*sic*] has fought a peace [*sic*] meal war."[9] It is important to note that the changed perspective that led Westmoreland to submit a second troop request was based on Wheeler's speculation about what the North Vietnamese were going to do following the Tet Offensive. There was no change on the ground justifying the difference between the two Westmoreland submissions, and no intelligence was entered into the record to support the speculation about what the North Vietnamese would do in the future. The closest to that was a statement by CIA Director Richard Helms, prompted by the president. Asked, "Dick, how do you feel about all of this?" Helms said, "I have been meeting this morning with twelve of my top CIA people who have been in Vietnam. They believe the war is in a critical phase. They think Westmoreland should get the troops if he needs them." Although "if he needs them" could be read as a hedging phrase, there is no reason to think that Helms intended it that way. He clearly believed that Westmoreland *did* need the additional troops.

Even more strongly convinced was General Maxwell Taylor, who alone among the participants had interpreted Westmoreland's *first* request as alarming. Now he said, "In my view, this is an urgent situation." After saying that Westmoreland seemed to think he had the necessary time to open blocked roads and take other defensive measures, Taylor emphasized, "I do not. This [anticipated enemy] offensive could open up today. We should assume in our planning that it will open up tonight."[10]

President Johnson, probably like the others in the room, understood the difference between Westmoreland's two communications not as evidence that Wheeler had put his thumb on the scales while in Saigon, but rather as evidence of how rapidly the military situation had changed. He told the group of senior advisers, "I hope all of you see what has happened during the last two weeks. Westy said he *could* use troops one day last week. Today he comes with an urgent request for them." Expanding on the theme that the situation could continue to change rapidly, the president added, "I want to anticipate that more will happen to us than we had planned. . . . Frankly, I am scared about Khesanh. . . . I have a mighty big stake in this. I am more unsure every day." He then asked, "Do all of you feel that we should send troops?"

McNamara, Rusk, Helms, Wheeler, Taylor, and Rostow each individually answered, "Yes." The president asked, "Is there any objection?" and
the meeting notes record, "There was no objection."[11]

Before the meeting broke up, President Johnson directed General
Wheeler and Secretary McNamara to figure out what units of reserves
should be called up to meet Westmoreland's request. "Let's not decide on that today," the president said. "Go back and agree on what
to call." Wheeler left the room so that he could "call now and get my
men drafting the order," but McNamara finally registered his dissent:
"My position on Vietnam is very clear. I do not think it wise to go to
the Congress asking for additional legislation. I do not think the call
up is necessary." Johnson dismissed this dissent with "Well, if you can
not agree with the Joint Chiefs on what is needed, then submit to me a
minority viewpoint and your separate recommendations."[12]

In short, the outcome of this crucial meeting on February 12 was
to approve Westmoreland's request for a large infusion of American
troops in Vietnam, based on Wheeler's assertions about how the situation on the ground had drastically changed after Tet and the anticipation of additional major communist offensives in the coming weeks and
months. The precise number of additional troops Westmoreland would
need had not yet been determined, but the assumption was that meeting his request would require calling up units of the reserves.

Ironically, one of the factors leading to this set of conclusions was
the timing. Previously, when Westmoreland had requested additional
troops, Defense Secretary McNamara often traveled to Vietnam to review the general's recommendation with him before it became public.
McNamara would whittle down Westmoreland's request to a number
that he thought would be politically acceptable and present *this* number
to the president, who would then accept this reduced number, claiming that he had provided Westmoreland with "whatever he needs." This
time, however, McNamara was in his final weeks in office, and his successor, Clark Clifford, had not yet been sworn in, so it was not appropriate for either of them to make the trip. That left only General Wheeler,
who had made several trips to Vietnam but was not well versed in the
political or diplomatic dimensions of troop requests, and his visit produced what Hoopes calls an "undiluted military judgment." Schandler
points out that the issue with previous requests was how many troops

could be provided *without* calling up the reserves, whereas now the possibility of a reserve callup was the very point at issue.[13]

Westmoreland followed Wheeler's advice to "think big" and to plan not only for the immediate needs in Southeast Asia but also for a longer-term strategic reserve. Accordingly, he and Wheeler developed a plan for "nationwide attacks on Vietcong and [North Vietnamese army] units and supply bases in the South; accelerated bombing of the North, including the port of Haiphong; cutting the Ho Chi Minh Trail in Cambodia and Laos; and launching an amphibious hook across the DMZ." This range of actions would give the lie to the notion that Vietnam was a limited war. As Woods concludes, "Such a strategy would require many more troops and would lead to a general call-up of reserves. Either the administration would mobilize the nation for war or it would not."[14] As we have seen, the decision makers initially were disposed to grant the troop request, if not to launch all these preemptive moves, then in order to defend against anticipated new enemy offensives. Before long, however, the magnitude of the troop request would backfire and lead the president and his advisers in a very different direction.

One might wonder what Wheeler's motivation was for encouraging Westmoreland to submit a request of such large magnitude, especially after seeming to claim initially that he did not need any more troops. The references to a call-up of the reserves may provide the answer. Wheeler and the Joint Chiefs had been urging Johnson to call-up the reserves, placing the country on a more substantial war footing. Reservists presumably were better trained and made better soldiers than draftees, so calling up the reserves would "harden the war effort," as Vandiver puts it. According to this theory, Wheeler had, in Karnow's phrasing, taken advantage of the situation created by the Tet Offensive in order "to coax Westmoreland" into submitting a very large troop request, which in turn would allow the Joint Chiefs to convince Johnson to mobilize the reserves.[15] This would explain why Wheeler initiated the troop request from his office in Washington even before arriving in Saigon, presumably to size up the situation.[16]

But just as consistently, Johnson had declined previous requests to call-up the reserves. He did so, in part, because putting the country on a war footing was precisely what he did *not* want to do. He probably could have persuaded Congress to go along, but he feared—with reason—that

Congress next would move to cut his valued Great Society programs on the grounds that they were luxuries the country could not afford when it was mobilized for war. Besides, calling up the reserves would bring the reality of the war into the families of a number of members of Congress and their leading supporters who had sons in the reserves. That, in turn, predictably would swell the growing ranks of antiwar advocates and create additional political problems for the president, who, as far as the Joint Chiefs and anyone else knew, was gearing up to run for reelection.

So, the theory goes, Wheeler (and probably Westmoreland) thought he had found a way to pressure Johnson to do what he did not want to do: to call-up significant numbers of reserves, with all the positive and negative consequences of taking that step. Wheeler, in Schandler's terms, "emphasized the dire nature of the situation in South Vietnam" and "put the worst possible case forward as though it represented the current situation in South Vietnam."[17] And while the *New York Times* reported on February 29 that "officials stressed that any proposal by General Wheeler for reinforcements would be tentative and would not constitute a formal request for a specific number of men,"[18] in fact Wheeler on February 27 had submitted a very specific proposal: to bring the total number of US forces in Vietnam to 731,756 by the end of 1968. The proposal called for an increase of 206,000 over the level currently scheduled and an increase of 225,000 over the number actually in Vietnam. Wheeler met with President Johnson and others on February 28 and painted an even more dire picture. Johnson asked what the alternatives to such a large increase were, and Wheeler replied that the United States would need to abandon the two northernmost provinces of South Vietnam. The Joint Chiefs supported Wheeler, stating "that only a huge expansion of the American force in Vietnam could turn the situation around."[19] These dire warnings came after the unquestioned military success in repelling the Tet Offensive.

Although many expected Johnson to approve something like the Wheeler–Westmoreland request, an alternate hypothesis advanced by Robert Buzzanco is that "the generals knew perfectly well that Johnson would neither send large reinforcements nor mobilize the reserves but that they made those requests so that when things later went badly in Vietnam, they would be able to blame Johnson for not having given Westmoreland the troops he needed."[20] This view has the aura of 20–20 hindsight. Given the uncertainties of the situation after Tet, it seems more plausible to assume that the troop request would have been granted, or at least approximated, than it was to have assumed that the request would have been turned down. Later, Wheeler and Westmoreland insisted that their requests were not formal requests at all, but "merely contingency plans developed to meet the various uncertainties that loomed ahead." Westmoreland described the request as "a contingency plan based on the assumption of a decision," a plan he thought would remain secret until Johnson reached an a priori decision about the force level he wanted. He called it a "prudent planning exercise designed to generate the military capability to exercise tactical and strategic options if permitted by a reappraisal of national policy." Wheeler tried to put the onus on Westmoreland for authoring the request, and Westmoreland "sharply rebuked Wheeler" for this act of dissembling.[21]

Since the existence of the troop request was not yet public knowledge, neither was the administration's response. In fact, despite the discussion at the meeting of February 12 recounted above, which took place before the magnitude of the troop request was known, President Johnson at no time seriously considered accepting the Wheeler–Westmoreland request, directing at once that a search be undertaken to find alternatives to it. But that is getting ahead of the story.

Consideration of the requested troop increase included arguments for and against the proposal. Perhaps the most prominent argument in its behalf, as noted above, was that it was needed to counter a change in strategy on the part of the North Vietnamese forces. The evidence for that strategy change apparently was the Tet Offensive itself. Seemingly fighting a struggle of attrition, and arguably on their last legs according to much of the American publicity, communist forces had succeeded in coming in from the rural areas to the cities, launching simultaneous attacks across South Vietnam and enjoying dramatic, if temporary, military success. Such a surprising result must be evidence of strategic change by the enemy. One could project that new approach forward and imagine a range of major strategic challenges that the United States had to be prepared in advance to meet because by the time they presented themselves, it would be too late. An ominous warning was a late March announcement by the CIA that since November 1, 1967, some 35,000 to 40,000 North Vietnamese army soldiers had been infiltrated into South Vietnam, where they were poised to do significant damage.[22] The alleged change in enemy strategy called for additional US troops, it was argued, both "to pursue the enemy's defeated units so they don't have time to recover" and "to exploit enemy weaknesses uncovered as a result of his unsuccessful [Tet] offensive."[23] What these weaknesses were was left unspecified.

Closely related was the argument that Westmoreland needed more troops in order to rebuild his strategic reserve, units that could be deployed quickly and flexibly wherever the need arose. The strategic reserve had been badly depleted by the need to commit forces to the area around Khe Sanh and by the need to move units back into cities and towns in order to protect the population in the aftermath of Tet.[24] Both of these moves left American forces inadequately prepared to respond quickly to unexpected attacks elsewhere, should they materialize.

A less defensive argumentative move was to suggest that additional forces would enable Americans to seize the moment and possibly exploit the enemy's weakness. Ambassador Bunker offered this recommendation, as did National Security Adviser Walt Rostow. Rostow concurred with Westmoreland's request for more troops and argued, "If enemy actions reflect his desperation, these additive forces can assist in delivery of a decisive blow." Rostow did not specify how this would be done. Hedging his bets, he added that if he were wrong and the enemy strength had been underestimated, additional forces would be needed "even more."[25] President Johnson characterized the argument in his memoirs, although he did not support it, by saying, "With forces of that size, Westmoreland believed he could not only resist anything the enemy attempted but could move quickly to the offensive and take advantage of heavy Communist losses suffered during the first weeks of the Tet offensive."[26] It is notable that all these articulations were at a high level of generality and did not explain how the addition of substantial numbers of American troops would bring about the predicted results.

Finally, it was argued that committing large numbers of new troops would capture public support. Walt Rostow, at the end of a memorandum in which he frankly acknowledged the difficulties in meeting the Wheeler–Westmoreland request and conceding that he was not an expert on public opinion, nevertheless predicted that support for a troop increase would be forthcoming. His reasoning was that the public was on balance hawkish but frustrated by the fact that the war was at an impasse and yet desiring to do something about that situation. Rostow also thought that public opinion would follow military results and that approving the troop increase would enhance the prospects for these results. He wrote, "If the war goes well, the American people are with us. If the war goes badly, they are against us. The only way for us to answer this is for the military situation out there to come out alright [*sic*]."[27] In a paper on "US Public Opinion," presumably drafted by William P. Bundy, one finds a similar argument: There would be support, at least initially, for a troop increase because the public is hawkish but frustrated. Otherwise, the call to "win or get out" would intensify, people would be willing to "wash our hands of the whole matter," and the public would "more and more question the capacity of an Administration which is unable to achieve a victory."[28] This description of American public opinion probably was accurate as recently as six months previously, but by March of 1968, with attitudes in such flux, one no longer could be so sure. Interestingly, both Rostow and Bundy relied on their intuitive sense of American public opinion rather than offering empirical support for their claims.

The arguments advanced against the troop increase were more numerous and elaborated. This may have been because Johnson, from the moment he received the Wheeler recommendation, instructed his aides to search for alternatives to it. It may have been because previous escalations, though in much smaller increments, generally had been frustrating. It may have been because both the outgoing and incoming secretaries of defense, Robert McNamara and Clark Clifford, were strongly opposed. Arguments ranged from the belief that more troops were not needed to the prediction that they would not be effective, to the concern that they would introduce worse problems, to the proposal of alternate solutions, and to the concern that adding more troops would be inconsistent with the expectations and frames of reference that had been established by the military success in defeating the Tet Offensive. These attacks on the proposal spoke to almost all the *topoi* or "stock issues" that arise in discussing policy proposals.

Even Westmoreland, back in the fall of 1967, had maintained that 525,000 troops would be enough. He told the Joint Chiefs, "For the first time I will have enough troops to really start grinding them [the enemy] down."[29] Of course, he believed that Tet had completely changed the situation, but, as noted, Clifford had countered by saying that forces elsewhere in Vietnam could be redeployed to areas of need. Probably more potent, though, were arguments questioning the effectiveness of supplying more troops. A *Wall Street Journal* article referred generally to the fears of "many military men" that Westmoreland could be supplied with any large number of troops fast enough to affect the military balance. More specifically, a draft paper in early March, probably prepared by the Public Affairs Office of the Defense Department, maintained that committing 205,000 additional troops "would not significantly improve our military operations, would only add to the already heavy human and economic costs of our efforts and would in fact make less likely the accomplishment of our objective in Vietnam."[30] One reason this was so was articulated by Henry Cabot Lodge, former ambassador to South Vietnam, who wrote that military action on the ground would not get to the heart of the guerrilla leadership. Therefore, Lodge recommended sending more troops "in numbers sufficient *only* to enable us to keep faith with our troops in exposed positions, as in the northern end of South Viet-Nam."[31]

Others noted the futility of assuming that the United States could add troops unmatched by those of North Vietnam and thereby gain superiority on the ground. *Newsweek* was hardly alone in judging that "the major cause of the present US military dilemma in Vietnam has been the administration's continuing faith in the efficacy of escalation. But each time we have escalated, North Vietnam has matched it, and they appear likely to continue to be able to do so for the foreseeable future."[32] Civilians in the Pentagon expressed the fear that an increase in American troops "will bring a matching increase by North Vietnam, thereby raising the level of violence without giving the allies the upper hand." On March 4, Clifford, referring to Westmoreland's proposal, reported to the president, "There is no assurance that this very substantial additional deployment would leave us a year from today in any different military position" because communist forces would match it and the fighting would continue, just at a higher level. Most specific was a CIA analysis suggesting that communist losses during the Tet Offensive could be made up within six months, and that if the United States put in an additional 200,000 troops, the People's Army of North Vietnam could infiltrate an equal number within no more than ten months.[33] This line of argument, of course, directly countered supporters' claim that a major escalation would overcome the sense of frustration born of military stalemate. Based on past experience and CIA analysis, it seemed at least as likely that escalation would re-create frustration at a higher level. As Berman put it, "The reinforcements would bring the total American military commitment in ground forces to three-quarters of a million—yet the United States would be no closer to victory than in 1965 at the outset of the Americanization of the war."[34] This would be the same condition Walter Cronkite famously described on his CBS News program on February 27: stalemate.

Furthermore, critics suggested that the proposed escalation would embolden North Vietnam while weakening the South. Zbigniew Brzezinski wrote that the message sent to Hanoi by an increased US military presence was "our impatience and our desire to get the war over with. Hence it reinforces Hanoi's will to continue as long as we are not able to defeat its forces." He went on to state that the absence of American victory then becomes not a stalemate but an American defeat, because we permit it to be defined that way. And concerning the South, *New York Times* reporter Max Frankel referred to "ever louder criticism that American troops are supplanting the South Vietnamese Army and making the war wholly their own."[35] The criticism was that there was no incentive for South Vietnam to put up a strong defense if it knew that the United States would shoulder the burden, and that North Vietnam could be free to engage in a struggle of wills, knowing at the outset that the American will was limited and weak.,

Gardner also cited Rusk and Clifford to the effect that enlarging the troop commitment to Vietnam would weaken our commitments to NATO because there were not enough troops to go around.[36] Moreover, concentrating such a large force in Vietnam would leave the United States unprepared to cope with a contingency that might develop simultaneously somewhere else in the world. "The Case Against Further Significant Increases in US Forces in Vietnam," dated March 3, which was unsigned but probably prepared in the Defense Department, cited that fear as well as the prospect of the United States being unable "to maintain in Europe a level of military preparedness sufficient to deter Soviet adventurism." While ultimately supporting the troop commitment, Rostow noted that a reservation "goes deep in State and Defense" that a disproportionate commitment to Vietnam would jeopardize America's strategic interests elsewhere in the world.[37] Then there were criticisms growing out of the likelihood that any increased troop commitment would be unilateral because allies of the United States would decline to participate.[38] Unconvinced by the underlying American rationale, European and Asian nations nominally supportive in Vietnam would be unwilling to raise their own ante.

Supporters of the troop commitment thought that it would catalyze US public opinion in their favor, but critics believed just the opposite. Phil Goulding, assistant secretary of defense for public affairs, was especially vocal on this point. In a nuanced analysis, he suggested that "mobilization/deployment" would hurt public opinion, whether it was accompanied by intensified bombing or even by a bombing pause. In the former case, it would isolate doves but antagonize some moderate supporters; in the latter, it would alienate hard-liners and divide the doves, who would welcome a bombing pause but still oppose mobilization. In fact, Goulding concluded, the only course that would be acceptable from the standpoint of public opinion would be *both* to deny Westmoreland and Wheeler's request for more troops *and* to undertake new peace initiatives. Otherwise, as Hoopes characterizes Goulding's view, "the shock wave would run through the entire American body politic."[39] This was quite different from the Rostow prediction that, by relieving the frustration of the hawks, an intensified troop commitment would capture the support of the American people. Of the two predictions, Goulding's was the more detailed and nuanced, based on analysis of individual segments of the public. Rostow's took the form of general impressions that easily could be regarded as wishful thinking.

The proposed increase was designed to deal with certain specific situations, primarily the need to keep a large force to defend Khe Sanh, which had been under intermittent siege since the week before the Tet Offensive. If the siege had intensified, the risk was that Khe Sanh could become the American Dienbienphu. Wheeler had proposed the troop increase, in part, so that Westmoreland could deploy troops elsewhere as needed while still keeping Khe Sanh protected. But there was an obvious alternative, noted by no less a military figure than Maxwell Taylor (who generally supported the deployment): "My review of Westy's cables does not convince me of the military importance of maintaining Khe Sanh at the present time if it still is possible to withdraw. Whatever the past value of the position, it is a positive liability now."[40] The value of Khe Sanh was symbolic: that it *not* become America's Dienbienphu, portending withdrawal or loss of the war. This value was especially important when decision makers had thought that Khe Sanh would be the site of the major communist attack in 1968, with Tet only a sideshow rather than the other way around. What made Khe Sanh into a liability was that the enemy could keep American troops tied down indefinitely to respond to a siege that never was undertaken in earnest, rendering those troops unavailable for possible use elsewhere. As it happened, General Creighton Abrams, who succeeded Westmoreland in June 1968 as commander of American forces in Vietnam, shut down the US base at Khe Sanh on July 5 after a siege that had lasted seventy-seven days but generally was inconclusive.

As suggested above, acceding to the request for the troop increase would have required a large-scale call-up of the reserves. Arguably, this was Wheeler's objective and the reason he encouraged Westmoreland to request such a large increment. Rostow advised the president to respond positively to the suggestion to call-up the reserves, believing that it would reassure allies nervous about the posture of the United States since Tet had shaken public opinion at home and abroad, and since the South Vietnamese government was "teetering on the brink of insolvency." Eisenhower and Maxwell Taylor, Berman reports, also supported calling up the reserves.[41] But there were serious concerns specifically related to the prospect of calling up the reserves. McGeorge Bundy thought there was no military case for calling them up and that doing so would thwart what he regarded as the widespread public desire to have the Vietnamese take over more of the fighting. He concluded a letter to the president acerbically, "I hate to see my President held to ransom by military men, and their Congressional friends, who really do not know what to do with the troops they are asking for."[42] In meetings with his senior foreign policy advisers, Johnson asked Defense Secretary McNamara whether he favored sending the 82nd Airborne to Vietnam if Westmoreland were to request it. McNamara replied in the negative because "We are carrying too much of the war there now. All this would do is to shift more of the burden on us." Johnson noted that, for his part, he would be reluctant to send the 82nd Airborne because it might be needed to deal with civil disorders in the United States.[43] After the four "long, hot summers" that had wracked the United States over issues of race, this was not an unreasonable or unjustified fear.

Calling up the reserves also entailed major political problems. On several previous occasions, the Joint Chiefs had proposed it and Johnson had resisted, mindful of these difficulties. He wanted to minimize the war's impact on the civilian population, particularly so that his domestic programs would not be threatened, yet this might well be the price that Congress would extract in return for agreeing to partial or full mobilization. Clifford noted that "without strong support from the Hill, a large callup of the Reserves was impossible, and without this, a large troop increase would be virtually impossible."[44] There was also a class consideration, which Melvin Small addressed frankly: "as the war went on, the reserves were becoming more and more a haven from the draft for middle- and upper-middle-class college graduates," whose parents' political activities "carried far more weight than those of disproportionately blue-collar parents of draftees." He concluded, "The more unpopular and endless the war became, the more college students swarmed into the reserves, the less likely it was any president would take the political risk of calling them up."[45] Yet without calling up the reserves, there was no practical way to significantly increase the number of troops in Vietnam. So, arguing against the reserves call-up served as a powerful proxy for arguing against the troop increase itself.

Last, there was what may have been the most obvious of reason for opposing the troop increase: on the face of it, it was incompatible with the frame of reference created by the understanding that the Tet Offensive had been a military failure for the communists. Even with whatever nuance was supplied, it did not make sense. One does not celebrate the defeat of forces far stronger and more coordinated than one had expected, and then in the face of that great success decide that it is necessary to increase one's own army by 50 percent in order to stave off stalemate or defeat. In the terms used in the last chapter, that is an inappropriate scene–act ratio. The scene had been changed by the fact of the Tet Offensive and its utter military failure (at least as the Americans understood it), and the new scene called for an act quite other than what would have been the largest single escalation in the history of the war.

Almost immediately upon receipt of Westmoreland's formal request, Clifford, after proposing for the sake of argument that the US add 500,000 troops to Vietnam, took issue with the proposed 206,000 increase, which he said would create widespread problems with US and world public opinion: "Problem is, how do we gain support for major program, defense and economic, if we have told people things are going well?"[46] Clifford added that, while the people widely regarded the Tet Offensive as an American disaster and could reconcile a big troop increase with that point of view, Johnson and his military advisers maintained consistently that the communist forces had suffered an overwhelming setback. In that case, why did we need so many additional troops? Clifford persistently raised this question in meetings throughout February. In one case, Johnson improvised an answer. The problem, argued the president, was that Tet showed that the enemy had changed tactics and was going for broke. This rationale, bereft of any supporting evidence, appeared in many of the justifications for making reinforcements.[47] At one point, McGeorge Bundy tried to explain why he thought the public had turned so strongly against a large increase. "This is not because our people are quitters," he explained, "and [Eugene] McCarthy and [Robert] Kennedy did not create the shift. . . . What has happened is that a great many people—even very determined and loyal people—have begun to think that Vietnam really is a bottomless pit."[48] McNamara's last official act as secretary of defense was to oppose the troop increase request "on economic, political, and moral grounds."[49] Clifford took the same position, and there is no indication that Johnson ever favored the troop increase either. The Wheeler–Westmoreland request would be turned down, and the apparent strategy behind it—to put the president in a position where he had no alternative to calling up the reserves— had backfired. But what to do instead?

That question was argued in a second series of deliberations at the White House. Unlike the first round, right after the Tet Offensive, these were not characterized by a disposition to give Westmoreland whatever he needed. Rather, once he had said what he thought he needed, the advisers were more likely to be skeptical, question assumptions, and search for alternatives.

Westmoreland's request was considered at a breakfast meeting on February 28, after which Johnson charged a task force chaired by

Clifford to "develop by Monday morning, March 4, recommendations in response to the situation presented to us by General Wheeler and his preliminary proposals. I wish alternatives examined and, if possible, agreed recommendations to emerge which reconcile the military, diplomatic, economic, Congressional, and public opinion problems involved."[50] Two things are notable about these instructions. First, from the beginning the president characterized the proposed troop increase not as a formal request, which it was meant to be, but as a "preliminary" proposal. This would give Johnson the space to reject the proposal while claiming that he gave Westmoreland what he needed. Later, after the request became public, a *New York Times* reporter noted that the White House regarded the troop proposal "as a preliminary request and not a formal recommendation. . . . Such requests apparently become formal recommendations only after the President has told General Westmoreland how many troops he can have."[51] One can easily detect the circularity here. Johnson tells Westmoreland how many troops he can have, provides that number of troops, and then announces that he has met the general's needs, as if the general had determined the number in the first place rather than merely opened the discussion. The second notable feature of the charge to the Clifford task force is that Johnson did not charge the group to figure out how to meet even a trimmed-down Westmoreland request but rather to examine alternatives to it,

Both of these features were departures from what might have been anticipated by anyone who was paying attention. As recently as February 22, the president had told a press conference, "Over recent weeks I have been in close touch with General Westmoreland, and in recent days in very close touch with all of our Joint Chiefs of Staff to make sure that every single thing that General Westmoreland believed that he needed at the time was available to him."[52] In the earlier deliberations (before the full magnitude of the proposal was known), Johnson's recollection was that Rusk, McNamara, Clifford, Wheeler, Maxwell Taylor, CIA Director Richard Helms, and Rostow all favored meeting the general's request.[53]

At the February 28 meeting, Johnson asked Wheeler what would happen if his request were not approved, and the general claimed that refusing it would mean the loss of the two northernmost provinces of South Vietnam.[54] But Johnson had doubts from the beginning, and he realized that he was constrained by public expectations. He admonished, "We have to be careful about statements like Westmoreland's when he came back and said that he saw 'light at the end of the tunnel,'" conveniently forgetting that it was Johnson himself who had brought Westmoreland back for the specific purpose of helping to convince the public that things were going well in Vietnam and success was imminent."[55]

The Clifford task force reported on March 4. It did not explicitly endorse or reject the request but noted that meeting it would require increasing the total strength of the armed forces by approximately 511,000 men over little more than a year, which could be done by a combination of calling up more than 250,000 reservists, increasing draft calls, and extending terms of service.[56] Questioning by Clifford during the March 4 meeting made clear that even this large increment was not linked to any overall strategy that offered a reasonable prospect, much less assurance, of victory. The group recommended that there should be a modest increase of forces (Walt Rostow had penciled in the number 30,000) to take care of immediate needs over the next three months, but that "there should be a fresh review of our strategy in Viet Nam" before committing forces beyond that.[57]

Although he earlier had suggested maybe adding 500,000 troops, Clifford by March 4 was a confirmed skeptic that a major force increase would make a significant difference. He had dissented from earlier recommended troop increases, a fact Johnson was aware of when he appointed Clifford as secretary of defense. Although Clifford had a reputation as a hawk, it is not likely that his doubts about a troop increase struck Johnson by surprise.[58] Besides, Dean Rusk also did not regard Westmoreland's request as urgent, believing that the US already had enough troops to prevent a communist takeover of South Vietnam.[59]

According to his memoirs, on March 8 Johnson decided against approving anything like 206,000 more troops, claiming that his decision was influenced by the doubts Clifford and others raised in the meeting of March 4.[60] By the middle of March, it had become clearer that an intensified, sustained siege at Khe Sanh was unlikely and that American forces in South Vietnam could be deployed more flexibly. But Johnson did not announce any formal decision. He had Wheeler ascertain whether Westmoreland could live with a much smaller troop increase. On March 15, Johnson again postponed making a final decision. He

wanted to consult with the Treasury secretary about the financial impli-
cations. He also noted that Westmoreland planned a major offensive in
April to relieve Khe Sanh and figured that if the general was confident
enough to do that with his existing forces, he might not need a large
increment of troops.[61] Also on March 15, Johnson heard from Secretary
of State Dean Acheson, a well-known hawk, that he was being misled by
the briefers from the Joint Chiefs of Staff about the need for additional
troops.[62]

If not the full 206,000, there was general agreement among those engaged in the deliberations that *some* increase of forces was needed to
meet short-term contingencies. The question was how many. As noted
above, Rostow had penciled in the number 30,000. Wheeler also recommended that number from the limited options given to them. Johnson asked if any specific request from Westmoreland could justify that
number but was told that the lowest increment that Westmoreland had
mentioned was 90,000. Johnson decided on March 13 to deploy 13,000
more troops. But the next day, the secretary of the army countered that
30,000 would not be enough to meet emerging needs. Besides, he noted,
there was an immediate need for 13,500 troops to support the 10,500
additional combat troops that had been sent to Westmoreland in February. Those 10,500 had been part of the 525,000 previously authorized
to be sent, but the 13,500 would be an add-on to that number. So the
proposal for 30,000 more troops was abandoned, and discussion focused on the 13,500 support troops.[63] The combat troops had been sent
in the immediate aftermath of Tet to reinforce defensive lines and in
anticipation of another possible assault on Vietnamese cities, but the
support troops in the war zone and those to replenish the infantry reserves that would match those 10,500 troops had not yet been sent.[64]

By March 22, Johnson had settled on sending 13,500 support troops
to Vietnam and adding 48,500 to the ready reserve in the United States,
for a total of 62,000. Some of the early drafts of the speech used this
number, and some also added the recently sent combat troops. Early on
in the drafting process, however, a decision apparently was made to refer
only to the number of additional troops actually to be sent to Vietnam,
and subsequent drafts referred only to the number 13,500 and their
function as support troops. This also avoided confusion about whether
the earlier 10,500 had been included in the previous total of 525,000

or whether they were new. Depending on how one counted, the total number of troops authorized went from 525,000 to about 549,500—a number that would be approached in early 1969 but not actually met. There was no explicit mention of this number as a ceiling on US troop commitments, and the possibility of meeting Westmoreland's larger request was formally left open for later review. But there certainly was no promise, or even likelihood, that they would be granted, and the new figure sometimes was referred to as a cap.[65]

On March 24, Wheeler finally told Westmoreland that he would not be receiving the big increase that he had requested. In that case, said Westmoreland, he could get by with the 13,500 that had been proposed.[66] This, then, became the general's formal request, enabling the president to say that Westmoreland had been given everything he had requested. The denied request for 206,000 troops was recast as only a preliminary proposal. But reviewing this chain of events also helps to make clear how the addition of 13,500 troops could be considered a move to de-escalate the war, by not being the much larger increment that had been widely expected.

The reason it was widely expected has to do with the fact that the 206,000 request had become public knowledge. Although the Clifford task force review and subsequent deliberations were intended to be private, the New York Times leaked the story on Sunday, March 10. The source of the leak was unknown, but the suspects included civilians in the Defense Department's public affairs office, who had played a major role in convincing Clifford to oppose the views of the Joint Chiefs.[67] Westmoreland later said that when he read the story in the New York Times, he did not remember what the 206,000 figure referred to, and then he realized "that this was the plan that was put in the context of General Wheeler's request." He added, "In any case, I never considered the plan developed by General Wheeler and me to be a demand per se for the deployment of additional forces or an 'emergency' request for battlefield reinforcements. Rather, I considered it a prudent planning exercise."[68] Nevertheless, Time indicated in early March that "[a]ll the signs indicate that Johnson is once more going through the process of preparing the nation for news of a major notch-up in the war." Johnson noted in his memoirs that throughout March, "rumors of a large-scale increase in our troop commitment spread on the Hill and generated additional criticism." Johnson was particularly perturbed because he already had decided against the troop increase but felt that he could not say so for fear of making a seemingly political statement at the time of the New Hampshire primary.[69]

The leaked story stimulated fears of higher balance-of-payments deficits and aggravated pressures on gold, to be discussed shortly. It also stimulated congressional demands for prior consultation, lest the president usurp the congressional power to declare war. Even before the story leaked, Senate Foreign Relations Committee Chair J. William Fulbright led the critics demanding that Congress be consulted before additional troops were sent to war. A bipartisan group of twenty-two House members introduced a sense-of-the-Congress resolution opposing the dispatch of any more troops to South Vietnam, and another group of seventeen demanded, as a precondition for deployment, a proposal that the explicit consent by Congress and a clear justification by Johnson would be essential. The president commented on the Senate debate only to state falsely that he had received no recommendations about future troop levels. Dean Rusk, previously scheduled to testify on foreign aid before the Senate Foreign Relations Committee on March 12, conceded that Johnson would consult with Congress about sending additional troops to Vietnam, but pointedly did not promise that the consultation would take place in advance.[70]

The announcement of the troop increase in the March 31 speech was subdued. The bombing halt received top billing. Success on the battlefield was presented as an alternative to success in negotiations, but that section featured praise for the growing strength of the South Vietnamese army and the sacrifices made by the South Vietnamese. Johnson described the additional aid that the United States would provide to South Vietnam. Then, in the fiftieth paragraph—nearly halfway through the speech—he made reference to the recently deployed additional 11,000 combat troops, adding that "the artillery, tank, aircraft, medical, and other units that were needed to work with and to support these infantry troops in combat could not accompany them by air on that short notice." The fifty-first paragraph contained the recommendation of the Joint Chiefs of Staff that the support troops be sent immediately, some 13,500 men, and the fifty-second paragraph stated that some of these would come from the active reserve and some "from reserve component units which will be called up for service." That is all the mention that the troop increase received in the speech. The brevity and placement of this announcement clearly were designed to minimize its significance. Schandler writes that it "seemed almost a footnote to the dramatic statements that had preceded it."[71] Johnson never even said explicitly that he was adopting the recommendation of the Joint Chiefs and ordering the additional troops to Vietnam, although that is implicit in his mention of the sources from which they would come. Reading this brief treatment against the backdrop of an anticipated 206,000-man increase, we find it easier to understand how the addition of troops could be seen as a *de*-escalation, almost an afterthought, a move implicit in the prior action of adding about 11,000 combat troops, and not really a new commitment at all. This solved a problem that had troubled Johnson and his writers in the earliest drafts of the speech: how to put the bombing halt and the troop increase in the same speech without the message seeming incoherent.

Although Johnson did not state overtly that, with the increased troops, American forces in Vietnam had reached the limit, others, both at the time and since, were willing to say so. Clifford recalled, "As soon as Wheeler told me that Westmoreland would be satisfied with this relatively small increase [of 13,500], I decided I would support it, but try to ensure that it would be the last increase ever." He was true to his word, using a speech at the National Press Club on September 5 to describe the level of 549,500 as a hard limit, what Schandler called "the upper limit of American military commitment to the defense of South Vietnam." Clifford concluded that "the limit of force the American military could commit to Vietnam without mobilization" had finally been reached.[72]

What made the announcement of the small increase rhetorically possible was the celebration of the prowess of the South Vietnamese. Even though the Tet Offensive had been a military failure, it showed that the enemy was hardly on its last legs. So it could not be the case that the task had become simpler or the enemy less threatening—especially if the speech maintained elsewhere that the North Vietnamese had abandoned a strategy of attrition and had decided to go for all-out victory. Instead, what had changed was the ability of our ally to handle more of the work, so that we could carry less of a constant (or maybe even growing) burden. This is the origin of the idea that Richard Nixon would call "Vietnamization," that is, turning over a greater share of the fighting, at least on the ground, to the South Vietnamese forces.

To be sure, the fighting ability of the South Vietnamese *had* improved since the early days of the war. Yet the praise given to them in the speech seems more the result of its rhetorical functionality than of a military assessment of their capability. As noted at the beginning of this chapter, on February 11 Johnson had assumed, in discussion with his advisers, that the South Vietnamese lacked the capacity to do the job. It was on this assumption that he urged his advisers to consider whether the United States ought to send Westmoreland more troops. Now, when the president did not want to send large numbers of additional troops, he could justify his reluctance by saying that the South Vietnamese were up to the job. Frankly, it is unlikely that the readiness and capacity of the South Vietnamese army changed that much between February 11 and March 31. What *did* change was the situation Johnson faced.

The antecedent for relying more heavily on the South Vietnamese was a series of statements, even preceding the American escalation of the war, that South Vietnam must carry the primary responsibility for preserving its own freedom and that the American role was one of providing assistance to them. (The most prominent expression of this view was Johnson's statement during the 1964 campaign that American boys were not to be sent nine or ten thousand miles to do what Asian boys ought to do for themselves.) McPherson's Alternate Draft #1, for example, incorporated this belief as the introduction to a section on why the principal response to the Tet Offensive should come from South Vietnam.[73] This theme was reiterated in subsequent drafts.

When this approach was first suggested in early March, President Johnson regarded it as a major change in strategy. The United States would "tell the ARVN to do more fighting" and "tell them we will be *prepared* to make additional contributions but not unless they 'get with it.'" Using a sports metaphor, the president assessed the chances of success. "I frankly doubt you will get much out of them unless they have a good coach, the right plays, and the best equipment."[74] An early memorandum from Philip Habib in the State Department challenged this way of thinking, pointing out that if the assumption of South Vietnamese weakness was correct, "then virtually no level of US Force impact will hold any reasonable prospect of attaining present US objectives."[75] That clearly was an unacceptable outcome, so during March the estimate of South Vietnamese strength was "rehabilitated." Whereas in other situations the act was adjusted to fit the requirements of the scene, in this case the depiction of the scene was altered to make appropriate the constraints that dictated a limited act.

Henry Cabot Lodge, among others, proposed using the prospect of additional American troops as leverage on the South Vietnamese.[76] In the March 31 speech, Johnson enumerated additional efforts the South Vietnamese had made: building to a military strength of 800,000; drafting 19- and then 18-year-olds; increased volunteering; extending tours of duty; and undertaking a major effort to eliminate corruption and incompetence from the government. Once these additional steps were taken, it was appropriate for the United States to increase military aid and commit a small increment of troops. But clearly the major burden of the war would be shifting (back) to the Vietnamese. Kolko regards this shift as "the most prominent new proposal" in President Johnson's speech because it redefined the American objective as providing a shield behind which the Republic of Vietnam could grow—rather than any of the grandiose earlier proclamations of objectives. He writes, "It was this new American readiness to limit its commitments and later partially to disengage, however amorphously stated and defined at this time, that was the major outcome of the Tet offensive."[77]

In fact, the capability of the South Vietnamese army was largely unknown, as Rostow noted in his March 4 memo to the president. Another internal document from early March proclaimed, "The ARVN and the GVN [Government of Vietnam], while not near collapse, have been greatly weakened [by the Tet Offensive] and cannot make any substantial contribution to progress in SVN [South Vietnam] over the next few months."[78] It is also not clear how much the South Vietnamese government knew of Johnson's plans for them to assume a much greater role in the war. Herring concludes that the idea of Vietnamization was largely illusory. Essentially, it was a hope, grounded in wishful thinking, to buy time in order to get past the 1968 presidential election. Nevertheless, South Vietnamese President Thieu told Johnson in the summer of 1968 that "American troops could begin to leave in mid-1969,"[79] which is very close to the timetable Richard Nixon would follow.

The additional military aid and troops would cost money. In his speech, Johnson identified the cost as $2.5 billion in the current fiscal year and $2.6 billion in the one to come. These numbers seem trivial in today's context, as was the size of the federal budget deficit, estimated at $20 billion. In those times, however, the figures were quite significant. The reason was the complex interrelationship among the costs of the war, the US balance of payments, the willingness of foreign governments to hold dollar reserves rather than gold, and the role of the dollar in undergirding the world economy. The problems in these relationships came to a head in March of 1968, at the very time Johnson and his advisers were reaching their decisions about Vietnam. For some, the economics of the war proved the most significant of all these decisions.

There had been forewarnings of trouble. In August 1967, Marriner Eccles, a former chair of the Federal Reserve Board, had "called for immediate withdrawal from the war because of its impact on the economy and on national priorities."[80] The dollar was weakening, and the balance-of-payments deficit was growing, in both cases largely because of the cost of the war. Although Johnson had proclaimed that the nation could afford both the cost of the war and the development of domestic social programs, not to mention goods and services demanded by the private sector, that was wishful thinking. The growing federal budget deficits had begun to fuel inflation. The complex of problems created what Collins has called "the most serious economic crisis since the Great Depression," culminating in a speculative run on gold during the very month of March when seemingly unrelated Vietnam issues were pressing for decisions.

The problem began with the balance of payments. Although the United States had a healthy positive balance of *trade*, other overseas expenditures (including foreign aid and military expenditures) outweighed the trade surplus and produced balance-of-payments deficits for most years beginning in 1950. Small deficits were not harmful and actually helped international economic growth since other nations pegged their currencies to the dollar and agreed to hold dollars in their currency reserves. They were willing to do so as long as they retained confidence in American pledges, made at the 1944 Bretton Woods Conference, to convert dollars into gold at the fixed rate of $35 per ounce. Foreign governments held more dollars than there was gold to redeem them, so the system depended fundamentally on confidence in the fiscal prudence of the United States. The increasing direct cost of the war exacerbated the balance-of-payments problem, as did the increased volume of imports resulting from the inflation produced largely by the war. This increased the amount of dollars held by foreign governments and the danger they felt that the United States would be forced to devalue the dollar lest it run out of gold. (The problem was even more dire because of a legal requirement, finally repealed in March 1968, that the government also maintain a reserve of gold equal to 25 percent of the value of the money in *domestic* circulation, even though the convertibility of dollars into gold domestically had been halted in 1933.)

One way to address the problem was through increasing taxes. By removing funds from the private domestic economy, a tax increase presumably would reduce the demand for imports and thereby lessen the balance-of-payments deficit resulting from that source. At the same time, a tax increase would symbolize the government's determination to get its financial house in order. That, in turn, presumably would inspire other nations to continue to hold dollar reserves and weaken any disposition to convert dollars into gold. In December of 1965, the chair of the Council of Economic Advisers recommended that President Johnson propose a tax increase to pay for the growing cost of the war. But Johnson was reluctant to take this action and did not request action from Congress until August of 1967, when he proposed a 10 percent surtax on both individual and corporate taxes. Two main factors explain Johnson's reluctance. First, he knew that there was widespread public and legislative opposition to raising taxes. (As late as January 1968, polls showed that 79 percent of the population was opposed to raising taxes.)[81] Second, with good reason, Johnson feared that calling for a tax increase would trigger demands that Congress reduce spending, gutting the programs of the Great Society on the pretext that they were luxuries unaffordable in wartime.

When Johnson finally did request a surtax, it encountered precisely the sort of reaction he had feared, and he soon found himself at an impasse with Wilbur Mills, Democrat of Arkansas, the powerful chair of the House Ways and Means Committee. Mills insisted on a $6 billion reduction in expenditures as the price of considering the bill. Johnson refused, and each man held his ground. Meanwhile, inability to act on the bill was taken abroad as a sign of American unwillingness to get its house in order, and, at first in relatively small amounts, governments began to exchange dollars for gold, shrinking the US gold reserve.

By March of 1968, the trickle of dollars-for-gold exchanges had become something of a flood. The first warning sign was the devaluation of the British pound the previous November, which was followed by nervousness about the integrity of the dollar. Although US officials tried to convince the investing public that the dollar was secure, the steady drain on the balance of payments suggested otherwise. The reluctance of Congress to increase taxes to pay for the war was well known, so that when word leaked of Westmoreland's troop request, the reaction on the gold markets was little short of panic. Speculators were assuming the worst: that Johnson would approve the troop request but not convince Congress to raise the money for it. The three days of March 12, 13, and 14 saw the heaviest volume of purchases of gold. Finally, on March 14, Congress removed the "gold cover" requirement, ending the legal obligation to hold gold equal to 25 percent of the domestic currency in circulation and making it possible to use the entire gold reserve, if necessary, to defend against international threats to the dollar.

There is little doubt that the gold crisis constrained decision making about the troop increase. The president wrote in his memoirs, "It was clear that calling up a large number of troops, sending additional men overseas, and increasing military expenditures would complicate our problems and put greater pressure on the dollar." At the meeting of advisers on March 15, the president noted, Secretary of State Rusk explained that the effect new military actions would have on the US monetary position was his greatest concern about taking them.[82] Similarly, Schandler notes that Treasury Secretary Henry Fowler "was quite clear as to the serious economic costs" that would be entailed by meeting Wheeler's request for 206,000 additional troops. Preserving the stability of the dollar, he maintained, would require that these costs be fully offset by tax increases or budget cuts,[83] and this would have required action of much greater magnitude than the surtax that Congress was refusing to pass. Undersecretary of Defense Paul Nitze maintained on March 16 that "the gathering financial crisis" represented an additional reason to support the proposals advanced the previous day by United Nations Ambassador Arthur Goldberg: a complete bombing halt and denial of the request for additional troops.[84] The fact that most of the European nations who held large dollar reserves objected to escalating the war did not help matters. *New York Times* columnist Tom Wicker wrote on March 17 that because of the gold crisis, "it has become an economic impossibility to meet the request of General Westmoreland for 206,000 additional troops."[85]

Although exacerbated by the costs of the war, the gold crisis had an underlying structural cause. Supporting international economic expansion through the dollar as a reserve currency was no longer sustainable because the supply of dollars held by other nations called into question the ability or willingness to convert them into gold at a fixed price of $35 per ounce. As it happened, the leading finance ministers met in Stockholm in March to complete discussions of a proposal that had been in the air for some time—the creation of a paper asset, called Special Drawing Rights, which henceforth would finance economic growth, relieving the dollar of its singular responsibility in this regard and making continued foreign purchases of gold unnecessary. But this new system had not been ratified yet, and its viability depended on the credibility of nations' efforts to bring their revenues and expenditures into greater balance. As Arthur Okun, chair of the Council of Economic Advisers, put it, the Stockholm agreement was "futile unless we [could] get a tax increase."[86]

Financial exigency made its way into the drafts of the speech from the beginning, but not in its full detail. The early drafts do not refer to the gold crisis specifically. There is no discussion of international economics as a constraint preventing Johnson from meeting the request for 206,000 troops, for the simple reason that there is no discussion of that large an increase at all. Rather, the emphasis is on the need for the surtax because otherwise the budget deficit would be imprudently large. And there is a concession to Wilbur Mills in Johnson's stated willingness to implement spending cuts as well as seeking a tax increase—although the nature of that willingness would change over the course of the many speech drafts.

The emphasis on the urgency of the tax increase was carried over from the early drafts to the "Alternate" Drafts. In commenting on Alternate Draft #4, Okun suggested emphasizing the urgency of the tax increase. He also inserted a specific reference to the Stockholm agreement, writing, "It is our special responsibility to insure the success of this historic agreement by correcting our deficit."[87] This reference made its way into the final text, with Johnson saying that "we face the sharpest financial threat in the postwar era—a threat to the dollar's role as the keystone of international trade and finance in the world." He referred to the Stockholm meeting and warned that "to make this system work the United States just must bring its balance of payments to—or very close to—equilibrium."

What changed, however, was the nature of Johnson's reference to spending cuts. In the early drafts, he would say that we must cut the expenditure budget by deferring or delaying domestic programs— as opposed to eliminating them altogether. In the Alternate Drafts, McPherson would have Johnson say that, while he would have preferred reducing the deficit through taxation alone, Congress had forced him to include spending cuts as well. For instance, Alternate Draft #3, while deleting the statement that Congress had forced his hand, still said that he preferred relying on taxation to pay for the war, "so that the burden would be equitably shared, and so that the programs I believe our country needs—the programs we have begun with such promise in the past four years—could continue without diminishment or delay." But Johnson subordinated his preference to the necessity of deficit reduction because otherwise the effects "would strike hardest at those we are striving to help."[88] This indication of Johnson's preference for tax increases alone did not survive into the final speech.

One significant change in Alternate Draft #3 was suggested by Lady Bird Johnson. Referring to the surtax, the previous draft, after describing the need, had said, "Yet that action has not been taken." It was cast in the passive voice and identified no agent of the failure. Mrs. Johnson proposed changing the sentence to "Up to now Congress has taken no action,"[89] putting the sentence in the active voice and, more importantly, locating responsibility. Rather than casting inaction as the result of a stalemate between himself and Wilbur Mills, Johnson attributed failure to enact the surtax to the recalcitrance of Congress alone. In the final version of the speech, Johnson said starkly, "Yet Congress has not acted."

Deleted from this version was the notion that Congress had forced the president's hand regarding spending cuts. But in Alternate Draft

#4, McPherson turned the tables on Congress so that the burden of expenditure reductions rested on them as well. He would have Johnson acknowledge that Congress was reviewing appropriations requests, and then pledge, "As part of a program of fiscal restraint that includes the tax surcharge, I shall approve appropriate reductions in the January budget when and if Congress so decides."[90] Previously, the House Ways and Means Committee was demanding spending cuts by the president as a precondition for congressional approval of the surtax. Now the president was proclaiming that *if* Congress acted on the surcharge, then he would go along with spending cuts that *they* identified, as long as he deemed them to be "appropriate." Johnson was taking advantage of the political reality that cutting government spending was more popular in the abstract than with regard to particular programs, each of which had a constituency. By placing Congress in charge of enacting the cuts, Johnson reasonably could have thought that it would be less likely that cuts would ensue. In the final speech, he took a similar approach. After reviewing international efforts to strengthen the new Special Drawing Rights, Johnson said, "The passage of a tax bill now, together with expenditure control that the Congress may desire and dictate is absolutely necessary to protect this Nation's security, to continue our prosperity, and to meet the needs of our people." After making this offer to let Congress determine the cuts, Johnson moved assiduously to protect his most important programs. In mid-March, talk was of a cut of $8 billion or $9 billion in appropriations.[91] Congress finally approved the surtax in late June, along with a smaller total reduction in previously approved appropriations.

A few days after the speech, in a meeting with House and Senate leaders, Johnson made clear that he was placing the decision about spending reductions in their hands. He said that he would accept a package of tax increases and spending cuts acceptable to both houses of Congress. He would go along with whatever the Congress would cut out, and he said the question was "how much Congress really wants to cut." He was willing to follow their lead on cuts in order to achieve the greater good of the tax increase because failure to pass it would be "playing with disaster." He cited David Rockefeller to the effect that it would be worse than 1931. Backing him up was Senator George Smathers of Florida, who said the economic crisis, if not resolved, "would destroy this country." He cited Lenin, who, according to Smathers, said that the "best way to destroy [a] country is to debauch its currency."[92] An indication of what Johnson was up against is that, despite these warnings regarding the urgency of the matter, the surtax remained problematic in Congress. As noted, it did not pass for another three months—arguably too late to restrain inflation or to do much to control the fiscal imbalances to which it had been addressed. A *Wall Street Journal* writer noted that if, after all the effort in its behalf, the surtax could pass only if it was billed as a "war tax," then it might have lost its usefulness "as a signal to European central bankers that the US is earnest about restraining inflation that weakens the dollar."[93] The response to this concern, of course, was that a major cause of the inflation weakening the dollar was the cost of the war.

In sum, then, a variety of contextual factors made it clear that the commitment of additional troops was not so much an escalation of the war as a denial of calls for escalation. It does not read that way on the surface, primarily because of what it does *not* say. There is no mention in the March 31 speech of the Wheeler–Westmoreland request—not that it was considered, not that it was rejected, not even that it was submitted. Had the *New York Times* not leaked the story of this unprecedentedly large request, the speech would likely have been understood as a routine approval of a routine request for another modest escalation, similar to those of the past three years and arguably at odds with the thrust of the bombing halt proposal in the same speech. But the omission of the Wheeler–Westmoreland request was not the only sign in the speech that the president was up to something new. There was the emphasis on the improved performance of the South Vietnamese government and army, notwithstanding some of the damaging photographs of the Tet Offensive, that reduced the need for additional American troops and called for American military assistance instead. There was the fact that the anticipated intensification of the siege at Khe Sanh, which had worried the president into suggesting in early February that Westmoreland might need reinforcements even though he had not asked for them and had to be coached to do so, was not occurring. There was also the serious constraint of the gold crisis, which was discussed in the speech not as a reason to reject the request for 206,000 troops but as an exigence that must be met even for the modest increases the president was proposing, with a two-year budgetary impact of slightly over $5 billion.

These factors were generally unknown to the American people in advance of the speech, however. What was understood was that Westmoreland had submitted a very large request and that Johnson repeatedly had promised to give Westmoreland whatever he needed. It was a reasonable expectation, therefore, that Johnson would use the March 31 speech to announce a massive escalation of the war. The president did not help to enlighten the public when he was asked about the matter at a press conference on March 22: "Mr. President, have you reached a decision on the question of additional combat troops for Vietnam?" His answer was, "I have not. I have no specific recommendations at this point."[94] Although he might not have settled on a precise number, all the discussions since receipt of the Wheeler–Westmoreland recommendation had been about a fairly small range of numbers much below what the generals had recommended. As early as March 5, for example, Johnson had Wheeler send Westmoreland the message that no more than 22,000 additional troops could be provided at this time, although Wheeler emphasized that no decision had been made.[95] But the president chose to share neither the specific numbers nor the order of magnitude with the press or the public. Had he done so, the announcements in the March 31 speech would have been less dramatic.

Barrett describes a key meeting between Wheeler and Westmoreland that took place on March 24. This was when Westmoreland was told definitively that he would not receive the large troop increase. Barrett reports that Westmoreland "recognized the political division back home and agreed to change his 'request' to 13,500 men."[96] That way, Johnson could claim that his political and military advisers were agreed on the appropriate increment. And he could maintain once again that he was giving Westmoreland whatever he needed.

6

Withdrawal from the Race

THE ANNOUNCEMENTS OF the bombing halt and the troop commitment had major consequences for American goals in Vietnam. But what was most likely to be remembered from the March 31 speech was neither of those moves but Lyndon Johnson's announcement that he would not be a candidate for reelection.

About 90 minutes before the president was scheduled to speak, Press Secretary George Christian distributed an advance copy of the text to waiting reporters. It was missing a peroration. Noticing that the speech ended abruptly, the reporters were told that Johnson intended to ad-lib a brief section at the end. When the reporters asked what it would be about, Christian replied that it would concern "a matter of some importance."[1]

Only three other twentieth-century presidents had foregone the chance to run for a second full term: Theodore Roosevelt in 1908, Calvin Coolidge in 1928, and Harry Truman in 1952.[2] Like Johnson, they were all vice presidents who had succeeded to the presidency on the death of their predecessors. None of their nineteenth-century counterparts—John Tyler, Millard Fillmore, Andrew Johnson, and Chester A. Arthur—served even one elected term. Nevertheless, the conventional wisdom was that Lyndon Johnson would seek a second full term. It was one of the few near-certainties of American politics as the year 1968 began.[3] His announcement on March 31 that he would not seek or accept a nomination was met with shock and disbelief. When did he decide not to run for reelection, and why? And why announce it at this particular time? Did he really mean it?

In his memoirs, Johnson relates that he had considered serving only one term as early as 1965.[4] Indeed, he reportedly had discussed with Lady Bird that he might bow out of the *1964* election, even as that year's Democratic National Convention was meeting in Atlantic City, New Jersey.[5] Apparently, he sometimes thought that he was inadequate as a leader who could unite the country. But if he harbored any such doubts, the public was unaware of them. Writing late in 1967, the columnist Tom Wicker suggested that "it is as likely that Lyndon Johnson will get out of the White House and go back to Texas as it is that Dean Rusk will turn dove, Dick Nixon will stop running, or J. Edgar Hoover will retire."[6]

During the fall of 1967, however, Johnson and those close to him seriously considered the possibility of his withdrawing from the race. Lady Bird, eager for her husband to retire, had a long conversation about it with Abe Fortas, long a Johnson friend and confidant. The president spoke with Texas Governor John Connally, who was considering leaving his own office in 1968. He spoke about it with Congressman Jake Pickle, who occupied Johnson's old congressional seat. Aides George Christian and Horace Busby also were consulted about the matter. In his memoirs, Johnson recalls also discussing the issue with Dean Rusk, Robert McNamara, and Henry Fowler (secretaries of state, defense, and treasury, respectively), Generals Westmoreland and Wheeler, and his aide and assistant press secretary, Tom Johnson.[7]

Perhaps Johnson's most important conversation was with General Westmoreland. While the general was in Washington to contribute to the "optimism campaign" during November 1967 by making speeches and granting interviews, the president pulled him aside for a private conversation. How would the troops react, Johnson wanted to know, if he were to announce his retirement? He did not want to hurt morale, and he would not feel right asking the troops to die for their country if they thought that he was not doing his own job to the fullest. Westmoreland did not reply at first but subsequently told the president that a withdrawal announcement, even if it came as a surprise, would not in any way hamper the war effort.[8] In retrospect, Johnson would identify this conversation as the "turning point" in his thinking about retirement, But he was not yet ready to commit himself.

Wishing to keep his options open, the president not only talked with selected listeners about retirement but also encouraged aides to be thinking about the coming campaign. He gave men such as Lawrence O'Brien, John Roche, Jim Rowe, and Marvin Watson, who would play key roles in a campaign, every reason to believe that things were on track.[9] He was not yet ready to enter any presidential primaries—there were only fifteen of them in 1968, and victories would not be crucial—but he certainly was not ready to take himself out of the running.

In December, Johnson asked Press Secretary George Christian to draft a statement announcing his intention not to run, should he reach that decision. Both Christian and Horace Busby were consulted at the LBJ Ranch during the Christmas holidays of 1967, and both encouraged him to retire.[10] *US News and World Report* published a prediction that Johnson would win only twelve states with 110 electoral votes.[11] It is not known whether that had any influence on Johnson's thinking, and it was very early in the campaign season for polls to be at all reliable. Nevertheless, Johnson continued to think about withdrawal. He consulted again with Governor Connally, who urged him to do it and suggested that the forthcoming State of the Union address, scheduled for January 17, would be the perfect time to make the announcement.[12] About this time, Secretary of Health, Education, and Welfare John Gardner decided to resign his post because he could not support Johnson for reelection, owing to the president's position on the war. To Gardner's great surprise, reportedly Johnson told him that he was not planning to run and would announce that decision later in the spring.[13]

Busby produced his draft, which Johnson says he intended to take with him to the Capitol when he delivered the State of the Union address on January 17. But, he says, he forgot to put the Busby text into the pocket of his suit coat and was surprised to discover in the House Chamber that it was not there.[14] A more likely account is that Johnson decided to omit the announcement because he had concluded that it would undercut the thrust of the State of the Union message. Johnson once again had proposed an ambitious national agenda to Congress, and he would sacrifice much of the political leverage to get it through if he announced in advance that he would not be a candidate for reelection. Why should a member of Congress, especially one who was on the fence, cast a politically risky vote when the beneficiary was a lame duck with a limited ability to reward compliance or to punish disloyalty?

But Johnson recovered his text, gave it back to Busby, and told him to hold onto it because it might be needed on another occasion. And he bided his time.

Contrary to what might be expected, the Tet Offensive per se did not appear to have influenced Johnson's decision not to run, except insofar as it added to his fatigue and frustration. Nor did the evolving political scene influence his decision. The president was expected to have an easy renomination despite minimal opposition from antiwar Minnesota Senator Eugene McCarthy. The first primary was in mid-March and McCarthy showed surprising strength. But whatever happened in the primaries, Johnson had the support of almost all the state party leaders who would effectively decide the nomination. But the primary calendar did impose a constraint on the timing of Johnson's announcement. The second primary would be in Wisconsin on April 2, and by mid-March polls were predicting that the president would lose decisively. If that happened, and then Johnson subsequently withdrew from the race, it would be hard to avoid the implication that he was conceding political weakness and withdrawing for that reason.

All these factors must have weighed on Johnson's mind as he pondered what to do in Vietnam in the wake of the Tet Offensive. In his own mind, there was a presumption for withdrawal from the race, and probably had been since his meeting with Westmoreland back in November. Still, that presumption was rebuttable, and Johnson gave no public signal of his private thinking. In his memoirs he states that during a discussion of Rusk's proposal on March 5 for a unilateral, partial bombing halt, he began to wonder about what the effect would be if he were to couple such an action with an announcement that he would not run for another term—the first known instance of considering how each of these actions could affect the other. He reported that he then instructed his staff not to enter a surrogate against McCarthy in the forthcoming Massachusetts primary—the first public act that was arguably inconsistent with a run for a second term.[15]

Later in March, the president had lunch with his aides Joseph Califano and Harry McPherson. They talked about the major policy announcements that would be featured in Johnson's forthcoming speech, particularly the bombing halt and the call for the tax surcharge. Johnson then, without warning, let slip that he was thinking about not

running for reelection. Believing that the president was just expressing his frustrations, neither aide replied at once. But, according to
McPherson, Johnson persisted, asking for reasons that he ought to run
and then refuting them.[16]

Despite all the evidence that the president was seriously considering
withdrawal, it was difficult to believe. As he was working toward a decision, he could express either possibility with equal conviction. And he
was hardly transparent. A *New York Times* writer noted that it was "a for-
gone conclusion" that Johnson would run, but that, given his penchant
for secrecy, he would not be likely to reveal how he would campaign
until sometime in the summer.[17] Another source reported that Johnson had been telling associates that he intended to follow the model of
Franklin D. Roosevelt in 1940, remaining above the fray while focusing
his energy on the war.[18] And if anything might induce him to withdraw,
surely it would be counteracted by the entry of Robert F. Kennedy into
the race. The enmity between the president and the senator was well
known and had festered since the Democratic Convention of 1960. As
the *New York Times* writer concluded, "the Kennedy challenge made a
Johnson withdrawal unthinkable."[19] Indeed, through March Johnson
continued to act like a candidate. Dallek notes that on March 8, Johnson
gave his approval to his aides to begin organizing efforts on his behalf,
notwithstanding that he had just rejected putting a stand-in into the
race in Massachusetts, and that he continued to promote his candidacy
after Kennedy entered the race on March 16.[20]

For his part, Johnson was characteristically cagey about his political
plans. In a press conference on March 25, he was asked when he was going to announce his entry into the race—not whether but when—and
he replied, "When I get to that bridge I will cross it. I am not there yet."
And on March 30 a reporter asked, concerning the next day's speech,
"do you have any plans tomorrow to discuss your future role in this
campaign, or candidacy?" to which the president replied simply, "No."[21]
White House aides followed suit, reportedly laughing off rumors that
Johnson would not run.[22]

Horace Busby spent much of March 31 with Johnson. His memoir
and the White House logs make clear that Johnson did not make up his
mind definitely not to run until well into the afternoon. He met in the
morning with Vice President Humphrey, who was about to leave for

Mexico City, and showed him two versions of the speech—with and without the peroration announcing his withdrawal. Johnson's daughter Lynda argued vigorously that he should stay in the race. In the late afternoon, Dallek reports, Johnson asked aides to inform Cabinet officers and congressional leaders that he was not going to run—but to wait until he actually began the speech, in case he changed his mind at the very last minute.[23] In his memoirs, Johnson explains that no president really makes a decision until he announces it and thereby commits himself to it. Applying this rule, he said that he made the decision announced at 9:01 p.m. on March 31 at precisely 9:01 p.m., when he began to speak.[24]

In their euphoria immediately following the withdrawal announcement, antiwar protesters were quick to claim that it was their agitation that had driven the president from office. While this was a self-satisfying claim, it is very likely mistaken. It is hard to square with evidence that the president was seriously considering withdrawing as early as the previous fall, when—except for the March on the Pentagon—the antiwar movement was neither especially active nor influential. The "optimism campaign" had driven Johnson's approval ratings up, and twice as many people self-identified as "hawks" as called themselves "doves."[25] During this period Johnson, his spirits uplifted, may have briefly considered remaining in the race.

It appears that the biggest factor in Johnson's decision was concern for his health. Quite simply, he was exhausted—and that was before the Tet Offensive added to his burdens. Press Secretary Christian denied that the president made his decision for reasons of health, but Vaughn Davis Bornet has made a persuasive case otherwise.[26] Johnson had suffered a major heart attack in 1955; he was concerned that he might not survive another. And he knew that most of the men in his family, going back generations, had died young—most commonly in their early sixties. (Johnson would be sixty in 1968.) Concern for the president's health was undoubtedly foremost in Lady Bird's mind as she encouraged him to retire. Of course, this concern gains added weight from our knowledge of how things came out. Even without the second term, Johnson survived only two days beyond when it would have ended: he died on January 22, 1973, at the age of sixty-four, after suffering several smaller heart attacks before the one that was fatal.

Most likely, the other major factor in Johnson's decision not to run was the one he stated in the speech—the existence of deep divisions in the country. In Johnson's view, the way to heal those divisions was to end the war, and he pledged to devote all his time to succeeding in this objective. But if unity would follow from ending the war, it was also a precondition for ending it. As Johnson saw it, Ho Chi Minh was keenly aware of US domestic dissent and misread it as an indication that the American will to sustain the war was lacking. If that were so, he would have every incentive to hold out for the collapse of the war effort rather than to enter into negotiations in good faith. The flip side was Johnson's apparent belief that there was some point at which Ho would decide that continuing the fight was not worth it, and that if the country would stay united, Ho would be more likely to reach that point.

It was not that Johnson feared he could not be nominated or that he could not win. But the prospect of being renominated by a divided party and then winning a close election with a deeply divided country was unappealing to him. Furthermore, he had lost confidence that he would be able to heal the divisions even if he won, whether because his actions had contributed to the divisions or simply because they focused on him.[27] Moreover, even before the election, his every move during 1968 would be interpreted in partisan political terms, making it much harder to achieve the legislative or diplomatic results he needed.[28]

As Kearns pointed out, Johnson had a history of risk-aversiveness in campaign situations, where "the size of the audience was beyond the reach of his personal abilities and skills." He had written out withdrawal statements at least twice before: in his Senate campaign of 1948 and during the presidential race of 1964.[29] But this was different. Johnson was aware of his own health, and he read correctly the condition of the country. Under these circumstances, continuing in office posed even greater dangers than the risk that the presidential nomination might be captured by Robert Kennedy.

The decision about when to announce Johnson's withdrawal proceeded in tandem with the decision about *whether* to withdraw. Much of the advice Johnson received focused on the January 17 State of the Union speech. Unlike today, when for fund-raising purposes political campaigns often begin a full two years before the election, in 1968 the State of the Union message occurred before the political season had heated up. As a result, Johnson's decision, if announced then, probably would not be attributed to adverse campaign events. Harry Truman's situation in 1952 could be seen as instructive. He waited to withdraw from the race until late March, by which time he had lost the New Hampshire primary to Tennessee Senator Estes Kefauver. Whether or not accurately, this result was claimed to be part of the cause for Truman's decision.[30] A January announcement would avoid that risk.

In any case, George Christian had prepared a short statement as "a brief addendum to the State of the Union," also incorporating a draft Busby had submitted on January 15. Christian gave the statement to Johnson as he went to the White House residence to dress for the ride to the Capitol. The president gave the draft to Mrs. Johnson, and they discussed it in the residence. When he emerged for the trip to the Capitol, he did not have the statement with him.[31] This is the basis for the story that Johnson forgot to put the manuscript in the pocket of his suit coat. It is far more likely, as noted above, that during the conversation with Mrs. Johnson, he had decided that this was not the right occasion to announce his withdrawal.

The statement prepared for the State of the Union address was substantially different from that of March 31. The earlier statement said, "I do not believe any one man can carry on a political campaign through the spring, summer, and fall without leaving undone some of our responsibilities here and abroad. . . . For the next twelve months I will devote every waking hour and every ounce of energy to supporting our men in Vietnam, to seeking an honorable peace, and to meeting our critical challenges at home. . . . With the priorities thus divided and with due concern for the future of my country, I have prayerfully concluded that I will not be a candidate for reelection and will not allow my name to be placed in nomination at the Democratic Convention."[32] After the State of the Union, however, Johnson asked Press Secretary Christian to keep the statement up to date in case he wanted to use it at some point in the future. But in late March he asked Busby to try his hand at a redraft of Christian's "renunciation statement," and then he asked Christian to read it.[33] As Johnson was considering, as late as the afternoon of March 31, whether to make the announcement, he consulted again with Governor Connally. The Texas governor strongly urged the president to announce in his speech that night that he would not be running. It was pretty late to do this as it is, Connally advised, and we should not wait any longer.[34] In fact, March 31 was the last possible moment to announce if Johnson wished to avoid the criticism Truman faced—that he was giving up in the face of unfavorable developments in the campaign.

Since the drafting of the speech had begun on March 20, it was well underway by the time Johnson settled on including his withdrawal statement. The original peroration fit with the more hawkish speech of Drafts 1–6, but when the decision was made to use the alternate version instead, that peroration was no longer appropriate. McPherson had not yet gotten around to replacing it.

McPherson had drafted a peroration as early as February 27, in which Johnson spoke reflectively about why it was sometimes necessary for young men to go to war. It said that "human freedom must ultimately be defended by human beings." He substituted it for the placeholder, "Closing peroration," in the first draft of what would become the March 31 speech, to the approval of William P. Bundy.[35] This version made its way into the first "alternate" version as well, where McPherson added a plea to "strengthen the arms of those who are fighting for us in Vietnam" and made a plea for national unity: "Let them know that all America stands with them. Divided, we are in danger. Together we cannot and will not fail."[36] In subsequent conversations, it was thought that the peroration should be a forceful rallying cry to resist aggression. At this point, Clifford began arguing that with the incorporation of proposals for a bombing halt now in the speech, such an assertive peroration would be out of place. Clifford suggested a version that acknowledged doubts and uncertainties.[37] The final version of the "Vietnam peroration" summarized the speech, prayed that North Vietnam would not reject the peace initiative, and asked for Americans' support.[38] There was no reference to the current political campaign. But as noted earlier, Johnson told McPherson not to worry about the peroration; he might have one of his own.

While McPherson was working on the body of the speech, Johnson had asked Busby to update the peroration that he had not used in January. In turn, he asked Press Secretary George Christian and his assistant Tom Johnson to polish this text.[39] The unused draft from the State of the Union was largely set aside. It had celebrated the legislative achievements of the Congress and had reminded listeners that there were many problems yet to be addressed even beyond winning the war. It also proclaimed that "no man wants peace more than I." Then, as quoted above, it strongly suggested that the task was too great for any one man and announced the "prayerful conclu[sion]" that he would not run.[40] This was a generalized statement and was not tied specifically to any specific issue or policy. In effect, it said that the presidency had become too large a job to permit anyone to campaign. This was an unlikely claim, and it left unanswered the obvious question of what had changed since 1964, when an obviously less experienced Lyndon Johnson had done precisely that. Moreover, if Johnson had made the withdrawal announcement in January, he would have given up the political leverage he would need to get his ambitious legislative program passed. Besides, of course, in March Johnson could not ignore the effect that Tet had had on the American people, although his initial draft peroration focused on the deep divisions in its aftermath rather than the military conflict itself.

For March 31, Busby produced a five-page handwritten draft in which one can find the origins of Johnson's final statement. Acknowledging that no one could say that no more would be asked of Americans, it asserted that now, as in 1961, in the words of President Kennedy's Inaugural Address, "this generation of Americans" was willing to "pay any price, bear any burden, meet any hardship, support any friend, oppose any foe, to assure the survival and the success of liberty." This reference not only cast Johnson as fulfilling Kennedy's promise, as he often sought to do, but none too subtly cast aspersions against Robert F. Kennedy, who was campaigning against the Vietnam War and arguably (according to Johnson) was traducing against his brother's legacy.[41] The quotation certainly was not out of place, but neither was it essential to Johnson's argument here, especially since he already had called for fidelity to our commitments earlier in the speech.

The Busby text had the president say, "whatever the tests before us," the ultimate strength of the American country and the American cause lies "not in ultimate weapons or infinite resources or boundless wealth—but in the unity of our people." To be sure, he did not mean absolute conformity but, rather, broad agreement on national goals and a commitment to pursue them. The contrast to national unity was Lincoln's metaphor of the "house divided," and the president concluded, "unfortunately, there is division in the American house now." He decided that he should not involve the presidency in "the partisan divisions that are developing." Accordingly, Johnson was to conclude, "I shall not seek—and I will not accept—the nomination of my party for another term as your president." The text then would claim that during Johnson's presidency the country had kept its commitments, that the reward "will come in the life of freedom and peace and hope that our children will enjoy through ages ahead," but that "what has been won in unity, should not now be lost in division."[42]

Johnson made three changes in this handwritten text. First, he clarified the word "more," out of concern that his secretary might not be able to read Busby's handwriting. Second, where Busby had referred to "the partisan divisions of this political year," Johnson rewrote it as "divisions that have developed in this political year" and changed it to the present tense, noting "divisions that are developing." Finally, Busby had Johnson pledge that he "will not accept" the Democratic nomination. Johnson changed "will" to "would," reportedly explaining that the term had to be cast in the subjunctive because he could not accept or reject a nomination until it was tendered. "Would," however, made the pledge seem less unequivocal, as would be noted later in the day.

Interestingly, the draft contained an error that neither Busby nor Johnson noticed at the time. Referring to the president's tenure in office, Busby would have him say, "Sixty-four months and ten days ago, in a moment of tragedy and trauma, the duties of this office fell upon me." Busby had given him an extra year in office; as of March 1968, Johnson had served slightly over four years, not five. This error persisted in further drafts but was caught before the speech was delivered.

Having received no advance notice of what Johnson wanted, Busby had been working on the draft at the White House during the morning of March 31. A note attached to the draft explains what happened to it:

When mf [Johnson's secretary, Marie Fehmer] was called to the Treaty Room at 2:06p, the President was sitting there at a small oval marble-topped table, with felt pen in hand, making changes. . . . He went over the entire draft, editing it and reading it aloud.

The Treaty Room table looked as if Busby had been there for some time. There was a coffee urn on a tray with just one cup, and an ash tray filled w/ cigarette remains.

After finishing reading aloud the entire draft and adding his handwriting to the draft, the President told mf to go to the office, type it, "make several copies, count the words, and show it to no one."[43]

She did so.

Fehmer took the draft to the president at about 2:42 p.m. He was in the dining room having lunch with Mrs. Johnson, his daughter and son-in-law, Luci and Pat Nugent, old friends, Mr. and Mrs. Arthur Krim, and Busby. Johnson took Fehmer's original and began reading it aloud to the group. At some point, Busby returned to the Treaty Room and continued to refine the draft. At about 6:30 p.m., Busby called again to say that he had another draft—actually, inserts and changes to the one previously typed. "mf went to the Treaty Room, and Busby began to explain the inserts and changes." Johnson came in and, noting that time was getting tight, asked to see what Busby had and began to make changes in his own handwriting. At one point, he took Fehmer's short-hand notebook and began to write himself, but he ultimately did not use these words because Busby "came up with an alternate suggestion" that he dictated to the president. Johnson copied it as an insert on one of the longhand pages that Busby had intended to insert into the earlier text. Fehmer made the changes and took a new. clean text back to Busby for review. He approved it. As Fehmer was leaving the second floor, she met the president at the elevator. He took the text and made some addi-tional edits, leaning over a desk in the hallway.

It was on this draft that Busby corrected his arithmetic, changing "sixty-four months" to "fifty-two months." And Johnson changed "would" back to "will," saying that he "will not accept" the Democratic nomination. The president made a few other "wordsmithing" changes, adding a few words here and there. For example, he enlarged "divi-sion among any of our people" to "suspicion distrust and selfishness among any of our people." (He would make a few more such changes ad lib when delivering the speech. For example, "an hour of my time" became "an hour or a day of my time" and "this office" became "this office—the presidency of your country.")[44] With these changes made, the president released the text to the teleprompter operators, first the first two pages and then, at 8:15 p.m., the third page, the one con-taining the "shall not seek" announcement. The text of the peroration

thus was ready only forty-five minutes before the speech was scheduled for delivery.

Events in the White House closely paralleled the drafting of the new
peroration, as Busby's posthumously published memoir makes clear.
On Saturday morning, unknown to anyone in the White House, Johnson called his former aide to ask him to work on the ending.[45] Over
the weekend, the president saw in the newspapers a newly released Gallup Poll showing that his approval ratings had reached a personal low
point. Only 36 percent supported his job performance overall, and only
26 percent supported his handling of the Vietnam War in particular.[46]
That news surely did not deter him from the decision he planned to
announce Sunday night.

Busby remained in the White House, close to the president, throughout the day on Sunday. Invited to have lunch with the Johnson family
and their good friends the Krims, Busby found himself the target of
protests and questions from those present—not including Lady Bird—
who did not want Johnson to step down. The president referred the
questions to Busby and nodded approvingly after his former aide answered them.[47] While Busby went back to the Treaty Room to polish the
ending so that it would sound more like Johnson, the president was trying out the idea of withdrawing on aides in the West Wing. He learned
that all were opposed, but that did not dissuade him.[48] He asked for a
copy of Truman's 1952 announcement,[49] although, as noted earlier, his
situation and Truman's were dissimilar in most respects. Later in the
afternoon, Busby had a conversation with Press Secretary George Christian and urged him to remain on the family floor of the White House,
lest someone come in at the last moment and talk Johnson out of his
decision. Indeed, within the next hour, Johnson summoned Busby to
his bedroom, where he was about to take a nap, to tell him that someone had suggested that he delay the announcement until the following
Thursday, April 4, when Johnson was scheduled to address a political
dinner; perhaps a political announcement would be more appropriate on that occasion. No, Busby replied. Television would be covering
the event, and cameras undoubtedly would pan the audience for reactions to the surprise announcement. Some of Johnson's critics would
be shown applauding, which would suggest that Johnson had capitu-
lated to them[50]—giving precisely the impression that the speech text

was careful to avoid. The text had presented the policy changes as the fruits of American success, not as the acknowledgment of errors. Apparently convinced, the president left the announcement in the speech that was now less than five hours away. After his nap, Busby reports, Johnson read the withdrawal announcement to a group of his friends and staff. They reacted with taut faces, emotional tears, gasps, and then shocked silence, but "the president disregarded the reaction." The verbal rehearsal of the news he would soon announce to the nation appeared to have a liberating effect on him; Busby wrote that "the president himself seemed to be a changed man."[51]

It was when Busby heard the speech read aloud that he realized he had wrongly reported the length of time Johnson had been in office. His memoir reports that he had written "49 months and ten days ago," but, as noted above, the drafts clearly indicate that he had given Johnson an *extra* year, having written "sixty-four months and ten days ago." The president, glad that Busby had caught the error, asked what his tenure really had been. Both men took pencils and recalculated; Busby then revised the manuscript to read "fifty-two months and ten days ago."[52]

The penultimate change made to the text, as the president was giving it to aide Jim Jones to take to the teleprompter operators, was to change "any partisan causes" to "any personal partisan causes." Johnson did not want to forego the opportunity to campaign on behalf of Vice President Humphrey if, as the president expected, Humphrey entered the race. The last alteration was to change "would" back to "will." Busby had written it that way in the first place but, as noted above, Johnson had changed it to the subjunctive "would" because he thought he could act only once a nomination had been tendered. But Busby persisted, arguing that "would" was not emphatic enough and seemed to leave Johnson too much "wiggle room" to change his mind. According to Busby, the president "grudgingly" agreed to make the change.[53]

Johnson had compiled a list of officials and private citizens to be notified of his impending announcement. But he did not want them to be notified until he had begun to speak. That way, no one could get through to him, either upsetting him or convincing him to change his mind, at the very last minute. The secrecy meant that no one would have the time to prepare a fitting response. They largely combined generalized expressions of support, sadness that the president was stepping down, and hope that he might change his mind. Those supporting Johnson's decision to withdraw generally did so not because of the reasons he had offered for it—he wanted to spend all his time trying to achieve a peace in Vietnam that would heal national divisions—but rather because he deserved relief from all the stress he had endured for the past years (stress, it was sometimes said, that had been intensified by those very divisions and by the antiwar movement in particular).

Larry Temple, one of the aides assigned to make these calls, recorded the responses (possibly a sanitized version of them). Most thanked Temple for calling. Many expressed shock.

A distraught Secretary of Agriculture Orville Freeman said, "Good Lord! I'm astounded." Newly installed Commerce Secretary C. R. Smith exclaimed, "My God! That is a very shocking announcement!" Labor Secretary Willard Wirtz called out, "Good Heavens!" and Interior Secretary Stewart Udall said, "Knocks me flat." Another Johnson aide, Barefoot Sanders, reported on his calls. Senator Richard Russell of Georgia argued, "Think he's making a helluva mistake. Great mass of American people are for him. All this hurrahing comes from a small minority." House Speaker Carl Albert said he would issue a statement saying that the American people will demand the president's renomination. Senate Majority Leader Mike Mansfield said that Johnson had given the greatest speech of his career except for the final two minutes, which he deeply regretted. Senator Phil Hart remembered that he had always said that the president wanted peace more than anyone else; this speech proved it. Marvin Watson, the postmaster general, also was one of the callers. He reached Tennessee Governor Buford Ellington, who said, "I cannot believe it. What will we do?" Chicago Mayor Richard J. Daley exclaimed, "He will not. By God. Oh oh. OK." But Illinois Congressman Roman Pucinski was far more specific: "He is Whistling Dixie in the grave yard. He will be drafted. He will be nominated. He will be elected. He will serve. We are going to twist his arm and going to give him the LBJ treatment."[54]

Weeks later, Johnson aide James R. Jones requested a tabulation of mail responses to the March 31 address. The File Room indicated that there had been 22,973 favorable responses and only 500 to 550 unfavorable ones.[55] Of course, it was not clear what counted as a favorable or unfavorable response, or whether the writers were commenting on specific sections of the text or on the speech as a whole. A frequent theme in the letters was that history would upgrade the stature of the Johnson presidency and that citizens would realize how lucky they were to have had Johnson in the role.

More organized measures of public response on file in the Johnson Library follow similar patterns. A survey of fifty-seven major editors and columnists between April 1 and April 19 found that forty-three generally approved of the speech and that forty fully approved of the bombing limitation.[56] A report of "a quick telephone poll of voters in every section of the country"—no more information is provided as to its reliability—found a slightly different pattern. Excluding those who were undecided, 72 percent approved of the bombing pause but 62 percent opposed the surtax. Meanwhile, 75 percent supported the president's decision not to run.[57] Furthermore, the stock market jumped twenty points the day after the speech, in the heaviest trading day in the history of the New York Stock Exchange. As Charles J. Ella noted, this seemed superficially as though the market were "bidding President Johnson an exuberant 'good riddance,'" but it is more likely that the market was responding to the improved prospects for peace in Vietnam as a result of Johnson's efforts to de-escalate the conflict.[58]

Newspaper editorials weighed in with praise of the president for his statesmanship and willingness to rise above partisan politics. The *Minneapolis Tribune* called the speech "statesmanship on a plane commensurate with the traditions and ideals associated with the nation's highest office" and judged that Johnson "placed the needs of the nation above partisan advantage to himself" or his party.[59] The *Nashville Banner* saw the speech as evidence of "a nobility of man that rises above considerations of ambition, pomp, and circumstance." The *Jackson Citizen Patriot* averred, "This may be President Johnson's finest hour. . . . he is adopting a statesmanlike method of attempting to put an end to the deep divisions which are threatening America." And the *Wisconsin State Journal* declared, "For his attempt to bring peace, unify the nation, and end the ugly mood of America, Lyndon Johnson became another profile in courage Sunday night."[60] To the degree that such views became the frame of reference for assessing the president, it became much harder for him to change his mind later and decide to run, after all.

Politicians, whether supporters or opponents of Lyndon Johnson, also weighed in with fulsome praise, some of which already has been quoted. Robert F. Kennedy sent Johnson a telegram expressing fervent hope that the peace efforts would succeed, noted the magnanimity of Johnson's removing himself from the race, and requested the opportunity to meet.[61] George McGovern called the speech "one of the most stirring and deeply moving experiences in our national history" and told the president, "You have placed the well-being of our Nation and the peace of the world above every other consideration. That has assured you a high place in history."[62] Edward Kennedy sent a telegram telling Johnson, "You met the difficult challenges with great strength and commitment, and you gave much to your country and the people who looked to your leadership."[63] Eugene McCarthy said that Johnson deserved the "honor, respect and approval of the nation" for the decision to de-escalate the war, and added, "He left no doubt about his commitment to peace by announcing he would not be a candidate."[64] House Minority Leader Gerald Ford hoped that "all Americans unite behind the President in his moves toward peace in Vietnam," and Senator J. William Fulbright, one of Johnson's most persistent critics on the war, called his decision "the act of a very great patriot."[65] General Earle Wheeler told the president that the speech of March 31 was "the most powerful public utterance which I have ever heard you make."[66] Similar statements can be found throughout the folders of responses from prominent citizens on file at the Johnson Library, to say nothing of the thousands of responses from ordinary citizens who praised the president for his courage and patriotism.

Antiwar activists, who had rallied behind the candidacy of Senator McCarthy and who were on the cusp of carrying him to victory in the Wisconsin primary, were elated. Flush with the euphoria of the moment, they took credit for driving Johnson from the race by bringing him to the brink of defeat. In retrospect, it appears that the possible outcomes of the presidential primaries had nothing to do with Johnson's decision. There also were some concerns in Asia that Johnson's withdrawal would be bad for the allied cause; there was more approval in Latin America where neither the president nor the war had been very popular.[67] And Bornet raises the possibility that people such as

Eisenhower and Westmoreland, "who had been told that LBJ's retirement would be because of his health and longevity problems," would now suspect him of a massive bait-and-switch operation now that he "offered the American people his nation-serving but false explanations about retiring to help end the war."[68] Bornet acknowledged, though, that he was raising a hypothetical question. Any such concerns about Johnson's character were lost in the wave of adulation that immediately followed the speech.

In his memoirs, Johnson stated that he expected that his announcement would surprise the country. He wrote sarcastically, "I believed that because of the 'informed guidance' the press had given the people, all the nation—except a dozen or so individuals—would be shocked and surprised."[69] No one seemed more surprised than "television and radio commentators, who usually rank high for instant loquacity." Many of the news executives were attending the National Association of Broadcasters convention and rushed to return home.[70] Surely their own surprise crept into their news reports. Surprise was one of Johnson's typical means of keeping control over the country. As Sylvan Fox put it, "He surprised everybody, the way he always likes to do, and it probably pleased him most that the news did not leak out until he announced it himself."[71]

Once recovered from its collective surprise, the press began to inquire about when the decision was made. Unnamed White House sources claimed that Johnson firmed up his decision in the day or two before the speech but had been thinking about it for several months.[72] This appears to be correct. However, these sources did not indicate that the motive for Johnson's decision was not the war per se, much less the Tet Offensive (which had not even happened yet when he began seriously to consider withdrawal). Rather, it appears that he was driven by deeper concerns about his health and longevity. Later in the spring, investigative reporter Drew Pearson tried to piece together the story of the withdrawal. He made several errors, including the statement that Johnson's staff was opposed to the decision. Press Secretary George Christian noted in a memorandum to Pearson, "Only 2 or 3 staff people knew he was even considering this, and I assured you I favored the ultimate decision."[73] Johnson himself, as has been noted, wrote in his memoirs that he never could be said to make a decision until he publicly announced and acted upon it. Accordingly, he made the decision only when he began speaking on March 31.[74]

Regardless of when Johnson made this decision, it was a great benefit for him to announce it on March 31, in the same speech in which he announced new initiatives in Vietnam and sought a constructive response from North Vietnam. Simply put, it gave those initiatives heightened credibility by testifying to their sincerity. In the absence of the withdrawal announcement, it would have been easy to dismiss them as political ploys to pick up votes, either in the Wisconsin primary or in the general election. Thus characterized, there would have been no reason for the North Vietnamese to respond encouragingly or for anyone to take the initiatives seriously. Conversely, if Johnson had announced earlier his intention not to run, there would have been no political power to back up the new measures; they could have been dismissed as irrelevant efforts to mask the rapidly receding power of a "lame duck" while everyone was waiting to see what his successor would do. In contrast, making the announcements simultaneously conveyed that the war moves were genuine and sincere, precisely because Johnson was demonstrating that he was willing to lay down his political career for them. If such a move were made by such a committed politician, it must be for real.

Johnson himself recognized this connection. Later at night on March 31, he said, "I would hope that by what I did tonight, we can concentrate more of our energies on trying to bring about peace in the world and that we would have a better chance to do it."[75] Senator Fulbright expressed his concurrence that Johnson's withdrawal "adds a great deal of credence" to the offer to limit the bombing of North Vietnam.[76] These opinions were widely shared. The *Christian Science Monitor* reported on a nationwide telephone survey indicating a major shift in national opinion regarding Johnson's handling of the war: 75 percent of its sample now believed that he was doing all he could to settle the war, whereas only 11 percent disagreed.[77] These figures represented significant improvement that could be attributed to the speech. The reason for these results was that the coupling in the same speech of the bombing halt and the withdrawal announcement separated the peace proposals from politics and thereby removed a convenient rationale for turning them down. Senator McCarthy recognized this when he said that it was clear that the halt of the bombing was not an attempt to gain political advantage.[78] Quite to the contrary, it converted Johnson's personal reasons for withdrawing—concern for his health and mortality—into a matter of high principle, or as Doris Kearns put it, coupling the two elements "gave him a way to withdraw without appearing to be a coward."[79]

The motivation of the North Vietnamese cannot be known, but it seems reasonable that they would be more likely to accept Johnson's proposal with his withdrawal than without it. To be sure, they could interpret it as another sign of American weakness. They could note (correctly) that it did not meet their stated precondition for talks: a complete and unconditional bombing halt. Yet it was not incompatible with that goal, and the nature of Hanoi's response to this offer could influence what further moves the United States might make. Besides, by combining a unilateral conciliatory move with the withdrawal announcement, Johnson had moved the United States beyond its calcified positions of the past; perhaps that would create a new environment in which Hanoi should act differently as well.

On the other hand, Johnson's strategy in coupling the two moves did not depend on a positive response from North Vietnam. Many were skeptical that there would be one. But in that case, Johnson, having demonstrated his bona fides and having taken partisan politics out of the equation, would have considerably more freedom to maneuver. In particular, it would be easier for him to justify escalation after having offered the olive branch. An unsigned *New York Times* article quoted an unnamed administration official noting that "it was often said that [Johnson] could hardly order a substantial call-up [of the Reserves] in an election year. But now that the President has announced he will not run for another term, he's really free to do anything he feels is in the best interest of the country. He can make peace or level North Vietnam. His options, suddenly, are almost unlimited."[80] Henry Gemmill, a *Wall Street Journal* reporter, put it more starkly: "a sword hangs over them— that North Vietnam can be smashed in ways not hitherto attempted." Hanoi would find such threats "thoroughly credible coming from a noncandidate," though they might not be plausible coming from a president "seeking re-election by war-weary voters."[81] Once he decoupled the war from his personal political future, then, Johnson put himself in a win–win situation insofar as Vietnam was concerned. No matter the enemy's response, Johnson could end up in a better position than if he had remained in the race.

It even seemed that other logjams might be broken as a result of the flexibility Johnson had gained. *Chicago Tribune* reporter Philip Warden mentioned the cautious prediction of Democratic legislative leaders that the president's action had improved the chances for passage of legislation.[82] McGeorge Bundy, engaging in wishful thinking, wrote the president, suggesting that he was now in a position to replace two or three "bureaucrats who are generally supposed to be politically invulnerable." At the top of his list was Selective Service Director General Lewis B. Hershey, "whom I would hold personally responsible for about 75 percent of the feeling against the Administration among people of draft age and their families." Bundy would also replace FBI Director J. Edgar Hoover, even though "I have great respect for him and do not share the violent views of some of my liberal friends," because "the FBI bureaucracy is much too tightly grown in on itself."[83] Johnson did not act on this advice.

Not everyone, however, saw the withdrawal as good for Johnson. It flew in the face of conventional wisdom that the power of a "lame duck" dissipates rapidly, and some criticized the move for that reason. As Gemmill put it, "LBJ is launched on his greatest gamble: That a lame duck can do something more than limp."[84] To Clark Clifford, who had favored an earlier announcement, coupling the two statements made it seem that both had the same cause—the Tet Offensive. Clifford was worried that making the two announcements together would create the impression that Johnson's political career had been ended by Hanoi rather than by his own choice.[85] This concern was a distinct minority view, however. Likewise, while there was much concern raised in South Vietnam about the announcement (reporter Beverly Deupe wrote that it "created an atomic-bomb-sized political shock wave through the hawkish American and Vietnamese anti-communist communities in Saigon"[86]), President Thieu told Ambassador Ellsworth Bunker that, upon reflection, "he felt that the speech was unexceptional, flexible, and very carefully constructed, and that it would give him no difficulties."[87]

The other major effect of the withdrawal announcement was on the developing 1968 campaign. Perhaps the worst prophecy of the year was that of James H. Rollins of St. Louis, co-chairman with Dr. Benjamin

Spock of the National Conference on New Politics, who said that Johnson's withdrawal from the race "shattered plans of radical groups to dis-
rupt the Democratic National Convention."[88] But more generally, the
president's action introduced new confusion into an already unpredict-
able campaign. This was true, in part, because Johnson was not conceding defeat. Had he remained in the race, he almost certainly would
have been renominated, especially in a system in which there were only
fifteen presidential primaries and the state party organizations were
mostly controlled by Johnson loyalists. His departure created a vacuum
that others would try to fill.

The most obvious effect was to propel Hubert Humphrey into the
race as the Democratic frontrunner. He announced his candidacy on
April 27, too late to enter any primaries, and he occupied an anomalous
position. Kennedy and McCarthy were bidding for his long-time liberal supporters, while Humphrey was cast as the stand-in for Johnson,
tied to the president's unpopular policies, especially on Vietnam. Dallek
notes that Johnson "liked Hubert and believed he would be a staunch
advocate of the domestic programs they favored. But he also considered
him too soft or too much of a bleeding-heart liberal who would have
trouble making tough decisions."[89] Johnson's ambivalence would continue throughout the campaign.

The McCarthy and Kennedy campaigns also were thrown into dis-
array. It seemed in the moment that Johnson was abandoning policies
they opposed and adopting ones they favored, leaving them with nothing to campaign against. Kennedy's immediate response to Johnson's
speech was, "I don't know quite what to say,"[90] and that remark captured the uncertainty of the rhetorical situation his campaign was in.
McCarthy was heavily favored to win the primary in Wisconsin on April
2—Kennedy was not on the ballot, having entered the race too late to
qualify—but the president's withdrawal robbed the victory of virtually
all meaning. Johnson's Wisconsin campaign chairman, Representative
Clement J. Zablocki, nevertheless urged a large vote for the president to
avoid seeming to repudiate his new course, as did the state Democratic
chairman,[91] but it was not to be. And yet the vote could not legitimately
be understood as a complete and total rejection of Johnson's policies on
Vietnam. In Madison, the most liberal city in the state, a referendum
was on the ballot calling for "an immediate cease-fire and American

withdrawal from Vietnam." It failed by a margin of 58 to 42 percent.[92] Wisconsin ratified McCarthy as a serious candidate with staying power until the convention. But he and Kennedy would fight largely on competing personal styles and the question of which was more electable.

George Wallace, running as the candidate of the American Independent Party, does not seem to have been affected much by Johnson's withdrawal from the race. His strategy remained to pick up enough votes to force a deadlock in the Electoral College, which he then could end by dealing with one or the other of the major parties to relax civil rights laws and to adopt other legislation to his liking, in return for his support.

Some Republicans mourned the loss of Johnson as a target for attack. Richard Nixon remained the frontrunner, although Nelson Rockefeller was reconsidering his decision, which he had just announced on March 22, to stay out of the race. The feeling among Republican politicians was that Johnson's withdrawal had improved Nixon's chances in the general election, if he could capture the Republican nomination.[93]

In all these ways, Johnson's withdrawal contributed to reshaping the 1968 presidential race. But there was still the nagging question: Did he mean it?

On the face of it, the president's statement of March 31 seemed quite definite, especially after he changed the subjunctive "would" back to "will." He had said that he "shall not seek" and "will not accept" the nomination of his party (although he joked later that he had not ruled out accepting the *Republican* nomination). Was there any way that this statement, just like the Vietnam announcements in the speech, might be strategically ambiguous? The answer is yes, and the explanation relates to the political concept of "drafting" a candidate. Like the military draft, this would be a form of conscription. It would involve having the convention nominate a candidate without first obtaining his or her consent (and possibly without his or her knowledge). Confronted with the fait accompli of a nomination, the candidate presumably would have no choice but to stand for the office and, if elected, to serve. In the lore of American politics, a "draft" would even override words as strong as Johnson's.[94] The way to eliminate this possibility was to make what was called a "Sherman statement," named after the Civil War General William Tecumseh Sherman, who was being considered as a possible candidate for the presidency in the 1880s. Sherman said, according to political lore, "If nominated, I will not run; if elected, I will not serve." Johnson's statement, strong as it seemed, stopped short of that.

Talk of a possible Johnson "draft" was in the air. As noted above, some of his allies *proposed* this idea as a way to get the president back into the race. Others, more skeptical or cynical about Johnson's motivations, charged or implied that he was actively planning and organizing such an effort. His role model in this was said to be Franklin D. Roosevelt, who throughout the spring of 1940 was publicly disclaiming interest in a third term while working behind the scenes to arrange a "draft" at the Democratic National Convention that year.

Shortly after March 31, Chicago's Mayor Daley said that at that time Kennedy was the favorite of state party leaders, but he did not exclude the possibility of a Johnson draft. Senator Mansfield on April 1 said he thought Johnson might "change his mind" if a draft movement developed at the convention. And columnist Tom Wicker cited the precedent of Roosevelt in 1940.[95] There was a certain degree of hopefulness in these statements. But others were far more cynical. Conservative columnist James J. Kilpatrick regarded Johnson's withdrawal as a strategic ploy, writing on April 4, "Many of us will not believe it. We will not believe that Johnson really 'will not accept' renomination until we see another man's hand raised in victory at Chicago."[96] Reporting on a survey of political leaders in sixteen Midwestern states, Howard James found "surprising cynicism on the part of many Democrats who see this as a political gambit on the part of the president. There is speculation that he is using it as a device to win sympathy for his cause and to prove his sincerity."[97] Both *LeMonde*, in Paris, and TASS, the official Soviet press agency, also thought it likely that Johnson was maneuvering.[98]

How could Johnson facilitate a draft? One possibility was to encourage a deadlocked convention by encouraging state party leaders to commit their delegates to "favorite sons," aspiring state-level politicians who were not serious presidential candidates but who captured their state's votes on early ballots in order to be in a position to negotiate with candidates for crucial votes on later ballots. (Party reforms after 1968 have since eliminated this practice.) Carl Oglesby, founder of the radical Students for a Democratic Society (SDS), imagined that if Johnson could properly handle the events of the spring and if Kennedy failed to receive enough votes to win on the first ballot, "we're quite likely to see Johnson reappearing as the binder of wounds in Chicago."[99]

Another possibility was that Johnson might change his mind, claiming that some change in the external environment made it necessary for him to override his pledge of March 31. Roosevelt had done that in 1940, maintaining that, while he still very much wanted to retire, developments in the war in Europe made it his duty to continue to serve if the American people chose him. Some commentators, unwilling to reveal their names, suggested that the course of events in Vietnam could force Johnson to change his mind. This could go either way. One "veteran analyst" hypothesized that if the war could be resolved—if the North accepted the call for talks and the negotiations produced a quick result—Johnson might well change his mind since he would no longer need to avoid spending "an hour or a day of my time" on the campaign. (It is a sign of the optimistic mood after the March 31 speech that this scenario would be mentioned with any seriousness.) At the opposite extreme, "an unnamed Chicago attorney" imagined that if Hanoi *rejected* the peace feeler, "Johnson will go to Congress and ask for a declaration of war and bomb the hell out of North Vietnam." Under such circumstances, he added, "it would be difficult for the Democratic Party not to draft Johnson or for the country not to elect him."[100] (Although the possibility that North Vietnam might reject the peace feeler was real, this scenario was also unlikely.)

These scenarios border on the fanciful. The *Wall Street Journal*, while reporting them, editorialized that the possibilities "were so remote that even the most scheming man—and there are many who would so characterize Lyndon Johnson—would hardly depend upon it as a political maneuver." Johnson himself, in a press conference shortly after he delivered the March 31 speech, described his decision to retire as "completely irrevocable." And Press Secretary George Christian, asked about the possibility that Johnson could be "drafted" for renomination, asserted that that possibility was covered by the president's statement that he "will not accept" a nomination.[101] It would seem that the door was shut tight against any possibility that Lyndon Johnson would remain a candidate.

Yet, Johnson did consider the possibility of retracting his renunciation. He loathed Kennedy, saw McCarthy as a hopelessly quixotic candidate, was ambivalent about Humphrey, thought that Rockefeller had entered the race too late, and could not imagine turning the country over to Nixon. After Kennedy was assassinated, he briefly considered getting back into the race. He was dissuaded by his failure to gain traction with state political leaders, even in the South, who by now had rallied to Humphrey. And the polls were showing that he would do no better against Nixon than either Humphrey or McCarthy.

He thought about it at least once again, as the Chicago convention approached in August. He entertained notions of emerging as a dark horse in case the convention deadlocked. He reportedly imagined announcing from the rostrum a summit meeting with Aleksei Kosygin and being nominated on the wave of emotion from a peace spectacular. He secretly commissioned both a speech and a documentary film exalting his life.[102] In what seemed a happier time long ago, the convention had been scheduled to conclude on Johnson's sixtieth birthday. Perhaps a grand celebration might still be possible.

It was not to happen. The Vietnam War was still raging in August, even though talks were also underway. There was massive civil disturbance in Chicago to protest the convention, and the Soviet invasion of Czechoslovakia one week before the convention ended any prospect of the "peace spectacular." The birthday party was quietly scrapped. Lyndon Johnson ended up not going to Chicago at all. It was probably just as well.

Yet, even so seemingly ironclad a pledge as the withdrawal statement did not necessarily mean what it seemed clearly to say. Just as the Vietnam announcements could be read as continuity or change, acknowledgment of error or celebration of success, so the withdrawal announcement could be read either as an unconditional pledge or as a contingent prediction. It was another sign of the strategic ambiguity in the speech—a rhetorical resource that was attuned to the delicately balanced public opinion of the time and that reflected the need for flexibility in the face of sudden and drastic change.

On April 9, 1968, a memorandum was retrieved from the pocket of Johnson's suit coat. It contained the peroration as it stood before final editing on March 31, together with a note from Horace Busby encouraging the president to use it.[103]

7

The Afterlife of March 31

THE SPEECH STUNNED its audience like a bombshell, but not for the reasons it might have. Initially, the announcements regarding Vietnam attracted little notice, except perhaps for the young men who might have been among the 206,000 troops requested by General Westmoreland and who undoubtedly felt a great sense of relief. But what stunned the public was the last substantive paragraph of the speech in which the president withdrew from the 1968 election contest. Even today, the speech is widely referred to as Johnson's "withdrawal speech," "renunciation speech," or (erroneously) "resignation speech."

The public simply did not consider the possibility that Johnson, the supreme politician of his age, might willingly forego reelection. Of his twentieth-century predecessors, only Theodore Roosevelt (1908), Calvin Coolidge (1928), and Harry Truman (1952)—all of whom, like Johnson, came into office as a result of their predecessors' deaths—voluntarily relinquished the chance to seek a second elected term. In the more than fifty years since Johnson, no one else has done so.[1]

On college campuses, the first reactions to the speech were euphoric. Antiwar protesters, convinced that they were the ones responsible for driving Johnson from the race, celebrated late into the night. Many of them believed that the Democratic presidential nominee now would be either Eugene McCarthy or Robert Kennedy, either of whom would be an antiwar candidate. To the degree that protests against the war convinced the president that the country was so deeply divided that he could not possibly heal it, this self-congratulation was warranted. Otherwise, the protesters were exaggerating their own role in a decision that had been reached largely during the previous November because of concern for Johnson's health. But students were not the only ones pleased by the withdrawal. Though judging it to be fleeting, Bernstein proclaimed, "The immediate reaction to the President's speech from his friends, Congress, the press, and the public was very favorable."[2] Berman points out that "Johnson's colleagues, friends, and political observers" all regarded his decision not to seek reelection as "a positive, forward, and constructive step for national unity and peace in Vietnam."[3] It was as though the president, by leaving the race, could achieve the very results that had eluded him as long as he remained in it.

The decision to exit the race could be linked to the announcements regarding Vietnam in several ways. One was to imagine that the withdrawal freed Johnson from the constraints of domestic politics and allowed him to do what he had "really" wanted to do all along. Another was to suggest that, unburdened by the requirements of reelection, Johnson could "think anew" about the war and could recognize the need for new approaches to the subjects of bombing and troop levels. A third was to maintain that the withdrawal gave credibility to the Vietnam decisions that the president and his advisers had reached quite possibly for other reasons. These decisions could not be dismissed as political ploys or election-year "stunts" since Johnson no longer had anything to gain politically from them. These different approaches to linkage all suggested that the president had achieved the rhetorical goal of *kairos*—finding the opportune moment for the speech. His withdrawal statement achieved results in this speech, simultaneously with the Vietnam announcements, that it would not have achieved in the January 17 State of the Union address, nor during Westmoreland's visit, nor at any earlier time.

There is something valid in each of these theorized linkages, but they overstate the degree to which "lame-duck" officeholders are liberated from constraints. The forces that had stymied Johnson, particularly the nearly even division of the country between hawks and doves, did not disappear and would continue to be a consideration for the remaining ten months of his term. His inability to control the behavior of other nations was still a factor. Whatever he did would still be too much for some audiences and not enough for others. And even "lame ducks" are still speaking to history, trying to affect retrospective judgments of themselves and their actions that may long outlast their days in office. Even taking all these considerations into account, though, Johnson clearly enjoyed a degree of maneuvering room after the speech that he had not enjoyed before.

Several factors combined to "freeze" this interpretation of the speech, at least in the short run. First, initial reaction for the most part generously lauded President Johnson for his political courage or for his statesmanship in placing the national interest above his personal advancement. Such extremely favorable judgments of the president's character created the expectation that his actions would be seen as consistent with the judgments, in order to show that the judgments were warranted. This limited his flexibility to change his mind.

Second, and for many people unexpectedly, on April 3 North Vietnam responded positively to the invitation to participate in talks. Cynics, confident that the North Vietnamese would reject the invitation, might have gone along with Johnson's proposal in the belief that rejection would have justified further American escalation of the war. They might have thought that the communists, having turned down a reasonable alternative to escalation, had left Johnson with no other option. The North Vietnamese acceptance excluded that interpretation. Assistant Press Secretary Tom Johnson's notes of an April 3 White House meeting capture positive assessments of the effect of the March 31 speech on Hanoi. United Nations Ambassador Arthur Goldberg enthused that "for the first time they have been willing to meet to discuss circumstances for a complete pause," making the most of the fact that the North Vietnamese acceptance was limited to talks about how to obtain a complete halt to the US bombing, not to resolve the underlying issues of the war. Similarly, Defense Secretary Clark Clifford argued that "Hanoi responded in [a] manner beyond furthest dreams." He added, "The debate in [the] Senate has been washed away by events," prompting the president to respond, "It's easier to satisfy Ho Chi Minh than Fulbright."[4]

Third, the tragic assassination of Dr. Martin Luther King Jr. on April 4 took the March 31 speech story off the front pages after it had been there only a few days. In the last year of his life, starting with a speech at Riverside Church in New York exactly a year earlier, Dr. King had become a harsh critic of the war on moral grounds. There was talk of movement toward "a grand alliance between civil rights and antiwar forces."[5] The murder of Dr. King not only canceled that talk but also replaced the optimism triggered by the March 31 speech with a widespread sense of lamentation in the face of national tragedy. The March 31 speech would not again capture the national attention for some time.

Fourth, some of the principals involved in the Vietnam decisions began to speak out, either to emphasize their own role or to give weight to a particular perspective on what was a highly ambiguous speech. Foremost in this regard were the efforts of Defense Secretary Clifford. Schandler maintains that Clifford, after March 31, vigorously gave Johnson's remarks a particular interpretation, "so as to occupy ground that Johnson had not yet reached." For example, at an April 11 press conference, he interpreted the partial bombing halt, which he had not advocated in advance, as the first step in a graduated reduction in tensions, whereby a series of reciprocal unilateral moves "over the course of time . . . could lead to a substantial de-escalation of the fighting." As for the American commitment of troops, Clifford described the increment committed on March 31 as reaching the upper limit, a position not taken explicitly in the past but acknowledged by Johnson in early April.[6] Perhaps a bit harshly, Vandiver opined, "Clifford thought he has been the one that changed America's course in history and basked in his own reflections," and Schandler judged that "Clifford's tactics worked admirably" in that the press took his press conference statements as authoritative enunciations of a new strategy supposedly put forth in the president's speech of March 31.[7]

Not everyone interpreted the speech favorably, of course. The government of Japan, which had strongly supported American policy in Vietnam, was seen by its critics to be left hanging as a result of the reversals announced in the president's speech. South Vietnamese President Thieu, who appears not to have been consulted in advance, regarded the speech as "a complete reversal of American policy since July 1965."[8] These, however, were minority viewpoints.

For the next several weeks, the judgment that Johnson acted positively by withdrawing from the race persisted. His aide Joseph Califano wrote on May 2, "For the past month we have been moving with increased power and ability to get things done, as well as an increased sense of confidence because the American people believe you are doing whatever you do without any ax to grind and only because it is right. This has all resulted from you pulling out of the race."[9]

Over time, however, it seemed that these early positive assessments of the speech were based more on atmospherics than substance. Disillusionment was symbolized by the fact that, although talks did get underway, they were almost completely unproductive, consumed for several weeks by disagreements over the shape of the negotiating table. Moreover, it did not appear that the Johnson administration's worldview or ideological framework had changed. Herring concluded that the decisions announced on March 31, "however drastic, represented a perpetuation of the old approach rather than a new departure and did not get near the heart of the problem." He theorized that US military successes in thwarting the Tet Offensive strengthened the belief "that an independent, noncommunist South Vietnam could yet be salvaged from the rubble of war," and he characterized Johnson's decisions as seemingly "designed to buy time to attain this result."[10]

The judgment that Johnson's speech did not herald any change in policy was offered by some even as the speech was delivered and by others, even when it was still in preparation. Immediately after the speech, Tennessee Senator Albert Gore noted that "the President did not reveal a change in war policy tonight. He discussed only tactics."[11] Within the administration, Rusk, Rostow, and General Wheeler all saw the president's announcements not as the marks of a new policy but "as a means to rally public support in order to continue the war much as before," and Herring likewise maintained that the speech was designed as "a quest for domestic consensus, "as much to quiet the home front as anything else"—an effort in which he judged that Johnson ultimately failed."[12]

To critics of this stripe, negotiations at Paris could not possibly succeed. The incompatibility of the American and North Vietnamese objectives had not changed. As Ambassador Averell Harriman left for Paris, Rusk instructed him not to use the talks "to pressure Washington to move from its initial goals." On this basis, of course, as Gardner noted, "there was likely to be little progress." Bernstein reached the same conclusion, calling the Paris talks "window-dressing"and the American belief that Johnson's speech marked the turning point of the war, "a fiction."[13]

Nor did the fighting on the ground mark a turning point. President Thieu understood that the Americans were leaving and tried to gain weapons and other military aid, but the performance of the South Vietnamese remained uneven.[14] American estimates of enemy troop strength were shown to be seriously low and were quickly revised upward.[15] Although the major communist attack on Khe Sanh had failed to materialize, the possibility of a continuing presence of a North Vietnamese attacking force tied down American troops, at least until the would-be attackers were thought to have faded away into Laos.[16] The North retained sufficient forces to mount a second wave of attacks on the same targets that had been hit during Tet, but this time the communist forces suffered a more serious military setback.[17] Even as Johnson focused on talks, he increased military pressure against the communists in the wake of this unsuccessful "Tet II."[18]

This was a sign of a general increase in American aggressiveness in the weeks following the March 31 speech. By April and May, the number of bombing attacks against North Vietnam was far greater than they had been in February and March; they just were concentrated in the part of North Vietnam from which Johnson had not excluded them in the March 31 speech.[19] Any letup in bombing was offset by increased activity on the ground. Even while he was preparing to announce a complete bombing halt in late October, Johnson wrote to General Creighton Abrams, who had succeeded Westmoreland as commander of US forces, "Keep the enemy on the run. Don't give them a minute's rest. Keep pouring it on. Let the enemy feel the weight of everything you've got."[20] Casualty rates in the year following the Tet Offensive were the highest of the war.[21] In the context of these military moves, the announcements in the March 31 speech seem disingenuous, if not downright hypocritical.

The likely reality is that Johnson was of two minds. He knew that there was no likelihood of American military victory in a traditional sense, yet he was determined not to be the first president to lose a war. He saw the damage the war was doing to his priorities foreign and domestic, yet he continued to believe in the Cold War ideological assumptions that had led him and his countrymen to this point. He held both of each pair of beliefs and lived his life in the tension between them. While he correctly diagnosed that the country was deeply divided, he seemed to be unaware that he embodied those deep divisions in his own person. Accordingly, Clifford believes, for the remainder of his term Johnson "sent conflicting signals and possibly lost the opportunity to end the war during his term in office."[22]

In his memoir, Clifford noted that this tension was baked into the March 31 speech itself. He noted that "none of the policy announce-ments were entirely new" but that "the tone and rhetoric of the speech, especially coupled with his withdrawal, was significantly more moder-ate than any other [Johnson] Presidential statement or speech."[23] Of course, Clifford himself had much to do with creating the ambiguity. In the process of drafting and revising the speech, he was one of the major figures arguing that the announcements in the speech were of a nature that *required* the tone that prevailed—a position he seems to have dis-avowed in his memoir by saying that the policies were not new. Then, after the speech had been delivered, he was the major figure advocating that it be interpreted in a particular way, as a major turning point in US policy.

Despite his closeness to the scene, Clifford's acknowledgment of the tension in the speech was not exactly right. He hedged his bets by not-ing that the policy announcements were not *entirely* new, but he failed to take note of the subtle but significant ways in which they *were* new—in their context as de-escalatory moves, in comparison to alternatives that were considered but rejected; in their unilateral nature; and in their overt invitation to the other side to respond reciprocally. Moreover, the ambiguity was not between the speech's content and tone; Clifford himself had done much to harmonize them. Rather, the ambiguity was within each of the policy announcements itself: What exactly did it mean? How would it be carried out? Was it a symbol of strength or of weakness, of continuity or of change?

This view of Johnson as embodying contradiction is at odds with the judgment of other writers. Herring describes him as seemingly op-erating from no convictions at all, merely desiring to reach prudent, satisfactory decisions. Herring concludes that "the tactics Johnson fash-ioned in 1968 were even less well calculated to achieve the illusive [sic] objectives than those of 1965. As before, he improvised, splitting the difference between those who wanted to escalate in pursuit of victo-ry and those, including Clifford, who wanted to scale down American military involvement and political objectives and seek the most graceful withdrawal possible."[24] Knowing that Johnson characteristically held his cards close to the vest, and reading the notes of White House deliberations in which Johnson would decide both that the speech should be "all troops and war" and also that Dean Rusk should "really get your horses on that" in pursuit of a bombing halt, one might easily conclude that Johnson did not care what was done as long as *something* was done. But such a view is out of line with the man who took combat deaths personally, who wanted to be awakened in the middle of the night with reports on the results of bombing runs, or who told his advisers, "I want war like I want polio." Rather than being stymied by failures at satisficing in the absence of convictions, Johnson was thwarted by the fact that he held contradictory convictions sincerely and could not find a way to fulfill them both.

Another critic, Gabriel Kolko, holds an opposite view, finding Johnson to be so firm in his convictions as to be unshakeable. He writes, "Clifford and those who wanted to redefine national policy and scale down the war knew that the President would never agree with them, whatever they said." Therefore, Kolko concludes, all that these well-intentioned advisers could do for the rest of 1968 was to "try to keep Johnson tied to what they regarded as a schizoid policy and prevent it from becoming something even worse."[25] But neither Clifford nor Johnson was so set in his view as this claim suggests. The defense secretary came to his post with hawkish convictions and began to favor de-escalation only when he discovered that the military could not promise victory no matter what the troop level. Moreover, Clifford believed he was breaking a logjam, not creating one, by setting in motion what he hoped would be a series of reciprocal moves. Johnson, far from being intransigent, was making a choice to reject escalation when he picked the Alternate Draft of the speech rather than the competing, more hawkish draft. In the same way, he was making a choice when he peremptorily dismissed Westmoreland's request for 206,000 troops even in advance of the complete policy review which the request had prompted him to order. It seems more likely that Johnson was acting from the deep wellsprings of competing motivations and was thwarted because he could not have it all.

Ambiguity is usually thought to be a liability in a message. Some theorists go so far as to label it a fallacy. When a term or phrase has multiple possible meanings and it is not clear which meaning is being used in a given case, there is always the danger that the participants in an exchange will use it differently, agreeing or disagreeing with one another not on the merits but merely as an artifact of the meanings each has chosen to use. For this reason, interactants often are admonished to be clear and to be sure that they are using the same terms in the same way.

But there is an exception to this general advice. Sometimes, whether intentionally or not, ambiguity can be strategic; that is, it contributes to outcomes that are in the interest of one or more of the participants in discourse. A simple example would be a situation such as an election canvass, in which candidates seek a consensus of support or opposition to a particular measure without regard to the reasons anyone has for his or her view. Ambiguous symbols into which individuals can read their diverse interests seem to satisfy this need. For example, a campaign may proclaim that its candidate is in favor of "securing the border" and seek support on that basis. To one potential supporter, "securing the border" might mean stationing more troops near the border; to another, speeding up the processing of applicants for immigration; and to another, building a physical barrier such as a wall along the border. It does not matter that they all support different actions, as long as they all identify their policy proposals with "securing the border."

It does not matter, that is, in the short run, when the campaigner's goal is to get elected, or to obtain appropriations, or to lambaste one's opponent for not truly being committed to the cause. But it is in the nature of strategic ambiguity that it often serves to "kick the can" further down the road. A time will arise when it will be necessary either to choose among the proffered options or else to invent another strategically ambiguous term or phrase that will permit further postponement of a decision. Strategic ambiguity opens windows for maneuvering toward a decision; it does not hold them open indefinitely.

Strategic ambiguity was built into American rhetoric and politics from the beginning. The Constitution clearly recognized the existence of slavery but declined to use the term; did that make it a proslavery or an antislavery document? The integrity of the Union depended on leaving the matter ambiguous, until the circumstances of the late 1850s demanded a resolution. Likewise, it did not seem to matter where sovereignty ultimately lay—with the states or the federal government—until the nullification crisis of the 1830s and the secession crisis of the 1860s made clear the need for a decision. Lincoln insisted that it did not matter whether or not the seceded states really had left the Union, as long as everyone agreed in 1865 that they were safely back in. It did not matter, that is, until one had to choose between a harsh and a lenient approach to Reconstruction. What the Supreme Court meant in saying that corporations were legal persons could be left ambiguous until some contended that the Court in the Gilded Age stretched the meaning beyond the intent of the Fourteenth Amendment's reference to "persons." What counted as equal in the phrase "separate but equal" could be left ambiguous until the civil rights movement of the 1950s awoke the conscience of the nation; what counted as "all deliberate speed" could not remain ambiguous for nearly so long. In the realm of foreign affairs, what counted as an "entangling alliance" to be avoided could be left ambiguous from Thomas Jefferson's First Inaugural Address in 1801 until the formation of NATO in the late 1940s. And with specific reference to Vietnam, what constituted "aggression" could be left ambiguous until it became clear that the answer determined whether the United States was engaged in an international conflict or was intervening unjustifiably in a civil war. The point is that US history can be understood as a continuing dialectic between tolerance for strategic ambiguity and forced choices that purchase clarity at the price of unity.

As the earlier chapters have suggested, there were key elements of strategic ambiguity throughout President Johnson's address of March 31. Concerning the bombing halt, what area was covered? Was it a de-escalatory move? What behavior by the North Vietnamese was necessary for them to obtain the complete bombing halt on which they insisted? Concerning the troop increase, was it an expansion or a limitation of the war? Did it imply a cap on the total number of US troops? Was the proposal to shift the burden to the Vietnamese realistic? Was it justifiable? Even concerning Johnson's withdrawal from the race, did he really mean what he said, or was it some kind of stunt? Was March 31 Johnson's final statement on the subject, or might he change his mind later?

These elements of strategic ambiguity were useful in the short run. They enabled Johnson's advisers to articulate post-Tet policies regarding Vietnam and to solicit support for them as new. Particularly after the favorable North Vietnamese response, they encouraged a mood of optimism that bought them time. They might have permitted some breakthrough proposal had one emerged. But the patience of the American people had worn thin by 1968 and could not be buoyed for long. The central ambiguity regarding the March 31 speech, as stated by Herring, was whether it had been "intended to extricate the United States from a war now conceded unwinnable" or whether "it [had] been designed to achieve at a lower cost the goal of an independent, noncommunist South Vietnam?"[26] Agreeing with this basic formulation of the question, Clifford noted that by the late spring of 1968 the Johnson administration had split into two factions. Supporting Herring's first interpretation of the speech's goal were Averell Harriman, Cyrus Vance, Nicholas Katzenbach, Arthur Goldberg, Paul Nitze, Paul Warnke, and Clifford himself. Herring's second view was supported by Dean Rusk, Walt Rostow, Ellsworth Bunker, Maxwell Taylor, Abe Fortas, and the entire military command.[27] Johnson, who at a fundamental level supported both views and did not want to choose between them, was left in the same difficult position that he had occupied before March 31. If he could not unite his own advisers, how could he hope to unite the country? The contribution that strategic ambiguity could make to resolving this predicament was limited.

Interestingly, there was one major section of the March 31 speech that so far has escaped analysis and that did not rely on strategic ambiguity. About two-thirds of the way through the speech, Johnson began a discussion of what an eventual peace in Southeast Asia would look like. He celebrated moves toward peace and security that had been made throughout the region, and he asserted that the US presence in Vietnam had been the shield behind which many of these efforts had taken place. He then harked back to his 1965 speech at Johns Hopkins University, in which he had laid out his vision for economic development of the region and had invited North Vietnam to participate. He renewed his offer, and he claimed that the Vietnam policies he was announcing on March 31 should be understood as the first steps toward lasting peace among independent nations of Southeast Asia. He prayed that his initiative would not be rejected by the leaders of North Vietnam.

This section of the speech, like the Johns Hopkins address to which it referred, illustrates what Doris Kearns Goodwin in another context calls Johnson's "visionary leadership,"[28] his ability to articulate a utopian vision that would inspire his fellow Americans to take steps toward its achievement. She was referring to Johnson's moves in 1964 to obtain passage of the Civil Rights Act. But here Johnson was sketching out how a postwar Vietnam might take its place among the family of independent nations of Southeast Asia, to which the United States would be a valued partner. It was an attempt to remove Vietnam from the Cold War context in which he usually spoke of it. Yet, it was seldom mentioned in analysis and commentary of the March 31 speech, and there is little reason to believe that it was taken seriously by those who heard the speech. Like the Johns Hopkins speech, much to Johnson's chagrin, it largely fell on deaf ears.

Why? It would not be right to dismiss this section of the speech as fluff, for there is every reason to think Johnson sincerely believed it. He thought the ability of humans, and especially of Americans, to solve problems was limitless if only they had the will. Although he surely had political motives—the Johns Hopkins speech had been intended to coopt liberal critics, particularly Walter Lippmann[29]—this does not deny the sincerity of Johnson's appeal. Rather, the difficulty with this section of the March 31 speech is that it does not speak to any of the factors that called for strategic ambiguity. It could be attached to any of the policy options Johnson was considering and to any of the questions of interpretation about the options he chose. It could be portrayed as the objective of limited or of expanded bombing, and of a cap on the number of troops or a surge in the number of troops, and just about anything in between. On its face, it might therefore seem like the ultimate case of strategic ambiguity. But there is nothing especially ambiguous about the vision itself, except perhaps for the details of what an independent Southeast Asian community might look like. The vision, however, was not offered at a time when the audience might be receptive to it. Unlike his decision not to run, Johnson had not found the kairotic moment for sharing this vision. A nation impatient with the war and

eager to end it one way or another was not in the mood for a long-term
enticement toward peace that had not worked yet. Johnson's utopian vision did not receive much attention because it did not contribute much
to meeting the needs of the moment.

The March 31 speech brought the two sides in the war into something of a dialogue, and it did not result in 206,000 more troops being
sent to Vietnam, but those were about the limits of its immediate effect. The war went on. But it played a relatively small part in the emerging presidential campaign, probably because any candidate would face
the same dilemma Johnson had: the public was deeply split; any stance
that favored hawks would alienate doves, and vice versa. Eugene Mc-
Carthy and Robert Kennedy continued to campaign as antiwar candidates, but they favored de-escalation rather than outright withdrawal.
In any case, it was not clear how much support they enjoyed beyond
their respective initial bases. Richard Nixon, who by now was the Republican frontrunner and who had canceled a speech on Vietnam he
had planned to make on March 31, subsequently announced that he
would "eschew 'comprehensive' discussion of Vietnam" in order to
give Johnson's peace moves every chance to succeed.[30] He maintained
a similar stance during the fall campaign, stating that he hoped Johnson's efforts would succeed but that, if the war had not concluded by
January 20, 1969, he had a plan to end it—a plan he could not divulge,
of course, lest he tip off the enemy.

Vice President Hubert Humphrey entered the race on April 27 with
an ill-timed appeal to the "politics of joy." He had the support of Democratic Party leaders throughout the country and would win the nomination without entering any of the fifteen primaries that were held that
year. He was widely perceived as identical to Johnson in his policy preferences. In fact, he occupied something of a middle ground between
Johnson and his challengers on the left. He had advised the president
against escalation in 1965 and was frozen out of the decision-making
circle as a consequence. By 1968, he had learned his lesson and was toe-
ing Johnson's line—at least in public. Yet, privately he sought a move
that might unite his fractured party, such as a total bombing halt. The
draft of the party platform was a ringing endorsement of Johnson's
policy. Humphrey appealed to the president for permission to deviate
from the party line by calling for a total bombing halt, but Johnson

turned him down flat.[31] Indeed, "as the Democratic National Convention approached, Johnson's resistance to appeals that he end the bombing of North Vietnam increased."[32]

Probably the dominant impression of the Democratic convention, however, was the simultaneous rioting in the streets of Chicago, which was shown on television screens inside the convention hall and elicited protest speeches supporting the demonstrators. The events would be called a "police riot," although public opinion supported the Chicago police. Any talk that Johnson might make a surprise visit to the convention to celebrate his birthday was quickly silenced. It seemed that if the party could not govern itself, surely it could not govern the country.

The Democrats emerged from the convention with the pro-Johnson plank, but it was a pyrrhic victory for Johnson and a net loss for Humphrey. The party left with the delegates badly divided and with Humphrey lagging significantly in the polls. There was even speculation that he might finish third in the popular vote, behind not only Nixon but also former Alabama Governor George Wallace, who was running as a third-party candidate. Humphrey's standing did not improve until September 30. On that night he delivered a speech in Salt Lake City, announcing that, as president, he would stop all bombing of North Vietnam, while reserving the right to resume it if the North took advantage of the situation. A gingerly step away from Johnson's position, it was understood at the time as a sharp break. Both Humphrey's poll numbers and campaign contributions rose dramatically during the campaign's last weeks, and the final popular vote was almost as much a nail-biter as 1960 had been.

By that time Johnson himself was prepared to order a complete halt to the bombing of North Vietnam. Gardner notes that, by mid-October, "even the most staunch hawks realized that the preconditions for stopping all bombing, as set out in the San Antonio formula, had been met."[33] True, North Vietnam had not pledged to refrain from "taking advantage" of a bombing halt. But, as the *New York Times* had editorialized back in the spring, if there were a North Vietnamese military threat while negotiations were underway, the United States undoubtedly would renew the bombing, so it was unnecessary to extract a pledge from the North Vietnamese in advance.[34]

At any rate, by late October, the president had secured the agreement—or so he thought—of North and South Vietnam, the Viet Cong,
and the United States to enter promptly into peace talks following a
complete bombing halt. Accordingly, on October 31 he announced
that all bombing of the North would cease.

Johnson's advisers were divided on the wisdom of pushing to get
peace talks underway in October of 1968. As Prados reports, "Clifford and Harriman might have been enthusiastic and General Abrams
resigned, but others were less amenable. Dean Rusk continued to be
reluctant, while Bunker took Thieu's side. The Joint Chiefs were un-
comfortable but willing to go along." Prados describes National Security Adviser Walt Rostow as playing "a complex game: on the one hand,
seeming to adopt the position of his boss, LBJ, who feared leaving office
having done nothing to jump-start talks; on the other hand, throwing
up obstacles."[35]

It is inconceivable that Johnson was unaware of the potential political impact of this announcement, coming just a few days before the
election and as Humphrey was moving rapidly to close the gap in the
polls between himself and Nixon. But it would be unfair to see it only
as a political stunt. It was the culmination of a diplomatic and military initiative within the administration. What made it seem like just a
political ploy was the disclosure by President Thieu of South Vietnam,
after Johnson had announced the bombing halt, that he was not willing to participate in the scheduled talks after all. His attitude toward
negotiations, as Prados describes it, "remained crystal clear: the only
acceptable settlement was one that removed the threat of Hanoi and
the National Liberation Front."[36] Not only did Johnson's proposal not
eliminate these groups, it invited them in as negotiating partners.

Thieu's refusal to participate might have seemed to be proof that
Johnson had halted the bombing prematurely, hoping only to help
Humphrey in the election. But it soon became known that Thieu had
been importuned to stay out by Anna Chennault, the widow of General Claire Chennault of the "Flying Tigers" during World War II. She
was now a Republican operative working on behalf of the Nixon campaign. Chennault told Thieu that if he held out now, he would get a
better deal from the Nixon administration later. Johnson knew of this
but could not reveal what he knew, having obtained his information

from illegal wiretapping. Humphrey chose not to make an issue of this episode in the closing days of the campaign because he had no proof of Nixon's direct involvement. There matters stood for many years—until 2017, when the historian John A. Farrell, doing research for a new Nixon biography, found evidence in the diaries of Nixon's chief of staff, H. R. Haldeman, strongly indicating that Nixon himself had given the order for Mrs. Chennault to make the overture to Thieu.[37] The last-minute Humphrey surge had begun to ebb even before this news had broken. Fate dealt him a very narrow loss.

In office, Nixon realized that he must respond to the people's growing impatience with the war, but he also knew that a hasty American exit would leave the South Vietnamese unable to sustain the effort on their own, notwithstanding the improvements they had made in their military capability. So Nixon played for time, announcing phased withdrawals of US troops while expanding the air war, including the secret bombing of Cambodia and Laos. Although Johnson had set a cap of 549,500 US troops, actual troop strength was below that level at the beginning of 1969. The number of American military personnel continued to grow until April 1969 and then began to decline gradually, taking six months to recede to the pre-Tet level.[38]

Nixon successfully pleaded for public support in a nationally televised speech on November 3, 1969. Asserting that only Americans could undermine the US war effort, he called upon "the great silent majority" to give him their support. The flood of favorable messages to the White House following the speech was later found to have been ginned up. Prados reports that "in testimony at a 1999 trial held to consider the fair market value of the original of this ["silent majority"] speech and its drafts, presidential aide Alexander M. Butterfield revealed that he had spent weeks prompting the response, arranging with labor unions, military retirees, the Veterans of Foreign Wars, the American Legion, millionaire entrepreneur H. Ross Perot, and others to generate it."[39]

Nevertheless, the combination of Vietnamization, the conversion of the military draft to a lottery system, and the replacement of the draft with an all-volunteer army, significantly reduced the risk of the war to individual Americans of draft age. As that happened, Small notes, there was "a slow but steady decline in the anti-war movement and anti-war opinion in the United States."[40] That, in turn, gave Nixon the time he needed to continue the war while the South Vietnamese presumably gained the strength and ability to take over on their own. The United States signed a truce in January 1973. The South Vietnamese government fell two years later.

Read from the perspective of over fifty years later, it may seem hard to see why President Johnson's speech of March 31, 1968, was regarded as so important. The changes announced in the speech were relatively modest; the agreement to talk it elicited from the North Vietnamese proved illusory; and the speech did not fundamentally alter the course of the war. Yet those who viewed the speech and stood to be affected by it are likely to recall it vividly—if only for Johnson's announcement of his withdrawal from the race—and to regard it as one of the more significant presidential speeches of the 1960s. Placing the speech in the context of its time, as this analysis has sought to do, reveals how its crafting, and particularly how its exploiting of the resources of strategic ambiguity, enabled Lyndon Johnson to respond to, and briefly to take control of, a highly constrained and complex rhetorical situation. The speech was masterful in its context, but unlike masterpieces of eloquence, it has not outlasted that context nor continued to speak meaningfully to us still.

On the other hand, it might yet. To understand the speech thoroughly, it must be set in the context of the Cold War of the 1950s and 1960s. If the ideological cold war between "freedom" and "communism" has faded, however, terrorism, cyberwarfare, and trade wars all have the potential to awaken a new cold war. Once again, policies might be based on motivations attributed to the other side, with or without evidence, and presidential credibility in conveying messages might be crucial to success. Another president, like Johnson, might conclude that the country is deeply divided and he (or she) cannot heal it. If that happens, the speech of March 31 will become most pertinent once again.

Notes

Chapter 1

1. Herbert Y. Schandler, *The Unmaking of a President: Lyndon Johnson and Vietnam* (Princeton, NJ: Princeton University Press, 1977), 340.

2. Schandler, *Unmaking*, 339.

3. John Prados, *Vietnam: The History of an Unwinnable War, 1945–1975* (Lawrence: University Press of Kansas, 2009), 21; Robert J. McMahon, "Harry S. Truman and the Roots of US Involvement in Indochina, 1945–1953," in *Shadow on the White House: Presidents and the Vietnam War, 1945–1975*, ed. David L. Anderson (Lawrence: University Press of Kansas, 1993), 25.

4. Prados, *Vietnam*, 20; McMahon, "Truman and the Roots," 32.

5. Anderson, *Shadow on the White House*, 45.

6. Anderson, *Shadow on the White House*, 47; Prados, *Vietnam*, 33.

7. Prados, *Vietnam*, 28.

8. Anderson, *Shadow on the White House*, 49.

9. Prados, *Vietnam*, 51.

10. Anderson, *Shadow on the White House*, 58.

11. "John F. Kennedy Speeches, Remarks of Senator John F. Kennedy at the Conference on Vietnam Luncheon in the Hotel Willard," Washington, DC, June 1, 1956, www.jfklibrary.org/Research/Research-Aids/JFK-Speeches/Vietnam-Conference-Washington-DC_19560601.aspx.

12. See Gregory A. Olson, *Mansfield and Vietnam: A Study in Rhetorical Adaptation* (East Lansing: Michigan State University Press, 1995), 42–43, 50–52, 118–19 on the role of religion in support for the Diem government.

13. Cited in Melvin Small, *At the Water's Edge: American Politics and the Vietnam War* (Chicago: Ivan R. Dee, 2005), 13.

14. Cited in Prados, *Vietnam*, 67.

15. Gary R. Hess, "Commitment in the Age of Counterinsurgency: Kennedy's Vietnam Options and Decisions," in *Shadow on the White House*, ed. Anderson, 67.

16. Small, *At the Water's Edge*, 20.

17. Hess, "Commitment," 79.

18. Schandler, *Unmaking*, 335.

19. David L. Anderson, "A Question of Political Courage: Lyndon Johnson as War Leader," in *Looking Back at LBJ*, ed. Mitchell B. Lerner (Lawrence: University Press of Kansas, 2005), 110.

20. Schandler, *Unmaking*, 333, 311.

21. Doris Kearns, *Lyndon Johnson and the American Dream* (New York: Harper and Row, 1976), 269; Prados, *Vietnam*, 161.

22. Anderson, "A Question of Political Courage," 111.

23. Cited in Prados, *Vietnam*, 83.

24. Cited in Prados, *Vietnam*, 167.

25. Cited in Edwin E. Moïse, *The Myths of Tet: The Most Misunderstood Event of the Vietnam War* (Lawrence: University Press of Kansas, 2017), 54.

26. Charles DeBenedetti, "Lyndon Johnson and the Antiwar Opposition," in *The Johnson Years*, ed. Robert A. Divine, vol. 2, *Vietnam, the Environment, and Science* (Lawrence: University Press of Kansas, 1987), 27.

27. Cited in Small, *At the Water's Edge*, 117.

28. Cited in Moïse, *The Myths of Tet*, 54.

29. Townsend Hoopes, *The Limits of Intervention: An Inside Account of How the Johnson Policy of Escalation in Vietnam Was Reversed* (New York: David McKay, 1969), 97.

30. Stanley Karnow, *Vietnam: A History* (New York: Viking, 1983), 546.

31. McGeorge Bundy, Memo to the President, March 21, 1968, 3/31/68 Remarks of the President to the Nation, the President's Oval Office, White House Central Files, Statements of Lyndon Baines Johnson, Box 274, Lyndon Baines Johnson Library.

32. Cited in Prados, *Vietnam*, 98.

33. Small, *At the Water's Edge*, 43.

34. Small, *At the Water's Edge*, 38.

35. www.americanwar library.com/Vietnam/vwatl.htm. Accessed May 10, 2018.

36. See, for example, Small, *At the Water's Edge*, 51; Prados, *Vietnam*, 151.

37. Prados, *Vietnam*, 140.

38. Robert Dallek, *Flawed Giant: Lyndon Johnson and His Times, 1961–1973* (New York: Oxford University Press, 1998), 376.

39. Dallek, *Flawed Giant*, 444.

40. CIA Memorandum, "Questions Concerning the Situation in Vietnam," March 1, 1968, Volume 4, Tabs C-M, National Security Files, National Security Council Histories, March 31st Speech, Box 48, Lyndon Baines Johnson Library.

41. Prados, *Vietnam*, 192.

42. Schandler, *Unmaking*, 335.

43. Cited in George C. Herring, "The Reluctant Warrior: Lyndon Johnson as Commander in Chief," in *Shadow on the White House: Presidents and the Vietnam War, 1945–1975*, ed. David L. Anderson (Lawrence: University Press of Kansas, 1993), 98.

44. Prados, *Vietnam*, 130.

45. Prados, *Vietnam*, 166.

46. Harry McPherson, Memorandum to the President, October 27, 1967, National Security File, Country File—Vietnam, Box 127, Lyndon Baines Johnson Library.

47. Prados, *Vietnam*, 158.

48. Cited in Anderson, *Shadow on the White House*, 184, 186.

49. Cited in Anderson, "A Question of Political Courage," 104.

50. Dallek, *Flawed Giant*, 453, 489.

51. DeBenedetti, "Lyndon Johnson and His Antiwar Opposition," 32.

52. Hoopes, *The Limits of Intervention*, 57.

53. Lyndon B. Johnson, Memorandum for the File, December 18, 1967, National Security File, Country File—Vietnam, Box 127, Lyndon Baines Johnson Library.

54. Schandler, *The Unmaking of a President*, 65.

55. Cited in Robert S. McNamara, *In Retrospect: The Tragedy and Lessons of Vietnam* (New York: Random House, 1995), 294.

56. Prados, *Vietnam*, 543.

57. Quoted in Prados, *Vietnam*, 213.

58. Robert McNamara, Memorandum to the President, November 1, 1967, National Security File, Country File—Vietnam, Box 127, Lyndon Baines Johnson Library.

59. Prados, *Vietnam*, 215.

60. Dean Rusk, Memorandum to the President, November 20, 1967, National Security File, Country File—Vietnam, Box 127, Lyndon Baines Johnson Library.

61. Abe Fortas, Memorandum to the President, November 5, 1967, National Security File, Country File—Vietnam, Box 127, Lyndon Baines Johnson Library.

62. Chart summarizing reactions to McNamara proposal, National Security File, Country File—Vietnam, Box 127, Lyndon Baines Johnson Library.

63. This was the memorandum of December 18, 1967 referred to in note 53.

64. Jim Jones, Memorandum to the President, n.d., November 2, 1967 Meeting with Foreign Policy Advisors on Vietnam, Meeting Notes File, Box 2, Lyndon Baines Johnson Library.

65. McNamara, *In Retrospect*, 306, 309.

66. DeBenedetti, "Lyndon Johnson and the Antiwar Opposition," 42.

67. Moïse, *The Myths of Tet*, 13.

68. Moïse, *The Myths of Tet*, 55.

69. Larry Berman, *Lyndon Johnson's War: The Road to Stalemate in Vietnam* (New York: Norton, 1989), 114.

70. Prados, *Vietnam*, 220.

71. Moïse, *The Myths of Tet*, 101, 34. See especially Chapters 2 and 3 for a

discussion of techniques to underestimate enemy strength.

72. Moïse, *The Myths of Tet*, 15.

73. Moïse, *The Myths of Tet*, 90.

74. Moïse, *The Myths of Tet*, Chapter 3.

75. Moïse, *The Myths of Tet*, 41.

76. Dallek, *Flawed Giant*, 490.

77. Herring, "The Reluctant Warrior," 101.

78. Herring, "The Reluctant Warrior," 102.

79. Small, *At the Water's Edge*, 95.

80. Schandler, *Unmaking*, 65.

81. Prados, *Vietnam*, 220.

82. Quoted in Dallek, *Flawed Giant*, 491.

83. Dallek, *Flawed Giant*, 499; Moïse, *The Myths of Tet*, 100–101; "Johnson's Rating on Vietnam Drops," *New York Times*, February 14, 1968, 4.

84. "Johnson's Rating on Vietnam Drops," 4.

85. Quoted in Moïse, *The Myths of Tet*, 99.

86. Robert G. Ginsburgh, Memorandum to Walt Rostow, January 31, 1968, National Security Council History, Volume 2, Tabs A to Z and AA to ZZ [part 1 of 2 parts], National Security File, National Security Council Histories, March 31st Speech, Box 47, Lyndon Baines Johnson Library.

87. Quoted in Moïse, *The Myths of Tet*, 104.

88. Zbigniew Brzezinski, Memorandum, "The War in Vietnam: For a Balance between US Goals and US Means," March 14, 1968, Memo's to Read [1], Papers of Clark Clifford, Vietnam Papers, Box 1, Lyndon Baines Johnson Library.

89. George C. Herring, "The War in Vietnam," in *Exploring the Johnson Years*, ed. Robert A. Divine (Austin: University of Texas Press, 1981), 51.

Chapter 2

1. The counts are from Clark Clifford with Richard Holbrooke, *Counsel to the President* (New York: Random House, 1991), 473.

2. Larry Berman, *Lyndon Johnson's War: The Road to Stalemate in Vietnam* (New York: Norton, 1989), 145.

3. Edwin E. Moïse, *The Myths of Tet: The Most Misunderstood Event of the Vietnam War* (Lawrence: University Press of Kansas, 2017), 144.

4. Cited in Clifford with Holbrooke, *Counsel to the President*, 473.

5. John Prados, *Vietnam: The History of an Unwinnable War, 1945–1975* (Lawrence: University Press of Kansas, 2009), 232; "The War: Double Trouble," *Time*, February 9, 1968, 15.

6. Cited in Bromley Smith, Memorandum to the President, January 30, 1968, Volume 2, Tabs A to Z and AA to ZZ [part 1 of 2 parts], National Security File, National Security Council Histories, March 31st Speech, Box 47, Lyndon Baines Johnson Library.

7. Lyndon Baines Johnson, *The Vantage Point: Perspectives of the Presidency, 1963–1969* (New York: Holt, Rinehart, and Winston, 1971), 382.

8. For examples and elaboration, see March 31st Speech, Volume 1, National Security File, National Security Council Histories, March 31st Speech, Box 47, Lyndon Baines Johnson Library.

9. Cited in Moïse, *The Myths of Tet*, 156.

10. For example, see Volume 2, Tabs A to Z and AA to ZZ [part 1 of 2], National Security File, National Security Council Histories, March 31st Speech, Box 47, Lyndon Baines Johnson Library.

11. Prados, *Vietnam*, 196, 230.

12. Prados, *Vietnam*, 195.

13. Cited in Prados, *Vietnam*, 193.

14. Stanley Karnow, *Vietnam: A History* (New York: Viking, 1983), 536.

15. Moïse, *The Myths of Tet*, 143.

16. Herbert Y. Schandler, *The Unmaking of a President: Lyndon Johnson and Vietnam* (Princeton, NJ: Princeton University Press, 1977), 71.

17. Moïse, *The Myths of Tet*, 129.

18. Quoted in Volume 2, Tabs A to Z and AA to ZZ [part 1 of 2 parts], National Security File, National Security Council Histories, March 31st Speech, Box 47, Lyndon Baines Johnson Library.

19. Notes on the President's Thursday Night Meeting on the Pueblo Incident, January 25, 1968, Tom Johnson's Notes of Meetings, Box 2, Lyndon Baines Johnson Library.

20. Clifford with Holbrooke, *Counsel to the President*, 469; Schandler, *Unmaklng*, 68.

21. Moïse, *The Myths of Tet*, 134.

22. Randall B. Woods, *LBJ: Architect of American Ambition* (New York: Free Press, 2006), 825; William P. Bundy, Draft Memorandum to the Group [the Clifford Task Force], February 29, 1968, Memos on Vietnam: February–March 1968, Papers of Clark Clifford, Vietnam Papers, Box 2, Lyndon Baines Johnson Library; "Westmoreland Asks for 206,000 More GIs; Stirs Debate," *Chicago Tribune*, March 10, 1968, 5.

23. Karnow, *Vietnam*, 546; John W. Finney, "Rusk Tells Panel of 'A to Z' Review of Vietnam War," *New York Times*, March 12, 1968, 1; Felix Belair Jr., "Aid Funds Facing Delay in Senate," *New York Times*, March 12, 1968, 1; Moïse, *The Myths of Tet*, 197.

24. Moïse, *The Myths of Tet*, 152; Ronald Sullivan, "Kennan Attacks Vietnam Policy as Massive, Unparalleled Error," *New York Times*, March 1, 1968, 25.

25. Moïse, *The Myths of Tet*, 153; Notes on the President's Meeting with Senior Foreign Policy Advisers, February 11, 1968, Tom Johnson's Notes of Meetings, Box 2, Lyndon Baines Johnson Library.

26. "Switches by Press on War Reported," *New York Times*, February 18, 1968, 9.

27. Notes of the President's Meeting with the Democratic Congressional Leadership, February 6, 1968, Tom Johnson's Notes of Meetings, Box 2, Lyndon Baines Johnson Library. President Johnson went on to urge Senator Mike Mansfield, the Majority Leader, to make a speech about Ho Chi Minh, saying, "nobody says anything bad about Ho. They call me a murderer. But Ho has a great image."

28. Schandler, *Unmaking*, 83.

29. Gladwin Hill, "Eisenhower Backs Course of War," *New York Times*, March 16, 1968, 15.

30. Cited in Moïse, *The Myths of Tet*, 153.

31. Harry McPherson, *A Political Education* (1972; rpt. Boston: Little, Brown, 1988), 424.

32. Joseph A. Califano Jr., *The Triumph and Tragedy of Lyndon Johnson* (New York: Simon and Schuster, 1991), 257.

33. Townsend Hoopes, *The Limits of Intervention: An Inside Account of How the Johnson Policy of Escalation in Vietnam Was Reversed* (New York: David McKay, 1969), 146.

34. Prados, *Vietnam*, 241.

35. Moïse, *The Myths of Tet*, 109.

36. Johnson, *The Vantage Point*, 380.

37. Johnson, *The Vantage Point*, 384.

38. Westmoreland is cited in George C. Herring, "The War in Vietnam," in *Exploring the Johnson Years*, ed. Robert A. Divine (Austin: University of Texas Press, 1981), 49. The Wheeler and Abrams statements are in Supplemental Notes on Meeting of the President with General Abrams, March 22, 1968, Tom Johnson's Notes of Meetings, Box 2, Lyndon Baines Johnson Library.

39. Moïse, *The Myths of Tet*, 186. See also Prados, *Vietnam*, 239.

40. Melvin Small, "Containing Domestic Enemies: Richard M. Nixon and the War at Home," in *Shadow on the White House: Presidents and the Vietnam War, 1945–1975*, ed. David L. Anderson (Lawrence: University Press of Kansas, 1993), 135; Clifford with Holbrooke, *Counsel to the President*, 474; Melvin Small, *At the Water's Edge: American Politics and the Vietnam War* (Chicago: Ivan R. Dee, 2005), 144. The major work alleging that the media treated Tet as a communist victory is Peter Braestrup, *Big Story* (New Haven, CT: Yale University Press, 1983). But Braestrup's argument has been heavily criticized by others such as Moïse, who claims that Braestrup's own research does not support it. See Moïse, *The Myths of Tet*, 178–87.

41. Woods, *LBJ: Architect of American Ambition*, 824.

42. William P. Bundy, Draft Memorandum to the Group [Clifford Task Force], February 29, 1968, Memos on Vietnam: February–March 1968, Papers of Clark Clifford, Vietnam Papers, Box 2, Lyndon Baines Johnson Library.

43. Clifford with Holbrooke, *Counsel to the President*, 474.

44. "Public Affairs," First Draft, March 3, 1968, Volume 7, Meeting with

President and Draft Memo [part 1 of 2], National Security File, National Security Council Histories, March 31st Speech, Box 49, Lyndon Baines Johnson Library.

45. Moïse, *The Myths of Tet*, 185; "The War: Thin Green Line," *Time*, February 23, 1968, 15–16; "Johnson's Rating on Vietnam Drops," *New York Times*, February 14, 1968, 4.

46. Cited in Vaughn Davis Bornet, *The Presidency of Lyndon B. Johnson* (Lawrence: University Press of Kansas, 1983), 272.

47. DeBenedetti, "Lyndon Johnson and the Antiwar Opposition," 43.

48. Karnow, *Vietnam*, 546; "Johnson Rating in Poll Hits Low," *New York Times*, March 31, 1968, 50; Tom Wicker, "In the Nation: Agonizing Reappraisal," *New York Times*, March 10, 1968, E15.

49. Hoopes, *The Limits of Intervention*, 125.

50. March 31st Speech, Volume 1, National Security File, National Security Council Histories, March 31st Speech, Box 47, Lyndon Baines Johnson Library.

51. William P. Bundy, Draft Memorandum to the Group [Clifford Task Force], February 29, 1968, Memos on Vietnam: February–March 1968, Papers of Clark Clifford, Vietnam Papers, Box 2, Lyndon Baines Johnson Library.

52. Schandler, *Unmaking*, 134; Lloyd Gardner, "Lyndon Johnson and Vietnam: The Final Months," in *The Johnson Years*, ed. Robert A. Divine, vol. 3, *LBJ at Home and Abroad* (Lawrence: University Press of Kansas, 1994), 201.

53. William P. Bundy, Draft Memorandum to the Group [Clifford Task Force], February 29, 1968, Memos on Vietnam: February–March 1968, Papers of Clark Clifford, Vietnam Papers, Box 2, Lyndon Baines Johnson Library.

54. Walt Rostow, Memorandum to the President, March 4, 1968, Volume 7, Meeting with President and Draft Memo, National Security File, National Security Council Histories, March 31st Speech, Box 49 [part 1 of 2], Lyndon Baines Johnson Library.

55. Schandler, *Unmaking*, 172.

56. Johnson, *The Vantage Point*, 398.

57. Quoted in Schandler, *Unmaking*, 174.

58. Notes of the President's Meeting with Senior Foreign Policy Advisers, March 4, 1968, Tom Johnson's Notes of Meetings, Box 2, Lyndon Baines Johnson Library.

59. Johnson, *The Vantage Point*, 406.

60. Schandler, *Unmaking*, 166–67.

61. Clifford with Holbrooke, *Counsel to the President*, 458.

62. David M. Barrett, *Uncertain Warriors: Lyndon Johnson and His Vietnam Advisers* (Lawrence: University Press of Kansas, 1993), 111.

63. Schandler, *Unmaking*, 329; Hoopes, *The Limits of Intervention*, 223; Johnson, *The Vantage Point*, 398.

64. Max Frankel, "Johnson to Talk to Nation Tonight on Vietnam War," *New York Times*, March 31, 1968, 1.

65. Prados, *Vietnam*, 248.

66. [Paul H. Nitze], Letter to the President from the Deputy Secretary of Defense, March 16, 1968, National Objectives, Resources, and Strategy vis-à-vis [Southeast Asia][part 1], Papers of Clark Clifford, Vietnam Papers, Box 1, Lyndon Baines Johnson Library.

67. Robert Dallek, *Flawed Giant: Lyndon Johnson and His Times, 1961–1973* (New York: Oxford University Press, 1998), 526; Doris Kearns, *Lyndon Johnson and the American Dream* (New York: Harper and Row, 1976), 338.

68. Alan L. Otten, "Deepening Dilemma: New Political Pressures Complicate President's Decision on Vietnam," *Wall Street Journal*, March 14, 1968, 1.

69. Kearns, *Lyndon Johnson and the American Dream*, 338.

70. Louis Harris, "How the Voters See the Issues," *Newsweek*, March 25, 1968, 26.

71. "Mechanics of Rebellion," *Time*, March 22, 1968, 19.

72. For a representative summary of Johnson's objections, see "Kennedy's Secret Ultimatum," *Time*, March 22, 1968, 18; Clark Clifford, Notes on Meeting with President Johnson, March 14, 1968, Notes Taken at Meetings [part 2], Papers of Clark Clifford, Vietnam Papers, Box 1, Lyndon Baines Johnson Library.

73. "To M'Carthy, Now, It's 'On, Wisconsin,'" *New York Times*, February 19, 1968, 22.

74. "The Presidency: Challenge & Swift Response," *Time*, March 29, 1968, 21.

75. "Newsweek Poll Finds Johnson 'Markedly Vulnerable' to Rivals," *Washington Post*, March 25, 1968, A2; Tom Wicker, "King Lyndon Commands the Waves," *New York Times*, March 28, 1968, 46.

76. Lyndon B. Johnson, "Remarks at a Ceremony Commemorating the 159th Birthday of Abraham Lincoln, February 12, 1968," in *Public Papers of the Presidents: Lyndon B. Johnson, 1968–69* (Washington, DC: US Government Printing Office, 1970), 1:219.

77. "The President's News Conference of February 16, 1968," in *Public Papers of the Presidents: Lyndon B. Johnson, 1968–69*, 1:235, 237.

78. "Remarks at El Toro Marine Corps Air Station, California, February 18, 1968," in *Public Papers of the Presidents: Lyndon B. Johnson, 1968–69*, 1:240.

79. "Remarks on the Flight Deck of the USS *Constellation*, February 18, 1968," in *Public Papers of the Presidents: Lyndon B. Johnson, 1968–69*, 1:242.

80. "Remarks at the National Rural Electric Cooperative Association Convention in Dallas, February 27, 1968," in *Public Papers of the Presidents: Lyndon B. Johnson, 1968–69*, 1:287. See also "US Reappraising Its Use of Troops in Vietnam War," *New York Times*, February 29, 1968, 1.

81. "Remarks at a Testimonial Dinner in Beaumont, Texas, for Representative Jack Brooks, March 1, 1968," in *Public Papers of the Presidents: Lyndon B. Johnson, 1968–69*, 1:318.

82. "Remarks at a Meeting of the National Alliance of Businessmen, March 16, 1968," in *Public Papers of the Presidents: Lyndon B. Johnson, 1968–69*, 1:404.

83. "Remarks to Delegates to the National Farmers Union Convention in Minneapolis, March 18, 1968," in *Public Papers of the Presidents: Lyndon B. Johnson, 1968–69*, 1:410.

84. "Remarks at the Conference on Foreign Policy for Leaders of National Nongovernmental Organizations, March 19, 1968," in *Public Papers on the Presidents: Lyndon B. Johnson, 1968–69*, 1:415.

85. Dallek, *Flawed Giant*, 510.

86. Dallek, *Flawed Giant*, 511.

87. Barrett, *Uncertain Warriors*, 140.

88. Cited in Gardner, "Lyndon Johnson and Vietnam," 209.

89. "Luncheon Meeting, March 22, 1968," Meeting Notes File, Box 2, Lyndon Baines Johnson Library.

90. This is the summary of Hoopes, *The Limits of Intervention*, 216. For notes on the meeting of the Wise Men, see "March 26, 1968–3:15 pm—Meeting with Special Advisory Group [the formal name for the Wise Men], Cabinet Room," Meeting Notes File, Box 2, Lyndon Baines Johnson Library.

91. "Summary of Notes, March 26, 1968" [the final briefing of the Wise Men], Tom Johnson's Notes of Meetings, Box 2, Lyndon Baines Johnson Library.

92. Barrett, *Uncertain Warriors*, 150.

93. Johnson, *The Vantage Point*, 416.

94. Clifford with Holbrooke, *Counsel to the President*, 518; "Summary of Notes, March 26, 1968," Tom Johnson's Notes of Meetings, Box 2, Lyndon Baines Johnson Library.

95. Reported in Karnow, *Vietnam*, 562.

Chapter 3

1. See especially George C. Edwards III, *On Deaf Ears* (New Haven, CT: Yale University Press, 2003). Edwards employs a narrow definition of both "presidential rhetoric" and "effect." He examines presidential speeches on matters of policy, and investigates changes in public opinion on the policy in question in the immediate aftermath of the speech. Rhetorical scholars often mention that these definitions are too narrow and that the causal connection between rhetoric and its consequences is not always known.

2. This function of the presidency is examined in Mary E. Stuckey, *The President as Interpreter-in-Chief* (Chatham, NJ: Chatham House, 1991).

3. Clark Clifford with Richard Holbrooke, *Counsel to the President* (New York: Random House, 1991), 483.

4. Larry Berman, *Lyndon Johnson's War: The Road to Stalemate in Vietnam* (New York: Norton, 1989), 199; Harry McPherson, *A Political Education* (1972; rpt. Boston: Houghton Mifflin, 1988), 423.

5. Walt Rostow, Memorandum to Dean Rusk, January 31, 1968, Volume 7,

Meeting Notes, National Security File, National Security Council Histories, March 31st Speech, Box 49 [part 1 of 2], Lyndon Baines Johnson Library.

6. [untitled file reporting Johnson's discussion with advisers], Tom Johnson's Notes of Meetings, Box 2, Lyndon Baines Johnson Library.

7. Agenda for Meeting with the President, Monday, February 12, 1968, 4:30 p.m., Volume 7, Meeting Notes, National Security File, National Security Council Histories, March 31st Speech, Box 49 [part 1 of 2], Lyndon Baines Johnson Library.

8. Moya Ann Ball, "Lyndon B. Johnson: From Private Deliberations to Public Declaration—The Making of LBJ's Renunciation Speech," in *Presidential Speechwriting: From the New Deal to the Reagan Revolution and Beyond*, ed. Kurt Ritter and Martin J. Medhurst (College Station: Texas A&M University Press, 2003), 239; Clifford with Holbrooke, *Counsel to the President*, 483–84; Walt Rostow, Memorandum to the President, February 23, 1968, Volume 3, Tabs A-Z and AA-QQ, National Security File, National Security Council Histories, March 31st Speech, Box 47, Lyndon Baines Johnson Library.

9. Lyndon Baines Johnson, *The Vantage Point: Perspectives of the Presidency, 1963–1969* (New York: Holt, Rinehart, and Winston, 1971), 406.

10. David M. Barrett, *Uncertain Warriors: Lyndon Johnson and His Vietnam Advisers* (Lawrence: University Press of Kansas, 1993), 135.

11. Johnson, *The Vantage Point*, 406.

12. Clifford with Holbrooke, *Counsel to the President*, 508.

13. Ball, "Lyndon B. Johnson: From Private Deliberations to Public Declaration," 113.

14. This interpretation differs from that of Hoopes, *The Limits of Intervention*, and other early writers who assumed that Johnson did undergo such a conversion under the influence of briefings from lower-level civilians in the Defense Department and changes of heart among the "Wise Men" at their meeting on March 25 and 26, discussed in the last chapter. That view assumes a susceptibility to persuasion on Johnson's part that does not seem credible. If any single event forced a reexamination on the president's part, it was more likely the receipt of Westmoreland's troop request, which Johnson immediately recognized as a political hot potato.

15. Harry McPherson, Notes of Meeting, February 27, 1968, White House Central Files, Statements of Lyndon Baines Johnson, Box 271, Lyndon Baines Johnson Library.

16. Lloyd Gardner, "Lyndon Johnson and Vietnam: The Final Months," in *The Johnson Years*, ed. Robert A. Divine, vol. 3, *LBJ at Home and Abroad* (Lawrence: University Press of Kansas, 1994), 199.

17. George C. Herring, "The Reluctant Warrior: Lyndon Johnson as Commander in Chief," in *Shadow on the White House: Presidents and the Vietnam War, 1945–1975*, ed. David L. Anderson (Lawrence: University Press of Kansas, 1993), 106. See also Berman, *Lyndon Johnson's War*, 191.

18. Ball, "Lyndon B. Johnson: From Private Deliberations to Public Declaration," 117.

19. Walt W. Rostow, Notes of March 14, 1968, suggesting insertions into the president's speech on Vietnam, White House Central Files, Statements of Lyndon Baines Johnson, Box 271, Lyndon Baines Johnson Library.

20. "A House Divided" [editorial], *Wall Street Journal*, April 2, 1968, 8.

21. Draft prepared February 5, 1968, for speech on both North Korea and Vietnam [drafted by McPherson, reviewed by Rostow], White House Central Files, Statements of Lyndon Baines Johnson, Box 270, Lyndon Baines Johnson Library; Harry McPherson, handwritten draft for proposed late February 1968 speech on Vietnam [folder dated February 25, 1968], White House Central Files, Statements of Lyndon Baines Johnson, Box 270, Lyndon Baines Johnson Library; Draft of speech dated February 27, 1968, White House Central Files, Statements of Lyndon Baines Johnson, Box 271, Lyndon Baines Johnson Library.

22. Harry McPherson, handwritten notes of March 20, 1968 meeting with the president and principal Vietnam advisers, White House Central Files, Statements of Lyndon Baines Johnson, Box 271, Lyndon Baines Johnson Library. Although Rusk made this comment on March 20, it accurately characterizes the earlier period when the concern was that the unexpected, surprise nature of Tet would shake the American will.

23. Dean Rusk (?), Draft, March 20, 1968, suggesting themes for President Johnson's speech, White House Central Files, Statements of Lyndon Baines Johnson, Box 271, Lyndon Baines Johnson Library.

24. Draft of speech material hand-carried from Bill Bundy's State Department office, March 20, 1968, #4 First Draft Folder 1, White House Central Files, Statements of Lyndon Baines Johnson, Box 271, Lyndon Baines Johnson Library.

25. Harry McPherson, Memorandum to the President, March 22, 1968, 3/31/68 Address to the Nation—March 21, 1968 #6 Third Draft Folder 1, White House Central Files, Statements of Lyndon Baines Johnson, Box 271, Lyndon Baines Johnson Library.

26. Notes of Meeting of March 20, 1968, Tom Johnson's Notes of Meetings, Box 2, Lyndon Baines Johnson Library.

27. Harry McPherson, Handwritten notes of March 20 meeting with the president and principal Vietnam advisers, White House Central Files, Statements of Lyndon Baines Johnson, Box 271, Lyndon Baines Johnson Library.

28. Harry McPherson, Handwritten Notes of March 20 Meeting; Notes of Meeting of March 20, 1968, Tom Johnson's Notes of Meetings.

29. Harry McPherson, Handwritten Notes of March 20 Meeting.

30. Johnson, *The Vantage Point*, 413.

31. Harry McPherson, Master Copy, marked "Saturday/March 30" on which are handwritten changes to the draft dated March 29, 1968, 2:30 p.m., 3/31/68

Address to the Nation, March 29, 1968, #12, Alternate, Draft 3, White House Central Files, Statements of Lyndon Baines Johnson, Box 273, Lyndon Baines Johnson Library.

32. Horace Busby, *The Thirty-First of March: An Intimate Portrait of Lyndon Johnson's Final Days in Office* (New York: Farrar, Straus, and Giroux, 2005), 200–201. This book was published posthumously.

33. Johnson, *The Vantage Point*, 365; "He Calls on Hanoi to Aid Peace Step," *New York Times*, April 1, 1968, 28.

34. March 31st Speech, Volume 1, National Security File, National Security Council Histories, March 31st Speech, Box 47, Lyndon Baines Johnson Library.

35. Berman, *Lyndon Johnson's War*, 189.

36. The drafts and the files containing comments, can be found in Statements of Lyndon Baines Johnson, March 31, 1968, White House Central Files, Boxes 271–74, Lyndon Baines Johnson Library. Drafts will be cited in the text by number but will not be referenced individually in the notes.

37. Clifford with Holbrooke, *Counsel to the President*, 509.

38. Notes of Meeting of March 20, 1968, Tom Johnson's Notes of Meetings, Box 2, Lyndon Baines Johnson Library.

39. Notes of Meeting of March 20, 1968, Tom Johnson's Notes of Meetings, Box 2, Lyndon Baines Johnson Library; Harry McPherson, handwritten notes of March 20, 1968 meeting, White House Central Files, Statements of Lyndon Baines Johnson, Box 271, Lyndon Baines Johnson Library. As noted above, the president was reflecting not a disinclination to consider peace proposals but an unwillingness to put them in the same speech with war measures.

40. Harry McPherson, handwritten notes on Clark Clifford's response to McPherson's March 20 draft, White House Central Files, Statements of Lyndon Baines Johnson, Box 271, Lyndon Baines Johnson Library.

41. McGeorge Bundy, Memorandum to the President, March 21, 1968, 3/31/68 Remarks of the President to the Nation, the President's Oval Office, White House Central Files, Statements of Lyndon Baines Johnson, Box 274, Lyndon Baines Johnson Library.

42. Doris Kearns, *Lyndon Johnson and the American Dream* (New York: Harper and Row, 1976), 339.

43. The reactions of Bundy, Goulding, and Mrs. Johnson are all in 3/31/68 Address to the Nation, March 25, 1968, #7, Fourth Draft, Folders 1 and 2, Statements of Lyndon Baines Johnson, White House Central Files, Box 272, Lyndon Baines Johnson Library.

44. Clark Clifford, Comments on 5th draft of the president's March 31 speech, with notes by Harry McPherson, 3/31/68 Address to the Nation, March 27, 1968 #9, Sixth Draft Plus "Peroration," Folder 1, White House Central Files, Statements of Lyndon Baines Johnson, Box 272, Lyndon Baines Johnson Library.

45. William P. Bundy, Memorandum to Harry McPherson, March 28, 1968,

3/31/68 Address to the Nation, March 27, 1968 #9, Sixth Draft Plus "Per-oration," Folder 1, White House Central Files, Statements of Lyndon Baines Johnson, Box 272, Lyndon Baines Johnson Library.

46. Frank E. Vandiver, *Shadows of Vietnam: Lyndon Johnson's Wars* (College Station: Texas A&M University Press, 1997), 328.

47. Johnson, *The Vantage Point*, 420.

48. Johnson, *The Vantage Point*, 420. Irving Bernstein, *Guns or Butter: The Presidency of Lyndon Johnson* (New York: Oxford University Press, 1996), 481 maintains that it was Clifford who suggested that the advisers not argue out the policy differences but present the president with two different drafts from which to choose.

49. Clifford with Holbrooke, *Counsel to the President*, 519.

50. Berman, *Lyndon Johnson's War*, 200. See also Hoopes, *The Limits of Intervention*, 218–19.

51. Hoopes, *The Limits of Intervention*, 220.

52. Prados, *Vietnam*, 249.

53. Walt W. Rostow, Memorandum to the [former] President, March 13, 1970, National Security File, Country File—Vietnam, Box 127 (part 1), Lyndon Baines Johnson Library.

54. Alternate Drafts #1 through #4 are found in Statements of Lyndon Baines Johnson, March 31, 1968, White House Central Files, Box 273, Lyndon Baines Johnson Library. They will be cited in the text by draft number but not referenced individually in the notes. The Teleprompter copy from which Johnson read the speech may be found in Box 274.

55. On a personal note, I was among this number who could breathe a sigh of relief at this point.

56. Johnson, *The Vantage Point*, 420.

57. Clark M. Clifford, Memorandum to [addressee unknown], March 29, 1968, 3/31/68 Address to the Nation, March 28, 1968, 3/31/68 Address to the Nation, March 28, 1968 #11, Alternate, 9:00 p.m., Draft #2, White House Central Files, Statements of Lyndon Baines Johnson, Box 273, Lyndon Baines Johnson Library.

58. Hoopes, *The Limits of Intervention*, 220.

59. Lady Bird Johnson, Comments on McPherson's alternate draft, March 29, 1968, 2:30 p.m., 3/31/68 Remarks of the President to the Nation, the President's Oval Office, White House Central Files, Statements of Lyndon Baines Johnson, Box 274, Lyndon Baines Johnson Library.

60. Arthur Okun, Comments on McPherson's March 30, 1968 draft, 3/31/68 Address to the Nation, March 30, 1968 #13, Alternate Draft #4, 4:00 p.m., White House Central Files, Statements of Lyndon Baines Johnson, Box 273, Lyndon Baines Johnson Library.

61. *Public Papers of the Presidents: Lyndon B. Johnson, 1968–69, 1*, 470–75. There are very minor variations among these texts. For a comparison of the

Public Papers version with the videotape as delivered, see the texts in David Za-refsky, "Lyndon Johnson's Withdrawal Speech," *Voices of Democracy* 9 (2014): 41–55 [electronic publication].

62. James Yuenger, "Lyndon Offers His Viet Plan Tonight," *Chicago Tribune*, March 31, 1968, 1.

63. The details of the day's schedule are in Daily log entries for Sunday, March 31, 3/31/68 Address to the Nation, Reactions to March 31st Speech, White House Central Files, Statements of Lyndon Baines Johnson, Box 274, Lyndon Baines Johnson Library. At the time, the United States did not yet have an official vice-presidential residence. The Naval Observatory would be dedicated to that purpose in the mid-1970s. Walter Mondale would be the first vice president to live there.

64. Walt Rostow, Memorandum for the Record, March 31, 1968, March 19, 1970 Memo to the [former] President, "Decision to Halt Bombing," with cop-ies of documents, I, 2, National Security File, Country File—Vietnam, Box 127, Lyndon Baines Johnson Library. The source of Johnson's percentages is unknown.

65. Jack Gould, "TV: Political Commentators Regain Their Aplomb," *New York Times*, April 1, 1968, 26.

66. "Some GIs Angry, Others Glad," *Chicago Tribune*, April 1, 1968, 13.

67. Hedrick Smith, "A Gradual Let Out Is Planned by US," *New York Times*, April 1, 1968, 26.

68. Gould, "TV: Political Commentators," 26.

69. Daily log entries for Sunday, March 31, 3/31/68 Address to the Nation, Reactions to March 31st Speech, White House Central Files, Statements of Lyndon Baines Johnson, Box 274, Lyndon Baines Johnson Library.

70. Hedrick Smith, "Decisions on War Reflect Appeals of Civilian Aides," *New York Times*, April 1, 1968, 26. See also "Johnson Says He Won't Seek or Accept Renomination; He Halts Bombing of North Vietnam Except for DMZ," *Wall Street Journal*, April 1, 1968, 3.

Chapter 4

1. Doris Kearns, *Lyndon Johnson and the American Dream* (New York: Harper and Row, 1976), 269; David Zarefsky, *Political Argumentation in the United States* (Amsterdam: John Benjamins, 2014), 222.

2. John Prados, *Vietnam: The History of an Unwinnable War, 1945–1975* (Lawrence: University Press of Kansas, 2009), 155.

3. Vaughn Davis Bornet, *The Presidency of Lyndon B. Johnson* (Lawrence: University Press of Kansas, 1983), 278.

4. Lyndon Baines Johnson, *The Vantage Point: Perspectives of the Presidency, 1963–1969* (New York: Holt, Rinehart, and Winston, 1971), 367–68.

5. See Herbert Y. Schandler, *The Unmaking of a President: Lyndon Johnson and Vietnam* (Princeton, NJ: Princeton University Press, 1977), 128.

6. "Rusk Says Hanoi Spurns US Terms for Negotiations," *New York Times*, February 15, 1968, 1; William P. Bundy, "Options on Our Negotiating Posture," 1st draft, February 29, 1968; Volume 3, Tabs RR-ZZ and a-d, Folder 2 of 2, National Security File, National Security Council Histories, March 31st Speech, Box 47, Lyndon Baines Johnson Library.

7. See Townsend Hoopes, *The Limits of Intervention: An Inside Account of How the Johnson Policy of Escalation in Vietnam Was Reversed* (New York: David McKay, 1969), 81.

8. Harry McPherson, Memorandum to the President, October 27, 1967, National Security File, Country File—Vietnam, Box 127, Lyndon Baines Johnson Library.

9. McPherson, Memorandum to the President, October 27, 1967.

10. Robert McNamara, Memorandum to the President, November 1, 1967, National Security File, Country File—Vietnam, Box 127, Lyndon Baines Johnson Library.

11. McNamara, Memorandum to the President, November 1, 1967, 5.

12. Walt W. Rostow, Memorandum to the [Former] President, March 19, 1970, National Security File, Country File—Vietnam, Box 127, Lyndon Baines Johnson Library. This is a comprehensive review of bombing halt proposals that Rostow prepared for Johnson and for the historical record after the president had left office. Many of those surveyed amplified their views in additional documents that are included as appendices to his report.

13. This memo is included as an appendix to Rostow, Memorandum to the [Former] President, March 19, 1970.

14. Rostow, Memorandum to the [Former] President, March 19, 1970, Tab N.

15. Harry McPherson, Notes of meeting, February 27, 1968, White House Central Files, Statements of Lyndon Baines Johnson, Box 271, Lyndon Baines Johnson Library.

16. Notes of the President's Meeting with Senior Foreign Policy Advisers, March 4, 1968, p. 15, Tom Johnson's Notes of Meetings, Box 2, Lyndon Baines Johnson Library.

17. Notes of the President's Meeting with Senior Foreign Policy Advisers, March 4, 1968, 8.

18. Rostow, Memorandum to the [Former] President, March 19, 1970.

19. Notes of Meeting of March 20, 1968, Tom Johnson's Notes of Meetings, Box 2, Lyndon Baines Johnson Library.

20. Walt Rostow, Cable to the President, March 16, 1968, Memorandum to the President, "Decision to Halt Bombing," March 19, 1970, with copies of

documents, I, 2 of 2; National Security File, Country File—Vietnam, Box 127, Lyndon Baines Johnson Library.

21. Hoopes, *The Limits of Intervention*, 184; David M. Barrett, *Uncertain Warriors: Lyndon Johnson and His Vietnam Advisers* (Lawrence: University Press of Kansas, 1993), 142–43.

22. Barrett, *Uncertain Warriors*, 143.

23. Johnson, *The Vantage Point*, 408.

24. See Johnson, *The Vantage Point*, 408; Harry McPherson, Handwritten notes of March 20, 1968 Meeting with the President and his Principal Vietnam Advisers, White House Central Files, Statements of Lyndon Baines Johnson, Box 271, Lyndon Baines Johnson Library.

25. Dean Rusk, Memorandum to the President, March 25, 1968, Volume 4, Tabs LL-ZZ and a-k, National Security File, National Security Council Histories, March 31st Speech, Box 48, Lyndon Baines Johnson Library; Barrett, *Uncertain Warriors*), 145. Schandler notes, however, that both McNamara and Rostow had made similar recommendations to Johnson in November 1967, so the idea was not new when it resurfaced in March of 1968. See Schandler, *The Unmaking of a President*, 188.

26. Cited in Johnson, *The Vantage Point*, 401.

27. Schandler, *The Unmaking of a President*, 306.

28. Schandler, *The Unmaking of a President*, 190; Johnson, *The Vantage Point*, 405.

29. In his memoirs, Johnson wrote that when he saw the language proposing a limited bombing halt, he knew it was what he wanted, "but I felt I still should not say so flatly for fear of another damaging press leak. I indicated that I did not want to comment further at that time." Johnson, *The Vantage Point*, 420.

30. Harry McPherson, Alternate Draft for March 31 Speech, March 28, 1968, 3/31/68 Address to the Nation, March 28, 1968, #10, ALTERNATE 6:00 pm, Draft 1. White House Central Files, Statements of Lyndon Baines Johnson, Box 273, Lyndon Baines Johnson Library.

31. Harry McPherson, Master Copy, marked "Saturday/March 30" on which are handwritten changes to the draft dated March 29, 1968, 2:30 p.m., 3/31/68 Address to the Nation, March 29, 1968, #12, Alternate, Draft 3, White House Central Files, Statements of Lyndon Baines Johnson, Box 273, Lyndon Baines Johnson Library.

32. Harry McPherson, Alternate Draft #4, 3/31/68 Address to the Nation, March 30, 1968, #13, Alternate Draft #4, 4:00 pm, White House Central Files, Statements of Lyndon Baines Johnson, Box 273, Lyndon Baines Johnson Library.

33. Hedrick Smith, "Decisions on War Reflect Appeals of Civilian Aides," *New York Times*, April 1, 1968, 26; Paul C. Warnke, Memorandum to Paul

Nitze, March 6, 1968, Memos on Vietnam: February–March 1968, Papers of Clark Clifford, Vietnam Papers, Box 2, Lyndon Baines Johnson Library.

34. Clark Clifford, with Richard Holbrooke, *Counsel to the President* (New York: Random House, 1991), 521; Schandler, *The Unmaking of a President*, 287; Johnson, *The Vantage Point*, 420n.

35. Notes on Tuesday Luncheon, April 2, 1968, Tom Johnson's Notes of Meetings, Box 3, Lyndon Baines Johnson Library; Notes on Cabinet Meeting, April 3, 1968, Tom Johnson's Notes of Meetings, Box 3, Lyndon Baines Johnson Library.

36. Notes on Cabinet Meeting, April 3, 1968, Tom Johnson's Notes; Notes on Tuesday Luncheon, April 2, 1968, Tom Johnson's Notes; both in Box 3, Lyndon Baines Johnson Library.

37. Dean Rusk, Telegram to Ellsworth Bunker, March 16, 1968, Volume 4, Tabs N-Z and AA-KK, National Security File, National Security Council Histories, March 31st Speech, Box 48, Lyndon Baines Johnson Library.

38. Johnson, *The Vantage Point*, 400.

39. On this point, see Schandler, *The Unmaking of a President*, 184.

40. See Charles E. Osgood, *An Alternative to War or Surrender* (Urbana: University of Illinois Press, 1962).

41. Kenneth Burke, *A Grammar of Motives* (1945; rpt. Berkeley: University of California Press, 1969), 3.

42. Hedrick Smith, "Decisions on War Reflect Appeals of Civilian Aides," 26; John Hughes, "Ho at 'point of no return'?" *Christian Science Monitor*, April 1, 1968, 4.

43. Schandler, *The Unmaking of a President*, 276.

44. Walt W. Rostow, Memorandum to the [Former] President, March 19, 1970, National Security File, Country File—Vietnam, Box 127, Lyndon Baines Johnson Library. The examples of what Clifford meant by reciprocity are in Johnson, *The Vantage Point*, 412.

45. Schandler, *The Unmaking of a President*, 244.

46. Cited in "The Administration: Clifford Takes Over," *Time*, March 8, 1968, 17.

47. Schandler, *The Unmaking of a President*, 193, 312. See also Frank E. Vandiver, *Shadows of Vietnam: Lyndon Johnson's Wars* (College Station: Texas A&M University Press, 1997), 320.

48. Clifford, *Counsel to the President*, 509.

49. Schandler, *The Unmaking of a President*, 250. Even when the proposal was inserted into the March 31 speech, it was not expected to produce a favorable response. See Schandler, *The Unmaking of a President*, 281; "North Vietnam Geography Defuses US Bombs," *Christian Science Monitor*, April 3, 1968, 3; "Mr. Johnson's Withdrawal," *Wall Street Journal*, April 1, 1968, 16.

50. Harry McPherson, *A Political Education* (1972; rpt. Boston: Houghton

Mifflin, 1988), 432.

51. Schandler, *The Unmaking of a President*, 187, 251.

52. Harry McPherson, Handwritten notes of March 20, 1968 meeting with the President and principal Vietnam advisers, White House Central Files, Statements of Lyndon Baines Johnson, Box 271, Lyndon Baines Johnson Library; Hedrick Smith, "Decisions on War Reflect Appeals of Civilian Aides," 26.

53. See Schandler, *The Unmaking of a President*, 192.

54. "Guest Editorials: Comment on Mr. Johnson's Withdrawal," *Chicago Tribune*, April 1, 1968, 26; Hedrick Smith, "Decisions on War Reflect Appeal of Civilian Aides," 26.

55. March 31st Speech, Volume 1, National Security File, National Security Council Histories, March 31st Speech, Box 47, Lyndon Baines Johnson Library.

56. George C. Herring, *LBJ and Vietnam: A Different Kind of War* (Austin: University of Texas Press, 1994), 162; Notes of the President's Meeting with Senior Foreign Policy Advisers, March 4, 1968, Tom Johnson's Notes of Meetings, Box 2, Lyndon Baines Johnson Library; Dean Rusk, Telegram to Ellsworth Bunker, March 16, 1968, Volume 4, Tabs N-Z and AA-KK, National Security File, National Security Council Histories, March 31st Speech, Box 48, Lyndon Baines Johnson Library.

57. Lloyd Gardner, "Lyndon Johnson and Vietnam: The Final Months," in *The Johnson Years*, ed. Robert A. Divine, vol. 3, *LBJ at Home and Abroad* (Lawrence: University Press of Kansas, 1994), 212.

58. "Significance of Bombing Campaign in North to Our Objectives in Vietnam," Volume 7, Meeting with President and Draft Memo, National Security File, National Security Council Histories, March 31st Speech, Box 49 (1 of 2), Lyndon Baines Johnson Library.

59. Harry McPherson, Handwritten notes of March 20, 1968 meeting with the president and principal Vietnam Advisers, White House Central Files, Statements of Lyndon Baines Johnson, Box 271, Lyndon Baines Johnson Library.

60. "North Vietnam Geography Defuses US Bombs," *Christian Science Monitor*, April 3, 1968, 3; Joseph C. Harsch, "The Long Road to Peace," *Christian Science Monitor*, April 4, 1968, 16.

61. "Bombing of N. Viet Ends as Lyndon Gives Speech," *Chicago Tribune*, April 1, 1968, 6; "Move Limiting North Vietnam Raids Once Vetoed," *Chicago Tribune*, April 4, 1968, 2.

62. Hedrick Smith, "A Gradual Let Out Is Planned by US," *New York Times*, April 1, 1968, 26.

63. "Johnson Says He Won't Seek or Accept Renomination; He Halts Bombing of North Vietnam Except for DMZ," *Wall Street Journal*, April 1, 1968, 3.

64. Notes of Meeting of March 20, 1968, Tom Johnson's Notes of Meetings, Box 2, Lyndon Baines Johnson Library.

65. Dean Rusk, Telegram to Ellsworth Bunker, March 29, 1968, Volume 4,

Tabs LL-ZZ and a-k, National Security File, National Security Council Histories, March 31st Speech, Box 48, Lyndon Baines Johnson Library.

66. "War Allies Urge Security for South Viet," *Chicago Tribune*, April 4, 1968, 2.

67. Barrett, *Uncertain Warriors*, 111; Johnson, *The Vantage Point*, 419.

68. Schandler, *The Unmaking of a President*, 303; Herring, *LBJ and Vietnam*, 163.

69. George C. Herring, "The War in Vietnam," in *Exploring the Johnson Years*, ed. Robert A. Divine (Austin: University of Texas Press, 1981), 53; Notes on Tuesday Luncheon, April 2, 1968, Tom Johnson's Notes of Meetings, Box 3, Lyndon Baines Johnson Library.

70. Hedrick Smith, "A Gradual Let Out," 26; Raymond H. Anderson, "Soviet Skeptical on Johnson Talk," *New York Times*, April 2, 1968, 32; Takashi Oka, "Relief Seen in Moscow at Viet Deescalation," *Christian Science Monitor*, April 1, 1968, 2.

71. "Big Opportunity, Big Test" [editorial], *Christian Science Monitor*, April 5, 1968, 3.

72. David K. Willis, "US Vietnam Allies Puzzle over Johnson Decisions," *Christian Science Monitor*, April 2, 1968, 20; Hedrick Smith, "A Gradual Let Out," 26; Juan de Onis, "Rejection Not Foreseen," *New York Times*, April 2, 1968, 26; Ellsworth Bunker, Telegram to Dean Rusk, March 20, 1968, Volume 4, Tabs LL-ZZ and a-k, National Security File, National Security Council Histories, March 31st Speech, Box 48, Lyndon Baines Johnson Library.

73. Vandiver, *Shadows of Vietnam*, 334.

74. Philip Dodd, "Fulbright Decides Johnson's Bombing Curb Is Significant," *Chicago Tribune*, April 3, 1968, 2.

75. Clifford, with Holbrooke, *Counsel to the President*, 529.

76. "War Allies Urge Security for South Viet," *Chicago Tribune*, April 4, 1968, 2.

77. "Hanoi's Nibble" [editorial], *Wall Street Journal*, April 3, 1968, 12; Frank Giles, "America Will Pay a High Price for Peace," *The Times* (London), April 7, 1968, 12.

78. Notes on Cabinet Meeting, April 3, 1968, Tom Johnson's Notes of Meetings, Box 3, Lyndon Baines Johnson Library.

79. Dodd, "Fulbright Decides," 2.

80. John Leo, "Leaders of Peace Movement Voice Skepticism," *New York Times*, April 1, 1968, 4.

81. John Allen May, "Britons See Hope for Peace," *Christian Science Monitor*, April 2, 1968, 2; "South Vietnam Official Fears Hanoi May Claim Victory," *New York Times*, April 1, 1968, 4; "War Allies Urge Security for South Viet," *Chicago Tribune*, April 4, 1968, 2.

82. Schandler, *The Unmaking of a President*, 284.

83. Schandler, *The Unmaking of a President*, 317–18.

84. "Bombing of N. Viet Ends as Lyndon Gives Speech," *Chicago Tribune*, April 1, 1968, 6; Hoopes, *The Limits of Intervention*, 228.

85. Edwin E. Moïse, *The Myths of Tet: The Most Misunderstood Event of the Vietnam War* (Lawrence: University Press of Kansas, 2017), 170.

86. Gardner, "Lyndon Johnson and Vietnam," 214–15.

87. Schandler, *The Unmaking of a President*, 297.

88. Max Frankel, "Johnson to Talk to Nation Tonight on Vietnam War," *New York Times*, March 31, 1968, 1.

Chapter 5

1. Lyndon B. Johnson, Memorandum for the file, December 18, 1967, National Security File, Country File—Vietnam, Box 127, Lyndon Baines Johnson Library.

2. These exchanges are recounted in David M. Barrett, *Uncertain Warriors: Lyndon Johnson and His Vietnam Advisers* (Lawrence: University Press of Kansas, 1993), 114; Lyndon Baines Johnson, *The Vantage Point: Perspectives of the Presidency, 1963–1969* (New York: Holt, Rinehart, and Winston, 1971), 383; Notes on the President's Meeting with Senior Foreign Policy Advisers, February 11, 1968, Tom Johnson's Notes of Meetings, Box 2, Lyndon Baines Johnson Library.

3. Larry Berman, *Lyndon Johnson's War: The Road to Stalemate in Vietnam* (New York: Norton, 1989), 164. The senior foreign policy advisers meeting on February 11 decided that Wheeler should visit Westmoreland in order to get first-hand information.

4. March 31st Speech, Volume 1, p. 12, National Security File, National Security Council Histories, March 31st Speech, Box 47, Lyndon Baines Johnson Library; Notes on the President's Meeting with Senior Foreign Policy Advisers, February 11, 1968, Tom Johnson's Notes of Meetings, Box 2, Lyndon Baines Johnson Library. Maxwell Taylor, one of the advisers present, read Westmoreland's cable differently, suggesting that he was "operating on a shoestring" and strongly recommending that Wheeler make a personal visit. Dean Rusk did not object to Wheeler's visit but noted, "If General Westmoreland is requesting troops in this cable he has a poor Colonel doing the drafting for him."

5. Edwin E. Moïse, *The Myths of Tet: The Most Misunderstood Event of the Vietnam War* (Lawrence: University Press of Kansas, 2017), 194.

6. William C. Westmoreland, Cable to Adm. US Grant Sharp and Gen. Earle Wheeler, February 12, 1968, Volume 2, Tabs a-z, National Security File, National Security Council Histories, March 31st Speech, Box 47, Lyndon Baines Johnson Library; Moïse, *The Myths of Tet*, 195. Schandler also suggests that the cable Wheeler sent in advance of his visit may have led Westmoreland to conclude that Johnson would be receptive to a request for a large increment of troops, shifting from the past practice of gradual escalation. See Herbert Y.

Schandler, *The Unmaking of a President: Lyndon Johnson and Vietnam* (Princeton, NJ: Princeton University Press, 1977), 105.

7. Randall B. Woods, *LBJ: Architect of American Ambition* (New York: Free Press, 2006), 828.

8. Notes on the President's Meeting with Senior Foreign Policy Advisors, February 12, 1968, Tom Johnson's Notes of Meetings, Box 2, Lyndon Baines Johnson Library.

9. Notes on the President's Meeting with Senior Foreign Policy Advisers, February 12, 1968, Tom Johnson's Notes of Meetings, Box 2, Lyndon Baines Johnson Library.

10. This and the preceding quotations are from Tom Johnson's Notes of Meetings, cited in notes 8 and 9.

11. These quotations and discussion are based on Tom Johnson's Notes of Meetings, cited in notes 8 and 9.

12. Tom Johnson's Notes of Meetings, February 12, 1968, cited in notes 8 and 9.

13. Townsend Hoopes, *The Limits of Intervention: An Inside Account of How the Johnson Policy of Escalation in Vietnam Was Reversed* (New York: David McKay, 1969), 163; Schandler, *The Unmaking of a President*, 138.

14. Frank E. Vandiver, *Shadows of Vietnam: Lyndon Johnson's Wars* (College Station: Texas A&M University Press, 1997), 300; Woods, *LBJ: Architect of American Ambition*, 828.

15. Vandiver, *Shadows of Vietnam*, 292; Stanley Karnow, *Vietnam: A History* (New York: Viking, 1983), 550.

16. Lloyd Gardner, "Lyndon Johnson and Vietnam: The Final Months," in *The Johnson Years*, ed. Robert A. Divine, vol. 3, *LBJ at Home and Abroad* (Lawrence: University Press of Kansas, 1994), 202.

17. Schandler, *The Unmaking of a President*, 112, 115.

18. "US Reappraising Its Use of Troops in Vietnam War," *New York Times*, February 29, 1968, 1.

19. Moïse, *The Myths of Tet*, 198.

20. Cited in Moïse, *The Myths of Tet*, 192.

21. George C. Herring, *LBJ and Vietnam: A Different Kind of War* (Austin: University of Texas Press, 1994), 156–57; Vandiver, *Shadows of Vietnam*, 300; Gabriel Kolko, *Anatomy of a War: Vietnam, the United States, and the Modern Historical Experience* (New York: Pantheon Books, 1985), 315.

22. Notes of the President's Meeting with His Foreign Policy Advisers, March 26, 1968, Tom Johnson's Notes of Meetings, Box 2, Lyndon Baines Johnson Library. (This is the president's meeting with the "Wise Men," who were being briefed primarily by General Wheeler.)

23. "An Outline Rationale for Partial Mobilization," Volume 7, Meeting Notes, National Security File, National Security Council Histories, March 31st Speech, Box 49 (1 of 2), Lyndon Baines Johnson Library.

24. Notes of the President's Meeting with the Joint Chiefs of Staff, February 9, 1968, Tom Johnson's Notes of Meetings, Box 2, Lyndon Baines Johnson Library; William Beecher, "High Pentagon Aides Urge Call-up of 30,000 Men," *New York Times*, March 13, 1968, 15.

25. Ellsworth Bunker, Cable to Dean Rusk, March 1, 1968, Volume 4, Tabs C-M, National Security Files, National Security Council Histories, March 31st Speech, Box 48, Lyndon Baines Johnson Library; Admiral US Grant Sharp, Cable to General Earle Wheeler, Volume 2, Tabs a-z, National Security File, National Security Council Histories, March 31st Speech, Box 47, Lyndon Baines Johnson Library.

26. Johnson, *The Vantage Point*, 389.

27. Walt Rostow, Memorandum to the President, February 29, 1968, Volume 7, Meeting Notes, National Security File, National Security Council Histories, March 31st Speech, Box 49 (1 of 2), Lyndon Baines Johnson Library; unnamed file reporting the president's discussion with advisers, Tom Johnson's Notes of Meetings, Box 2, Lyndon Baines Johnson Library.

28. William P. Bundy, "Asian Reaction to a Major US Force Increase," Draft, March 1, 1968, Volume 4, Tabs C-M, National Security Files, National Security Council Histories, March 31st Speech, Box 48, Lyndon Baines Johnson Library.

29. Cited in Woods, *LBJ: Architect of American Ambition*, 809.

30. "The Case Against Further Significant Increases in US Forces in Vietnam" (unsigned), March 3, 1968, Volume 7, Meeting with President and Draft Memo, National Security File, National Security Council Histories, March 31st Speech, Box 49 (1 of 2), Lyndon Baines Johnson Library; Alan L. Otten, "Deepening Dilemma: New Political Pressures Complicate President's Decision on Vietnam," *Wall Street Journal*, March 14, 1968, 1.

31. Henry Cabot Lodge, Memorandum to Dean Rusk, March 5, 1968, Volume 4, Tabs N-Z and AA-KK, National Security File, National Security Council Histories, March 31st Speech, Box 48, Lyndon Baines Johnson Library.

32. "The Military Dilemma: The New Math of Escalation Adds Up to One-to-One," *Newsweek*, March 18, 1968, 27.

33. Robert H. Phelps, "US to Put More Men in Vietnam," *New York Times*, March 17, 1968, 1; Unsigned Draft Memorandum for the President (probably from the Clifford Task Force), March 4, 1968, Volume 7, Meeting with President and Draft Memo, National Security File, National Security Council Histories, March 31st Speech, Box 49 (1 of 2), Lyndon Baines Johnson Library; CIA Memorandum, "The Communists' Ability to Recoup Their Tet Military Losses," National Objectives, Resources, and Strategy vis-s-vis SEA" [2]. Papers of Clark Clifford, Vietnam Papers, Box 1, Lyndon Baines Johnson Library; CIA Memorandum, "Questions Concerning the Situation in Vietnam," March 1, 1968, Volume 4, Tabs C-M, National Security Files, National Security Council Histories, March 31st Speech, Box 48, Lyndon Baines Johnson Library.

34. Berman, *Lyndon Johnson's War*, 181.

35. Zbigniew Brzezinski, Memorandum, "The War in Vietnam: For a Balance Between US Goals and US Means," March 14, 1968, Memo's [*sic*] to Read [1], Papers of Clark Clifford, Vietnam Papers, Box 1, Lyndon Baines Johnson Library; Max Frankel, "US Rushes 10,500 to Meet Threat of Vietnam Foe," *New York Times*, February 14, 1968, 1.

36. Gardner, "Lyndon Johnson and Vietnam: The Final Months," 205.

37. "The Case Against Further Significant Increases" (cited in note 30), 2; Walt Rostow, Memorandum to the President, March 4, 1968, Volume 7, Meeting with President and Draft Memo, National Security File, National Security Council Histories, March 31st Speech, Box 49 (1 of 2), Lyndon Baines Johnson Library.

38. For example, see William P. Bundy, "European and Other Non-Asian Reactions to a Major US Force Increase," draft, March 1, 1968, and "Asian Reaction to a Major US Force Increase," draft, March 1, 1968, both in Volume 4, Tabs C-M, National Security Files, National Security Council Histories, March 31st Speech, Box 48, Lyndon Baines Johnson Library.

39. Phil Goulding, "Possible Public Reaction to Various Alternatives," n.d. (sent to Paul Nitze and Clark Clifford March 2, 1968), National Objectives, Resources, and Strategy vis-à-vis SEA [2], Papers of Clark Clifford, Vietnam Papers, Box 1, Lyndon Baines Johnson Library; Hoopes, *The Limits of Intervention*, 179.

40. Maxwell D. Taylor, Memorandum to the President, February 14, 1968, National Security File, National Security Council Histories, March 31st Speech, Box 49 (2 of 2), Lyndon Baines Johnson Library.

41. Berman, *Lyndon Johnson's War*, 166.

42. McGeorge Bundy, Memorandum to the President, March 21, 1968, 3/31/68 Remarks of the President to the Nation, the President's Oval Office, White House Central Files, Statements of Lyndon Baines Johnson, Box 274, Lyndon Baines Johnson Library.

43. Notes of the President's Meeting with the Senior Foreign Affairs Advisory Council, February 10, 1968, Tom Johnson's Notes of Meetings, Box 2, Lyndon Baines Johnson Library; Notes of the President's Meeting with Senior Foreign Policy Advisers, February 11, 1968, Tom Johnson's Notes of Meetings, Box 2, Lyndon Baines Johnson Library.

44. Clifford, *Counsel to the President*, 499.

45. Melvin Small, *At the Water's Edge: American Politics and the Vietnam War* (Chicago: Ivan R. Dee, 2005), 52.

46. As noted by Harry McPherson, Notes of Meeting, February 27, 1968, White House Central Files, Statements of Lyndon Baines Johnson, Box 271, Lyndon Baines Johnson Library.

47. For example, Berman, *Lyndon Johnson's War*, 161; Notes of the President's Meeting with the Joint Chiefs of Staff, February 9, 1968, Tom Johnson's

Notes of Meetings, Box 2, Lyndon Baines Johnson Library; Notes of the President's Meeting with the Senior Foreign Affairs Advisory Council, February 10, 1968, Tom Johnson's Notes of Meetings, Box 2, Lyndon Baines Johnson Library.

48. McGeorge Bundy, Memorandum to the President, March 21, 1968, 3/31/68 Remarks of the President to the Nation, the President's Oval Office, White House Central Files, Statements of Lyndon Baines Johnson, Box 274, Lyndon Baines Johnson Library.

49. Reported in Robert S. McNamara, *In Retrospect: The Tragedy and Lessons of Vietnam* (New York: Random House, 1995), 315.

50. Draft, Charge to Rusk and McNamara (possibly written by Walt Rostow), February 28, 1968, Volume 3, Tabs RR-ZZ and a-d, Folder 2 of 2, National Security File, National Security Council Histories, March 31st Speech, Box 47, Lyndon Baines Johnson Library.

51. "Westmoreland Requests 206,000 More Men, Stirring Debate in Administration," *New York Times*, March 10, 1968, 1.

52. March 31st Speech, Volume 1, National Security File, National Security Council Histories, March 31st Speech, Box 47, Lyndon Baines Johnson Library.

53. Johnson, *The Vantage Point*, 386.

54. Woods, *LBJ: Architect of American Ambition*, 829; Barrett, *Uncertain Warriors*, 127.

55. Cited in Gardner, "Lyndon Johnson and Vietnam: The Final Months," 203.

56. Schandler, *The Unmaking of a President*, 167.

57. Walt Rostow, Memorandum to the President, March 4, 1968, Volume 7, Meeting with President and Draft Memo, National Security File, National Security Council Histories, March 31st Speech, Box 49 (1 of 2), Lyndon Baines Johnson Library. Rostow's memo also noted that the Clifford task force did not consider how the larger package would be presented to Congress and the country.

58. On this point, see Robert Dallek, *Flawed Giant: Lyndon Johnson and His Times, 1961–1973* (New York: Oxford University Press, 1998), 509; Gardner, "Lyndon Johnson and Vietnam: The Final Months," 203; Woods, *LBJ: Architect of American Ambition*, 830.

59. Cited in Schandler, *The Unmaking of a President*, 183.

60. Johnson, *The Vantage Point*, 402. See also Vandiver, *Shadows of Vietnam*, 315.

61. Barrett, *Uncertain Warriors*, 134; Johnson, *The Vantage Point*, 407.

62. Hoopes, *The Limits of Intervention*, 205.

63. Schandler, *The Unmaking of a President*, 231; Notes of the President's Meeting with Foreign Policy Advisers, March 11, 1968, Tom Johnson's Notes of Meetings, Box 2, Lyndon Baines Johnson Library; Beecher, "High Pentagon Aides Urge Call-up," 15.

64. Max Frankel, "US Rushes 10,500 to Meet Threat of Vietnam Foe" (cited in note 35), 1.

65. "60,000 Reservists Face Call in Next Few Months," *New York Times*, April 1, 1968, 10.

66. Vandiver, *Shadows of Vietnam*, 324.

67. In his memoirs, Johnson blamed lower-level civilians in the Pentagon for the leaks. See Johnson, *The Vantage Point*, 403.

68. Cited in Schandler, *The Unmaking of the President*, 230.

69. "The Administration: Clifford Takes Over," *Time*, March 8, 1968, 19; Johnson, *The Vantage Point*, 401; Vandiver, *Shadows of Vietnam*, 316.

70. John W. Finney, "Criticism of War Widens in Senate on Build-Up Issue," *New York Times*, March 8, 1968, 1; Hedrick Smith, "Bipartisan Group Acts," *New York Times*, March 13, 1968; John W. Finney, "Rusk Tells Panel 'We Will Consult' on Any Troop Rise," *New York Times*, March 13, 1968, 1.

71. Schandler, *The Unmaking of a President*, 284.

72. Clark Clifford, with Richard Holbrooke, *Counsel to the President* (New York: Random House, 1991), 511; Schandler, *The Unmaking of a President*, 316, 302.

73. Harry McPherson, Alternate Draft for the President's March 31 Speech, March 28, 1968, 3/31/68 Address to the Nation, March 28, 1968, #10, ALTERNATE 6:00 p.m., Draft 1, White House Central Files, Statements of Lyndon Baines Johnson, Box 273, Lyndon Baines Johnson Library.

74. Notes on Tuesday Luncheon with Senior Foreign Policy Advisers, March 5, 1968, Tom Johnson's Notes of Meetings, Box 2, Lyndon Baines Johnson Library.

75. Phil Habib, "Increasing the Effectiveness of Vietnamese Efforts in Conjunction with a US Troop Increase," draft, February (?) 3, 1968 [probably March 3], Volume 7, Meeting with President and Draft Memo, National Security File, National Security Council Histories, March 31st Speech, Box 49 (1 of 2), Lyndon Baines Johnson Library.

76. Henry Cabot Lodge, Memorandum to Dean Rusk and Nicholas Katzenbach, March 6, 1968, Volume 4, Tabs N-Z and AA-KK, National Security File, National Security Council Histories, March 31st Speech, Box 48, Lyndon Baines Johnson Library. See also Draft Memorandum for the President, March 4, 1968 (unsigned, probably from the Clifford Task Force), Volume 7, Meeting with President and Draft Memo, National Security File, National Security Council Histories, March 31st Speech, Box 49 (1 of 2), Lyndon Baines Johnson Library.

77. Kolko, *Anatomy of a War*, 321–22.

78. Walt Rostow, Memorandum to the President, March 4, 1968, Volume 7, Meeting with President and Draft Memo, National Security File, National Security Council Histories, March 31st Speech, Box 49 (1 of 2), Lyndon Baines Johnson Library; "Draft Memorandum for the President: Alternative Strategies

in Vietnam, 1 March 1968," Volume 8, Draft Memo for the President, National Security File, National Security Council Histories, March 31st Speech, Box 49 (2 of 2), Lyndon Baines Johnson Library, 1.

79. Herring, *LBJ and Vietnam*, 164; John Prados, *Vietnam: The History of an Unwinnable War, 1945–1975* (Lawrence: University Press of Kansas, 2009), 262.

80. For a historical analysis of the gold crisis, see Robert M. Collins, "The Economic Crisis of 1968 and the Waning of the 'American Century,'" *American Historical Review* 101 (April 1996): 396–422.

81. These events are discussed in Collins, "Economic Crisis," 402.

82. Johnson, *The Vantage Point*, 406.

83. Schandler, *The Unmaking of a President*, 139.

84. [Paul Nitze], Letter to the President from the Deputy Secretary of Defense, March 16, 1968, National Objectives, Resources, and Strategy vis-à-vis SEA [1], Papers of Clark Clifford, Vietnam Papers, Box 1, Lyndon Baines Johnson Library.

85. Tom Wicker, "In the Nation: Guns, Butter, and Folly," *New York Times*, March 17, 1968, E13.

86. Quoted in Collins, "Economic Crisis," 410.

87. Arthur Okun, Comments on McPherson's March 30, 1968 Draft, 3/31/68 Address to the Nation, March 30, 1968, #13, Alternate Draft #4, 4:00 p.m., White House Central Files, Statements of Lyndon Baines Johnson, Box 273, Lyndon Baines Johnson Library.

88. Harry McPherson, Master Copy (marked "Saturday/March 30") on which are handwritten changes to the draft dated "March 29, 1968, 2:30 p.m.," 3/31/68 Address to the Nation, March 29, 1968. #12, Alternate, Draft #3, White House Central Files, Statements of Lyndon Baines Johnson, Box 273, Lyndon Baines Johnson Library.

89. Lady Bird Johnson, Comments on McPherson's alternate draft (dated 29 March 1968, 2:30 p.m.), 3/31/68 Remarks of the President to the Nation, the President's Oval Office, White House Central Files, Statements of Lyndon Baines Johnson, Box 274, Lyndon Baines Johnson Library.

90. Harry McPherson, Alternate Draft #4, 3/31/68 Address to the Nation, March 30, 1968, #13, Alternate Draft #4, 4:00 p.m., White House Central Files, Statements of Lyndon Baines Johnson, Box 273, Lyndon Baines Johnson Library.

91. William Chapman, "Troops Will Be Boosted," *Washington Post*, March 17, 1968, A1.

92. Meeting with House and Senate Leaders, April 3, 1968, Tom Johnson's Notes of Meetings, Box 3, Lyndon Baines Johnson Library.

93. Richard F. Janssen, "Payments Gap Peril: Johnson's Bid to Cut International Deficit Faces New Difficulties," *Wall Street Journal*, March 12, 1968, 1.

94. "The President's News Conference of March 22, 1968," *Public Papers of the Presidents: Lyndon B. Johnson, 1968–69* (Washington, DC: US Government

Printing Office, 1970), I, 432.

95. Notes on Tuesday Luncheon with Senior Foreign Policy Advisers, March 5, 1968, Tom Johnson's Notes of Meetings, Box 2, Lyndon Baines Johnson Library.

96. Barrett, *Uncertain Warriors*, 146.

Chapter 6

1. Robert Young, "Stuns Nation at End of TV, Radio Speech," *Chicago Tribune*, April 1, 1968, 1. Trying to guess what Christian could be referring to, a group of NBC correspondents decided that Johnson would be announcing a forthcoming presidential trip to Vietnam. See "The Talk of the Town," *New Yorker*, April 6, 1968, 36.

2. "Coolidge, Truman Also Withdrew," *New York Times*, April 1, 1968, 26. Theodore Roosevelt sought another, nonconsecutive term in 1912 as a third-party candidate after failing to win the Republican nomination, but he had declined to run in 1908.

3. Theodore H. White, *The Making of the President 1968* (New York: Atheneum, 1969), 115.

4. Lyndon Baines Johnson, *The Vantage Point: Perspectives of the Presidency, 1963–1969* (New York: Holt, Rinehart, and Winston, 1971), 427–28.

5. Johnson, *The Vantage Point*, 92–95. It was a handwritten note from Mrs. Johnson, pinned to his pillow, that eventually convinced him to stay in that year's race, according to his account, but urged him to retire after having served one full term. This handwritten note is at the Lyndon Baines Johnson Library and is quoted in the president's memoirs.

6. Quoted in Frank E. Vandiver, *Shadows of Vietnam: Lyndon Johnson's Wars* (College Station: Texas A&M University Press, 1997), 331.

7. Johnson, *The Vantage Point*, 366; Robert Dallek, *Flawed Giant: Lyndon Johnson and His Times, 1961–1973* (New York: Oxford University Press, 1998), 523–24; Walter Trohan, "Report from Washington," *Chicago Tribune*, April 3, 1968, 14.

8. Cited in "Move Called 'Completely Irrevocable,'" *New York Times*, April 1, 1968, 28.

9. Dallek, *Flawed Giant*, 524.

10. Vaughn Davis Bornet, *The Presidency of Lyndon B. Johnson* (Lawrence: University Press of Kansas, 1983), 300.

11. Cited in Dallek, *Flawed Giant*, 524.

12. Dallek, *Flawed Giant*, 524.

13. Irving Bernstein, *Guns or Butter: The Presidency of Lyndon Johnson* (New York: Oxford University Press, 1996), 471.

14. Johnson, *The Vantage Point*, 430.

15. Johnson, *The Vantage Point*, 400.

16. Harry McPherson, *A Political Education* (1972; rpt. Boston: Houghton Mifflin, 1988), 427. See also Randall B. Woods, *LBJ: Architect of American Ambition* (New York: Free Press, 2006), 834.

17. "Johnson's Campaign Warm-Up," *New York Times*, February 25, 1968, E2.

18. "LBJ Retirement Rumor Is Deflated," *Washington Post*, March 22, 1968, A2.

19. "LBJ Retirement Rumor Is Deflated," A2. See also James Reston, "Washington: Johnson Is the Issue," *New York Times*, March 17, 1968, E12.

20. Dallek, *Flawed Giant*, 527–28.

21. The President's News Conference of March 25, 1968, and The President's News Conference of March 30, 1968, both in Volume 8, Excerpts and Taylor's Memo, National Security File, National Security Council Histories, March 31st Speech, Box 49 (2 of 2), Lyndon Baines Johnson Library.

22. "LBJ Retirement Rumor Is Deflated," A2.

23. Horace Busby, *The Thirty-First of March* (New York: Farrar, Straus, and Giroux, 2005); Dallek, *Flawed Giant*, 529.

24. Johnson, *The Vantage Point*, 424.

25. Godfrey Hodgson, *America in Our Time* (Garden City, NY: Doubleday, 1976), 384, citing data from the Gallup Poll.

26. "Lyndon Tells Nation He Will Not Seek Reelection," *Chicago Tribune*, April 1, 1968, 4; Bornet, *The Presidency of Lyndon B. Johnson*, 289, 298.

27. See "Mr. Johnson's Withdrawal" [editorial], *Wall Street Journal*, April 1, 1968, 16.

28. See Notes on Cabinet Meeting, April 3, 1968, Tom Johnson's Notes of Meetings, Box 3, Lyndon Baines Johnson Library; Johnson, *The Vantage Point*, 426–27.

29. Doris Kearns, *Lyndon Johnson and the American Dream* (New York: Harper and Row, 1976), 339.

30. See Memorandum from Horace Busby to the President, January 15, 1968, White House Central Files, Statements of Lyndon Baines Johnson, Box 274, Lyndon Baines Johnson Library. Truman's withdrawal on March 29, however, was cited by Johnson as one of the reasons for his own timetable. On the afternoon of March 31, he sent an aide to check the exact date of Truman's withdrawal in case he wanted to make reference to it. See Johnson's daily log reproduced in Busby, *The Thirty-First of March*. See also Johnson, *The Vantage Point*, 430. In all likelihood, the Truman–Johnson comparison was a red herring.

31. George Christian, Memorandum to Drew Pearson, May 15, 1968, 3/31/68 Address to the Nation, Reactions to March 31st Speech, White House Central Files, Statements of Lyndon Baines Johnson, Box 274, Lyndon Baines Johnson Library.

32. Draft manuscript attached to Memorandum from [Tom Johnson] to Bill Jorden, April 3, 1989, White House Central Files, Statements of Lyndon Baines

Johnson, Box 274, Lyndon Baines Johnson Library. The State of the Union version of the withdrawal announcement focused on the magnitude of the tasks, not the division within the country.

33. George Christian, Memorandum to Drew Pearson, cited in note 31; Johnson, *The Vantage Point*, 431.

34. George Christian, Memorandum to the President, March 31, 1968, 3/31/68 Address to the Nation, Reactions to March 31st Speech, White House Central Files, Statements of Lyndon Baines Johnson, Box 274, Lyndon Baines Johnson Library.

35. Harry McPherson, Memorandum to the President, March 27, 1968; William P. Bundy, Memorandum to Harry McPherson, March 28, 1968, both in 3/31/68 Address to the Nation, March 27, 1968, #9, Sixth Draft Plus "Peroration," Folder 1, White House Central Files, Statements of Lyndon Baines Johnson, Box 272, Lyndon Baines Johnson Library.

36. Harry McPherson, Alternate Draft for the President's March 31 Speech, March 28, 1968, 3/31/68 Address to the Nation, March 28, 1968, #10, ALTERNATE 6:00 p.m., Draft 1, White House Central Files, Statements of Lyndon Baines Johnson, Box 273, Lyndon Baines Johnson Library.

37. Harry McPherson, Memorandum to the President, March 30, 1968, 9:30 p.m., 3/31/68 Address to the Nation, March 30, 1968, #14, Alternate Draft #5, 7:00 p.m., White House Central Files, Statements of Lyndon Baines Johnson, Box 274, Lyndon Baines Johnson Library.

38. Harry McPherson, Draft Closing Remarks for March 31 Speech [March 30, 1968], White House Central Files, Statements of Lyndon Baines Johnson, Box 274, Lyndon Baines Johnson Library.

39. Johnson, *The Vantage Point*, 421. See also Moya Ann Ball, "Lyndon B. Johnson: From Private Deliberations to Public Declaration—The Making of LBJ's Renunciation Speech," in *Presidential Speechwriting: From the New Deal to the Reagan Revolution and Beyond*, ed. Kurt Ritter and Martin J. Medhurst (College Station: Texas A&M University Press), 126.

40. Memorandum from [Tom Johnson] to Bill Jorden, April 3, 1989, cited in note 32.

41. See "President Moves in the Name of Unity," *New York Times*, April 1, 1968, 27.

42. Horace Busby, Early Version of Closing Remarks for March 31 Speech, White House Central Files, Statements of Lyndon Baines Johnson, Box 274, Lyndon Baines Johnson Library.

43. Horace Busby, Peroration for March 31 speech [early draft], White House Central Files, Statements of Lyndon Baines Johnson, Box 274, Lyndon Baines Johnson Library.

44. These and the preceding details are related in Horace Busby, Subsequent drafts of the peroration for the March 31st Speech, White House Central Files, Statements of Lyndon Baines Johnson, Box 274, Lyndon Baines Johnson Li-

brary, in notes accompanying the various drafts.

45. Busby, *The Thirty-First of March*, 201.

46. Cited in Woods, *LBJ: Architect of American Ambition*, 836.

47. Busby, *The Thirty-First of March*, 210.

48. Busby, *The Thirty-First of March*, 212.

49. 3/31/68 Original Drafts, "Accordingly I Shall Not Seek—and Would Not Accept the Nomination of My Party for Another Term," White House Central Files, Statements of Lyndon Baines Johnson, Box 274, Lyndon Baines Johnson Library.

50. Busby, *The Thirty-First of March*, 215–16.

51. Busby, *The Thirty-First of March*, 220.

52. See Busby, *The Thirty-First of March*, 221.

53. Busby, *The Thirty-First of March*, 222.

54. These and other responses can be found in Comments from Cabinet members called during the early part of the speech, 3/31/68 Address to the Nation, Reactions to March 31st Speech, White House Central Files, Statements of Lyndon Baines Johnson, Box 274, Lyndon Baines Johnson Library.

55. William J. Hopkins, Memorandum to James R. Jones, April 29, 1968 (forwarded by Jones to the President), 3/31/68 Address to the Nation, Reactions to March 31st Speech, White House Central Files, Statements of Lyndon Baines Johnson, Box 274, Lyndon Baines Johnson Library.

56. News Analysis/April 1968, Papers of Lyndon Baines Johnson, File EX SP 3–236, 4/18/68–4/30/68, Box 198, Lyndon Baines Johnson Library. See also Ball, "Lyndon B. Johnson: From Private Deliberations to Public Declaration," 126.

57. Cited in an untitled, unsigned document dated April 2, 1968, File SP3–236, President's remarks to the nation, 3/31/68—Vietnam and renomination, White House Central Files, Papers of Lyndon Baines Johnson, GEN SP, Box 197, Lyndon Baines Johnson Library.

58. Charles J. Ella, "Peace Hopes, Not Exit of Johnson, Are Behind Big Rally, Analysts Say," *Wall Street Journal*, April 2, 1968, 1.

59. This editorial was transmitted to the president by Vice President Hubert H. Humphrey, Memorandum to Marvin Watson, April 5, 1968, SP3–236, President's remarks to the nation, cited in note 57.

60. "Guest Editorials: Comment on Mr. Johnson's Withdrawal," *Chicago Tribune*, April 3, 1968, 14; "Guest Editorials: Comment on Mr. Johnson's Withdrawal," *Chicago Tribune*, April 1, 1968, 26.

61. Robert F. Kennedy, Telegram to the President, March 31, 1968, 11:41 p.m., SP 3–236, President's remarks to the nation, 3/31/68—Vietnam and renomination, White House Central Files, Papers of Lyndon Baines Johnson, GEN SP, Box 197, Lyndon Baines Johnson Library.

62. George McGovern, Letter to the President, April 1, 1968, SP 3–236/ST 41, Papers of Lyndon Baines Johnson, Speeches File, EX SP 3–236, Box 200,

Lyndon Baines Johnson Library.

63. Edward M. Kennedy, Telegram to the President, April 1, 1968, SP 3–236/ST 21, Papers of Lyndon Baines Johnson, SP 3–236, 5/1/68–, Papers of Lyndon Baines Johnson, Speeches File, EX SP 3–236, Box 199, Lyndon Baines Johnson Library.

64. Quoted in E. W. Kenworthy, "M'Carthy Praises President on War," *New York Times*, April 2, 1968, 1.

65. Quoted in Ian McDonald, "Selfless Gesture Praised," *The Times* (London), April 2, 1968, 1.

66. Earle G. Wheeler, Letter to the President, April 1, 1968, SP 3–236, President's remarks to the nation, 3/31/68—Vietnam and renomination, White House Central Files, Papers of Lyndon Baines Johnson, GEN SP, Box 197, Lyndon Baines Johnson Library.

67. See, for example, John Hughes, "Ho at 'Point of No Return'?" *Christian Science Monitor*, April 1, 1968, 4; James Nelson Goodsell, "Americans Sight New US Era," *Christian Science Monitor*, April 1, 1968, 2.

68. Bornet, *The Presidency of Lyndon B. Johnson*, 301.

69. Johnson, *The Vantage Point*, 433.

70. Jack Gould, "TV: Commentators Stunned by President's Action," *New York Times*, April 1, 1968, 26.

71. Sylvan Fox, "Political Chiefs Stunned; Kennedy Sets News Parley," *New York Times*, April 1, 1968, 27.

72. "Lyndon Tells Nation He Will Not Seek Reelection," *Chicago Tribune*, April 1, 1968, 4.

73. George Christian, Memorandum to Drew Pearson, May 15, 1968, 3/31/68 Address to the Nation, Reactions to March 31st Speech, White House Central Files, Statements of Lyndon Baines Johnson, Box 274, Lyndon Baines Johnson Library.

74. Johnson, *The Vantage Point*, 424.

75. Quoted in "Withdrawal from Race Is Final: Lyndon," *Chicago Tribune*, April 1, 1968, 3.

76. Sylvan Fox, "Political Chiefs Stunned; Kennedy Sets News Parley," *New York Times*, April 1, 1968, 27.

77. "Shifts Seen in Johnson Support," *Christian Science Monitor*, April 4, 1968, 14.

78. Robert Weidrich, "Vote Today in Wisconsin," *Chicago Tribune*, April 2, 1968, 1.

79. Kearns, *Lyndon Johnson and the American Dream*, 344.

80. "60,000 Reservists Face Call in Next Few Months," *New York Times*, April 1, 1968, 10.

81. Henry Gemmill, "President Could Wring Some Significant Gains from Lame Duck Role," *Wall Street Journal*, April 1, 1968, 1.

82. Philip Warden, "Dems Predict LBJ Move Will Help His Bills," *Chicago*

Tribune, April 1, 1968, 8.

83. McGeorge Bundy, Letter to the President, April 2, 1968, SP 3–236, ST 32, 4/5/68–4/8/68, Papers of Lyndon Baines Johnson, Speeches File, EX SP 3–236, Box 200, Lyndon Baines Johnson Library. Hershey would be replaced by President Nixon in 1969. Hoover would die in office in 1972.

84. Gemmill, "President Could Wring Some Significant Gains," 1. See also "Guest Editorials: Comment on Mr. Johnson's Withdrawal," *Chicago Tribune*, April 1, 1968, 26; and "The President's Peace Drive," *Christian Science Monitor*, April 3, 1968, 5 for similar but more prosaic expressions of the same idea.

85. See Clark Clifford, with Richard Holbrooke, *Counsel to the President* (New York: Random House, 1991), 525.

86. Beverly Deupe, "Johnson Stuns Many in Vietnam," *Christian Science Monitor*, April 1, 1968, 17. See also "LBJ's Decision Causes Dismay in Viet Capital," *Chicago Tribune*, April 1, 1968, 3.

87. Ellsworth Bunker, Message to the President, April 4, 1968, Volume 6, Bunker Reports, National Security File, National Security Council Histories, March 31st Speech, Box 48, Lyndon Baines Johnson Library.

88. "Johnson Move Changes Plans, Radical Says," *New York Times*, April 2, 1968, 30.

89. Dallek, *Flawed Giant*, 544.

90. Quoted in Sylvan Fox, "Political Chiefs Stunned," 1.

91. "Urges Big Vote for Lyndon in Wisconsin," *Chicago Tribune*, April 1, 1968, 3; "Wisconsin Primary Today Loses Its Significance," *New York Times*, April 2, 1968, 10.

92. "Word from Wisconsin" [editorial], *Christian Science Monitor*, April 4, 1968, 16.

93. Cited in Warren Weaver Jr., "Impact on McCarthy," *New York Times*, April 1, 1968, 28.

94. Sylvan Fox, "Political Chiefs Stunned," 27.

95. James Reston, "Daley Withholds His Preference, Doesn't Rule Out Johnson Draft," *New York Times*, April 2, 1968, 30; Fred Panzer, Memorandum to Marvin Watson, April 5, 1968, SP3–236 President's remarks to the nation, 3/31/68—Vietnam and renomination. White House Central Files, Papers of Lyndon Baines Johnson, GEN SP, Box 197, Lyndon Baines Johnson Library.

96. Cited in Panzer, Memorandum to Marvin Watson (see note 95).

97. Howard James, "Contest Seen between Humphrey and Kennedy," *Christian Science Monitor*, April 1, 1968, 16. On a personal note, I recall that this was my reaction at the time. I thought that Johnson was following Roosevelt's playbook and that he would be back in the race by the time of the Democratic convention.

98. Dana Adams Schmidt, "President Given Generous Praise," *New York Times*, April 1, 1968, 32; Raymond H. Anderson, "Soviet Skeptical on Johnson Talk," *New York Times*, April 1, 1968, 32.

99. Quoted in John Leo, "Leaders of Peace Movement Voice Skepticism," *New York Times*, April 1, 1968, 4.

100. Quoted in Charles J. Ella, "Peace Hopes, Not Exit of Johnson, Are Behind Big Rally, Analysts Say," *Wall Street Journal*, April 2, 1968, 1; "Johnson Move Brings Heavy Stock Buying by Institutions; Small Investor Is Cautious," *Wall Street Journal*, April 2, 1968, 19.

101. "Mr. Johnson's Withdrawal" [editorial], *Wall Street Journal*, April 1, 1968, 16; "Move Called 'Completely Irrevocable,'" *New York Times*, April 1, 1968, 28; "Lyndon Tells Nation He Will Not Seek Reelection," *Chicago Tribune*, April 1, 1968, 4.

102. See John Prados, *Vietnam: The History of an Unwinnable War, 1945–1975* (Lawrence: University Press of Kansas, 2009), 259.

103. Horace Busby, Memorandum to the President, probably March 29 or 30, 1968, 3/31/68 Remarks of the President to the Nation, the President's Oval Office, White House Central Files, Statements of Lyndon Baines Johnson, Box 274, Lyndon Baines Johnson Library.

Chapter 7

1. Jimmy Carter and George H. W. Bush were defeated in their quest for a second term, and Gerald R. Ford went down to defeat in seeking his first elected term, but as of 2019 no one since Johnson has declined to run.

2. Irving Bernstein, *Guns or Butter: The Presidency of Lyndon Johnson* (New York: Oxford University Press, 1996), 492.

3. Larry Berman, *Lyndon Johnson's War: The Road to Stalemate in Vietnam* (New York: Norton, 1989), 202.

4. "3:07 p.m. Meeting [April 3, 1968]," Tom Johnson's Notes of Meetings, Box 3, Lyndon Baines Johnson Library.

5. See John Prados, *Vietnam: The History of an Unwinnable War, 1945–1975* (Lawrence: University Press of Kansas, 2009), 250.

6. Herbert Y. Schandler, *The Unmaking of a President: Lyndon Johnson and Vietnam* (Princeton, NJ: Princeton University Press, 1977), 313–14. For Johnson's acknowledgment that there would be no more than 549,500 troops in Vietnam, see Edwin E. Moïse, *The Myths of Tet: The Most Misunderstood Event of the Vietnam War* (Lawrence: University Press of Kansas, 2017), 199.

7. Frank E. Vandiver, *Shadows of Vietnam: Lyndon Johnson's Wars* (College Station: Texas A&M University Press, 1997), 334; Schandler, *The Unmaking of the President*, 314.

8. Robert Trumbull, "Foes in Japan Ask Sato Resignation," *New York Times*, April 1, 1968, 3; Lloyd Gardner, "Lyndon Johnson and Vietnam: The Final Months," in *The Johnson Years*, ed. Robert A. Divine, vol. 3, *LBJ at Home and Abroad* (Lawrence: University Press of Kansas, 1994), 213.

9. Joseph A. Califano Jr., Memorandum to the President, May 2, 1968, SP 3–236, 5/1/68–, Papers of Lyndon Baines Johnson, Speeches File, EX SP 3–236,

Box 198, Lyndon Baines Johnson Library.

10. George C. Herring, *LBJ and Vietnam: A Different Kind of War* (Austin: University of Texas Press, 1994), 163; George C. Herring, "The War in Vietnam," in *Exploring the Johnson Years*, ed. Robert A. Divine (Austin: University of Texas Press, 1981), 53.

11. Cited in "President Moves in the Name of Unity," *New York Times*, April 1, 1968, 27.

12. Rusk, Rostow, and Wheeler cited in Schandler, *The Unmaking of a President*, 304; George C. Herring, "The Reluctant Warrior: Lyndon Johnson as Commander in Chief," in *Shadow on the White House: Presidents and the Vietnam War, 1945–1975*, ed. David L. Anderson (Lawrence: University Press of Kansas, 1993), 102–3.

13. Gardner, "Lyndon Johnson and Vietnam," 214; Bernstein, *Guns or Butter*, 492.

14. Prados, *Vietnam: The History of an Unwinnable War*, 345, 394.

15. "The War: More Men, More Doubts," *Newsweek*, March 4, 1968, 19; Moïse, *The Myths of Tet*, 73.

16. "Foe Has Reduced Forces at Khesanh," *New York Times*, April 1, 1968, 26.

17. Prados, *Vietnam: The History of an Unwinnable War*, 254.

18. Moïse, *The Myths of Tet*, 169.

19. Gabriel Kolko, *Anatomy of a War: Vietnam, the United States, and the Modern Historical Experience* (New York: Pantheon Books, 1985), 321.

20. Cited in Gardner, "Lyndon Johnson and Vietnam," 225.

21. Ronald H. Spector, *After Tet: The Bloodiest Year in Vietnam* (New York: Free Press, 1993).

22. Clark Clifford with Richard Holbrooke, *Counsel to the President* (New York: Random House, 1991), 528.

23. Clifford with Holbrooke, *Counsel to the President*, 528.

24. Herring, "The War in Vietnam," 53.

25. Kolko, *Anatomy of a War*, 321.

26. Herring, *LBJ and Vietnam*, 164.

27. Clifford with Holbrooke, *Counsel to the President*, 528.

28. Doris Kearns Goodwin, *Leadership in Turbulent Times* (New York: Simon and Schuster, 2018), 306–43.

29. On the preparation of the Johns Hopkins speech to appeal to Walter Lippmann, see Kathleen J. Turner, *Lyndon Johnson's Dual War: Vietnam and the Press* (Chicago: University of Chicago Press, 1985).

30. Quoted in Clayton Knowles, "Nixon Delays War Statement; Lindsay Seeks G.O.P. Interest," *New York Times*, April 1, 1968, 1.

31. Melvin Small, *At the Water's Edge: American Politics and the Vietnam War* (Chicago: Ivan R. Dee, 2005), 112.

32. Gardner, "Lyndon Johnson and Vietnam," 221.

33. Gardner, "Lyndon Johnson and Vietnam," 223.

34. "Vietnam Peace Talks" [editorial], *New York Times*, February 11, 1968, E12.

35. Prados, *Vietnam: The History of an Unwinnable War*, 267.

36. Prados, *Vietnam: The History of an Unwinnable War*, 344.

37. John A. Farrell, *Richard Nixon: The Life* (New York: Doubleday, 2017), 342.

38. Moïse, *The Myths of Tet*, 170.

39. Cited in Prados, *Vietnam: The History of an Unwinnable War*, 313. Butterfield is the same aide who revealed the existence of the secret White House taping system at the time of the congressional investigations of Watergate in 1973.

40. Small, *At the Water's Edge*, 137.

Bibliography

Primary sources for this study are found at the Lyndon Baines Johnson Library in Austin, Texas. Two series in the White House Central Files are particularly useful: Statements of Lyndon Baines Johnson, which include all eleven drafts of the speech and notes, comments, and memos concerning the various drafts; and the Speeches File, further divided into General and Executive, based on the status of the respondents, which includes reaction to the speech and commentary about it.

Another especially valuable file series is the National Security File, which includes both the National Security Council Histories and the Country File—Vietnam. The former is a file of administrative histories that include a subseries on the March 31 speech in relation to national security issues. The content of the Country File—Vietnam is suggested by its title.

By 1968, Assistant Press Secretary Tom Johnson was the principal note-taker at meetings related to planning Vietnam policy. His handwritten notes of individual meetings are so detailed that they are almost transcripts of the discussions. There is a separate Meeting Notes File for notes by others (presumably when Tom Johnson could not be present).

The Papers of Clark Clifford, with a subseries of Vietnam Papers, were valuable in revealing Clifford's thinking as he conducted his review of Vietnam policy in early March and reached the conclusion that there was no plan for victory at any level of troop commitment.

The President's Appointments File with its Diary Backup is particularly useful in tracking the activities and meetings of the president during the last fifteen days in March as he worked toward a series of related decisions, including the decision not to run for reelection.

Johnson's public statements, including news conference transcripts and speeches to various organizations, are easily available in volume 1 of *Public Papers of the Presidents: Lyndon B. Johnson, 1968–69* (Washington, DC: US Government Printing Office, 1970).

For contemporaneous developments and news, I consulted five major newspapers, each of which had its own reportorial staff at the time: *New York Times, Washington Post, Wall Street Journal, Christian Science Monitor,* and *Chicago Tribune,* with occasional reference to *The Times* (London) and *Le Monde* (Paris). I also consulted two weekly newsmagazines, *Time* and *Newsweek,* for the spring of 1968.

Memoirs and secondary source materials that were valuable for this study are listed here.

Anderson, David L., ed. *Shadow on the White House: Presidents and the Vietnam War, 1945–1975.* Lawrence: University Press of Kansas, 1993.

Ball, Moya Ann. "Lyndon B. Johnson: From Private Deliberation to Public Declaration—The Making of LBJ's Renunciation Speech." In *Presidential Speechwriting: From the New Deal to the Reagan Revolution and Beyond,* edited by Kurt Ritter and Martin J. Medhurst, 108–36. College Station: Texas A&M University Press, 2003.

Barrett, David M. *Uncertain Warriors: Lyndon Johnson and His Vietnam Advisers.* Lawrence: University Press of Kansas, 1993.

Berman, Larry. *Lyndon Johnson's War: The Road to Stalemate in Vietnam.* New York: Norton, 1989.

Bernstein, Irving. *Guns or Butter: The Presidency of Lyndon Johnson.* New York: Oxford University Press, 1996.

Bornet, Vaughn Davis. *The Presidency of Lyndon B. Johnson.* Lawrence: University Press of Kansas, 1983.

Braestrup, Peter. *Big Story.* New Haven, CT: Yale University Press, 1983.

Burke, Kenneth. *A Grammar of Motives.* 1945; rpt. Berkeley: University of California Press, 1969.

Busby, Horace. *The Thirty-First of March: An Intimate Portrait of Lyndon*

Johnson's Final Days in Office. New York: Farrar, Straus, and Giroux, 2005. (Published posthumously.)

Califano, Joseph A., Jr. *The Triumph and Tragedy of Lyndon Johnson*. New York: Simon and Schuster, 1991.

Clifford, Clark, with Richard Holbrooke. *Counsel to the President*. New York: Random House, 1991.

Collins, Robert M. "The Economic Crisis of 1968 and the Waning of the 'American Century.'" *American Historical Review* 101 (April 1996): 396–422.

Dallek, Robert. *Flawed Giant: Lyndon Johnson and His Times, 1961–1973*. New York: Oxford University Press, 1998.

Divine, Robert A., ed. *Exploring the Johnson Years*. Austin: University of Texas Press, 1981.

—, ed. *The Johnson Years*. Vol. 2, *Vietnam, the Environment, and Science*. Lawrence: University Press of Kansas, 1987.

—, ed. *The Johnson Years*. Vol. 3, *LBJ at Home and Abroad*. Lawrence: University Press of Kansas, 1994.

Edwards, George C., III. *On Deaf Ears*. New Haven, CT: Yale University Press, 2003.

Farrell, John A. *Richard Nixon: The Life*. New York: Doubleday, 2017.

Goodwin, Doris Kearns. *Leadership in Turbulent Times*. New York: Simon and Schuster, 2018.

Herring, George C. *LBJ and Vietnam: A Different Kind of War*. Austin: University of Texas Press, 1994.

Hoopes, Townsend. *The Limits of Intervention: An Inside Account of How the Johnson Policy of Escalation in Vietnam Was Reversed*. New York: David McKay, 1969.

Johnson, Lyndon Baines. *The Vantage Point: Perspectives of the Presidency, 1963–1969*. New York: Holt, Rinehart, and Winston, 1971.

Karnow, Stanley. *Vietnam: A History*. New York: Viking, 1983.

Kearns, Doris. *Lyndon Johnson and the American Dream*. New York: Harper and Row, 1976.

Kolko, Gabriel. *Anatomy of a War: Vietnam, the United States, and the Modern Historical Experience*. New York: Pantheon Books, 1985.

Lerner, Mitchell B., ed. *Looking Back at LBJ*. Lawrence: University Press of Kansas, 2005.

McNamara, Robert S. *In Retrospect: The Tragedy and Lessons of Vietnam*. New York: Random House, 1995.

McPherson, Harry. *A Political Education*. 1972; rpt. Boston: Houghton Mifflin, 1988.

Moïse, Edwin E. *The Myths of Tet: The Most Misunderstood Event of the Vietnam War*. Lawrence: University Press of Kansas, 2017.

Olson, Gregory A. *Mansfield and Vietnam: A Study in Rhetorical Adaptation*. East Lansing: Michigan State University Press, 1995.

Osgood, Charles E. *An Alternative to War or Surrender*. Urbana: University of Illinois Press, 1962.

Prados, John. *Vietnam: The History of an Unwinnable War, 1945–1975*. Lawrence: University Press of Kansas, 2009.

Schandler, Herbert Y. *The Unmaking of a President: Lyndon Johnson and Vietnam*. Princeton, NJ: Princeton University Press, 1977.

Small, Melvin. *At the Water's Edge: American Politics and the Vietnam War*. Chicago: Ivan R. Dee, 2005.

Spector, Ronald H. *After Tet: The Bloodiest Year in Vietnam*. New York: Free Press, 1993.

Stuckey, Mary E. *The President as Interpreter-in-Chief*. Chatham, NJ: Chatham House, 1991.

Turner, Kathleen J. *Lyndon Johnson's Dual War: Vietnam and the Press*. Chicago: University of Chicago Press, 1985.

Vandiver, Frank E. *Shadows of Vietnam: Lyndon Johnson's Wars*. College Station: Texas A&M University Press, 1997.

White, Theodore H. *The Making of the President 1968*. New York: Atheneum, 1969.

Woods, Randall B. *LBJ: Architect of American Ambition*. New York: Free Press, 2006.

Zarefsky, David. "Lyndon Johnson's Withdrawal Speech," *Voices of Democracy* 9 (2014): 41–55. Electronic publication.

—. *Political Argumentation in the United States*. Amsterdam: John Benjamins, 2014.

Index

Abrams, Creighton, 40, 129, 179, 188
Acheson, Dean, 25–26, 55, 134
Aiken, George, 112
Albert, Carl, 162
ally recruitment efforts, 17
Alternate Draft #1, 76–81, 101, 109, 138, 156, 203n48
Alternate Draft #2, 81–82
Alternate Draft #3, 82–83, 101, 144
Alternate Draft #4, 83–85, 101, 143–45
Alternate Draft #5, 85–87
Alternate Drafts, not numbered, 104, 144, 156
ambiguity, role in rhetoric, 181–83
American Friends of Vietnam, 6–7
American Institute for Public Opinion Research, 11
Anderson, David L., 6, 11
antiwar movement: and ending of draft, 189–90; growth of, 1–2; Johnson's mindset about, 22–24; and Johnson's withdrawal from reelection, 153, 164; media coverage, 40; and New Hampshire primary, 48–49; public opinion, 12; as reserves call up factor, 122; responses to North Vietnam's negotiations offer, 112; and speech development discussions, 106. *See also* critics of war policy, overview
appeasement argument, 22
Arthur, Chester A., 148
Australia, 17, 112

balance-of-payments deficit, 47, 50, 140–41, 143–44
Ball, George, 20–21

Ball, Moya Ann, 60, 62
Bao Dai, 5
Barrett, David M., 54, 59, 98, 109, 147
Battle of the Bulge, 32–33
Bay of Pigs, 7
Berman, Larry, 27, 76, 127, 129, 175
Bernstein, Irving, 175, 178
bombing activity: and Gulf of Tonkin episode, 13; limitations of, 17, 93, 107–108; after March speech, 113, 179, 186–87; Nixon administration, 189; as nonverbal bargaining, 10, 90–91; and Pleiku attack, 15; public opinion, 42
bombing halt: Clifford's post-speech statements, 177; Clifford task force discussion, 96–97; Goldberg's proposal, 50, 97–98; Humphrey's proposal, 187; illusion of, 179; McNamara's recommendations, 24–25, 94–96; McPherson's suggestions, 93–94; October 1968 announcement, 188–89; post-March speech predictions about, 110–11; public opinion, 163; and reelection withdrawal announcement, 166–68; Rusk's proposal, 46, 59, 206n29
bombing halt, as negotiating tactic: during Christmas truce, 17–18, 92; and Johnson's belligerent speeches, 53; message complexity, 91–92; North Vietnam's demands, 18, 19; San Antonio speech, 19, 93
bombing halt, in speech development discussions: overview of debate arguments, 65–66, 98–104, 107–109; in

Alternate Drafts #1 through #4, 76–78, 81, 83–84, 104; in Drafts #1 through #6, 69, 70, 72, 76; in early unnumbered drafts, 60, 64; in final version, 86, 113; influencers summarized, 104–105; as public opinion appeal, 106–107; Rostow's recommendation, 58; sincerity intent, 114–15. *See also* peace negotiations
Bornet, Vaughn Davis, 92, 153, 164–65
Bradley, Omar, 55
Braestrup, Peter, 196n40
Britain. *See* Great Britain
Brzezinski, Zbigniew, 30, 127
Buddhist community, 6, 7, 8, 21
Bundy, McGeorge: on bombing campaign impact, 108; concerns about escalation effectiveness, 46; and Goldberg's bombing halt proposal, 98; Johnson's communication about Vietnam dilemma, 22; in March speech drafting, 71; and McNamara's bombing halt plan, 95; on optimism campaign, 13, 30; on public support, 13, 54; and reelection withdrawal announcement, 168; in troop commitment discussions, 129, 131; in Vietnam, 15; in Wise Men discussions, 25–26, 54–55
Bundy, William P.: and Clifford task force, 44, 45; public opinion arguments, 125; Tet Offensive memo, 35
Bundy, William P. (in speech development discussions): Alternate Draft #3, 82; bombing halt perspective, 106; Drafts #1 through #6, 70, 72, 73, 74, 75, 156; early unnumbered drafts, 64
Bunker, Ellsworth: in bombing halt debate, 95, 105, 107, 109, 110–11; October 1968 peace negotiations, 188; in optimism campaign, 28, 29, 37; and reelection withdrawal announcement, 168; in speech development discussions, 61; and Tet Offensive, 31, 33; troop commitments statement, 124
Burke, Kenneth, 103
Burma, in domino theory, 6
Busby, Horace, 67, 84, 85, 87, 149, 150–51, 156–59

Bush, George H. W., 223n1
Butterfield, Alexander M., 189, 225n39
Buzzanco, Robert, 122–23

Califano, Joseph, 37–38, 151–52, 177–78
California Poll, 51
Cambodia, 5, 6, 189
Carter, Jimmy, 223n1
Carver, George, 26
casualty statistics, 13, 23, 31, 32, 36
Catholic community, in Vietnam, 7
Chancellor, John, 16
Chennault, Anna, 188–89
Chicago Tribune, 35, 107, 108, 168
China, 3, 4, 74
Christian, George, 37, 148, 149, 150, 153, 155, 156, 160, 165, 172
Christian Science Monitor, 104, 106, 108, 110, 166
Christmas truce, 17
Churchill, Winston, 4
CIA, analysis reports: absence in Wise Men meeting, 26; enemy strength estimates, 28; North Vietnamese infiltration, 123–24, 126–27; peace negotiations probability, 93; troop commitments, 119; Vietnam withdrawal option, 23
Clifford, Clark: air power directive from Johnson, 44; early bombing halt perspective, 93; on entanglement of speechwriting and policy development, 57–58; Fulbright meeting, 46; and Goldberg's bombing halt proposal, 98; on Hanoi's negotiations offer, 111, 112; on Johnson's conflicting signals, 180; and Johnson's withdrawal from reelection announcement, 168; R. Kennedy's proposed policy review, 49; and McNamara's bombing halt plan, 95; on media coverage, 40; on North Vietnam's acceptance of negotiations, 176; October 1968 peace negotiations, 188; selection as Defense Secretary, 25, 43; Senate hearings, 46, 48; on Tet Offensive impact, 36, 41; Westmoreland's troops request, 44–45, 118, 126, 130, 131, 137; in Wise Men discussions, 25–26

Clifford, Clark (in speech development discussions): Alternate Drafts #1 though #4, 76–77, 80, 82–83, 84, 156, 203n48; bombing halt element, 60, 98, 102; Drafts #1 through #6, 69, 70, 71–73, 74, 75–76, 81; influence summarized, 104–105, 113; negotiations-oriented perspective, 61–62, 181; Tet Offensive response, 59; troop requests inconsistency, 63; on war/peace combination problem, 99–100, 156

Clifford task force, policy topics: assumptions problem, 60; bombing halt, 96–97; Haiphong Harbor mining, 45; peace possibilities, 45; strategic plan for war, 45–46; troop commitments, 44–45, 48, 59, 97, 131–33

closing peroration: in Alternate Drafts #1 through #4, 80, 82, 84, 156; Busby's drafting of, 87; in Drafts #1 through #6, 69, 70, 74, 75, 156; in final version, 156; Johnson's comments, 80, 156. *See also* withdrawal from reelection, Johnson's

Cold War logic, in speech development discussions, 62, 75

Cold War logic, Vietnam War origins: decision-making characterized, 1–2, 3; Eisenhower administration actions, 4, 5–6; Ho Chi Minh's appeal, 3–4; at Johnson administration beginnings, 9–10; Kennedy administration actions, 6–9; and nuclear weapons paradox, 2–3; Truman administration actions, 4, 21

Collins, Robert M., 140

communism threat. *See* Cold War logic *entries*, Vietnam War origins

Congress, U.S.: consultation demand about troop commitments, 136; gold cover requirement, 50, 142; Gulf of Tonkin response, 13, 21; as March speech element, 70, 71, 74, 84, 144–45; reserve call up authority, 17, 120, 121–22, 130; responses to North Vietnam's negotiations offer, 112; Senate Foreign Relations Committee hearings, 21,

44, 47–48; surtax proposal, 141–42, 145–46; Tet Offensive impact, 35–36; in Wise Men discussions, 26

Connally, John, 149, 150, 155–56

Constellation, USS, Johnson's speech, 52

Coolidge, Calvin, 148

Cooper, John Sherman, 101

corruption accusations, in South Vietnam, in speech development discussions, 83

costs of war, 23, 47, 139–43

critics of war policy, overview: congressional members, 21–22; government officials, 15, 20–21, 46; Johnson's mindset about, 22–24, 26, 51–54; opinion leaders, 19–20; Tet Offensive impact, 35–36, 41. *See also* antiwar movement

Cronkite, Walter, 127

Cuba, 7

currency worries, 47, 50, 140–41, 142–43

Cushman, Robert, 30

Daley, Richard J., 162, 171

Dallek, Robert, 17, 28, 53, 152, 153, 169

Danang, deployment of Marines, 15

DeBenedetti, Charles, 12, 22, 26–27, 42

Democratic National Convention, 51, 169, 171, 187

détente goal, Johnson's, 11

Deupe, Beverly, 168

Diem, Ngo Dinh, 5–6, 8

Dienbienphu, French defeat, 4

dividing of Vietnam, Geneva Conference, 5

Dobrynin, Anatoly, 87, 110

dollar problems, 47, 50, 140–41, 142–43

domestic agenda: and costs of war, 140, 141–42; in March speech development, 66–67, 69, 70, 71, 73–74, 144–45; and public debate avoidance, 11; and reelection withdrawal announcement, 168; as reserves call up factor, 121–22, 130; and troop announcement approach, 16–17; as war opposition factor, 19–20

domino theory, 6–7, 9. *See also* Cold War logic *entries*

draft, military, ending of, 189–90
drafting presidential candidates, process,
    170–71
Drafts #1 through #6, March speech,
    68–76, 81

Eccles, Marriner, 140
economic development proposal, 20, 87,
    184–86
Edwards, George C. III, 199n1
82nd Airborne, 129–30
Eisenhower, Dwight D. (and administra-
    tion), 4, 5–6, 37, 62, 129
elections, Vietnamese, 5, 90
Ella, Charles J., 163
Ellington, Buford, 162
El Toro Marine Air Station, Johnson's
    speech, 51–52
embassy, US, in South Vietnam, 31, 32,
    34, 38, 40
enemy strength, counting approach,
    27–28, 39
escalation steps: for air base protection,
    15; gradual nature, 15–16, 55–56; Gulf
    of Tonkin impact, 12–13; Johnson's
    purpose, 10, 43; North Vietnam's
    matching actions, 17, 126; pattern of,
    16–17; Pleiku attack impact, 13–14

Farrell, John A., 189
favorite son tactic, 171–72
Fehmer, Marie, 158–59
Field, Mervin, 51
Fillmore, Millard, 148
financial section, March speech develop-
    ment: in Alternate Drafts #1 through
    #4, 79, 84, 85, 143–44; in Drafts #5
    and #6, 74, 75; in final version, 86
Flaming Dart operation, 14–15
Ford, Gerald R., 22, 112, 164, 223n1
foreign aid bill, 35, 48
Fortas, Abe, 16, 24–25, 65, 95, 108, 149
Fowler, Henry H., 72, 142, 149
Fox, Sylvan, 165
France, 1–5, 17
Frankel, Max, 47, 115, 127
Freeman, Orville, 162
Fulbright, J. William, 21, 26, 46, 111, 136,
    164, 166

Gallup polls, 12, 41–43, 49, 51, 160
Gardner, John, 150
Gardner, Lloyd, 6, 127, 178, 187
Gavin, James M., 21
Gemmill, Henry, 167, 168
Geneva Conference, 4–5, 17
Germany, 17
Giap, Vo Nguyen, 33
Giles, Frank, 111–12
Ginsburgh, Robert G., 30
Goldberg, Arthur, 16, 50, 65, 97, 100, 176
gold issues, 47, 50, 140–41, 142–43
Goldwater, Barry, 4, 13
Goodwin, Doris Kearns, 10, 72, 91, 154,
    167, 185
Gore, Albert, 178
Gould, Jack, 88
Goulding, Phil, 73, 80–81, 83, 128
government dissenters, exclusion of,
    20–21
graduated and reciprocated initiatives
    theory, 103
Great Britain: and France-Vietnam con-
    flict, 4; as March speech element, 82,
    86; pound devaluation, 142; resistance
    to U.S. alliance, 17; responses to North
    Vietnam's negotiations offer, 112; and
    Vietnam War origins, 1–2
GRIT theory, 103
Gulf of Tonkin episode, 13–14, 21

Habib, Philip, 138
Haiphong, bombing of, 42, 69, 70, 94, 108
Haiphong Harbor, mining option, 42, 45
Haldeman, H. R., 189
Hanoi the city, bombing of, 69, 70, 94,
    108
Harriman, Averell, 61–62, 81, 86, 87, 110,
    178, 188
Harris, Lou, 48–49
Harris poll, 41–42
Harsch, Joseph C., 106
Hart, Phil, 162
Helms, Richard, 23, 26, 119, 120
Herring, George C., 29, 30, 107, 109–10,
    139, 178, 180–81
Hershey, Lewis B., 168
Hess, Gary R., 9

Ho Chi Minh: Johnson's views of, 10, 43, 154, 196n27; in March speech development, 85, 86; nationalist movement beginnings, 1, 3–4, 3–5

Ho Chi Minh Trail, 46

Hoopes, Townsend (writing about): bombing campaign, 113; combat levels, 23; Goldberg-Johnson argument, 98; March speech drafting, 77, 82, 200n14; public opinion, 47, 128; Tet Offensive, 38, 43; troop commitments, 120

Hoover, J. Edgar, 168

House of Representatives, Gulf of Tonkin response, 13. See also Congress, U.S.

Hue, Tet Offensive attacks, 31

Hughes, John, 104

Humphrey, Hubert: notification about March speech, 87, 152–53; and October 1968 negotiations announcement, 189; primary campaign, 161, 169, 172–73, 186–87; war policy dissent, 15, 46

Inaugural Address, Kennedy's, 69, 84, 85, 157

India, in domino theory, 6

Italy, 17, 18

Jackson, Henry, 111, 112

Jackson Citizen Patriot, 107, 163

James, Howard, 171

Japan, 1, 6, 17, 177

Johns Hopkins University speech, 20, 70, 184

Johnson, Andrew, 148

Johnson, Lady Bird, 73, 84–85, 87, 144, 149, 155, 159, 217n5

Johnson, Lynda, 87, 153

Johnson, Lyndon Baines: belligerent speeches, 52–54; death of, 153; and France-Vietnam conflict, 4; R. Kennedy's proposed policy review, 49–50; presidential goals, 10–11; and Tet Offensive, 32, 36–37, 51, 196n27; victory promises, 52–53; on Vietnam dilemma, 22; visits to Vietnam, 7–8, 29. See also specific topics, e.g., bombing *entries*; Clifford *entries*; March 31

speech *entries*; troop commitments/ requests

Johnson, Tom, 65–66, 69–70, 88, 111, 149, 156, 176

Joint Chiefs of Staff, 15, 108, 121, 130, 134, 136, 188

Jones, Jim, 25, 87, 161

Karnow, Stanley, 34, 42, 121

Katzenbach, Nicholas, 61–62, 95, 96, 102, 112

Kearns, Doris. *See* Goodwin, Doris Kearns

Kefauver, Estes, 155

Kennan, George, 21, 36

Kennedy, Edward, 162

Kennedy, John F. (and administration), 6–9, 21, 26, 62. *See also* Inaugural Address, Kennedy's

Kennedy, Robert F., 49–51, 131, 152, 157, 164, 169–70, 172–73, 186

Khe Sanh, 31, 32, 34–35, 119, 124, 128–29, 133, 134

Khrushchev, Nikita, 7

Kilpatrick, James J., 171

King, Martin Luther, 176–77

Kolko, Gabriel, 139, 181

Komer, Robert, 28

Krim, Mr. and Mrs. Arthur, 159, 160

Ky, Nguyen Cao, 107, 109

Laos: establishment of, 5; and Ho Chi Minh Trail, 46; Kennedy administration actions, 6, 7, 9; after March speech, 113; Nixon administration actions, 189

La Rocque, Eugene, 26

LeMonde, 171

Lincoln's birthday, Johnson's speech, 51

Lippmann, Walter, 20

Loan, Nguyen Ngoc, 38

Lodge, Henry Cabot, 9, 55, 126, 139

Lou Harris polls, 41–42

MACV (Military Assistance Command, Vietnam), 28, 92

Mansfield, Mike, 9, 109, 112, 162, 171, 196n27

March 31 speech, development discussions: Alternate Drafts #1 through #5, 76–85, 101, 138; conflicts and inconsistencies of advisors, 61–62, 184, 200n14; drafting procedures, 67–68; Drafts #1 through #6, 68–76; perseverance emphasis, 62; and policy development entanglement, 57–58, 59–60; Sixth Draft Alternative, 81, 82; war and peace combination question, 65–66. *See also* peace negotiations, in speech development discussions; troop commitments/requests, in speech development discussions

March 31 speech, Johnson's presentation: bombing halt consequences, 109–10; as conflicting message, 178–84; inattention to economic development section, 184–86; media coverage, 88–89; meetings during day of, 87–88; North Vietnam's response, 111; significance summarized, 190; transcript of, xv–xxvi; troop announcement section, 136–39; viewership of, 88; war policy interpretations, 178

March on the Pentagon, 23

Marigold, 18

Marine Air Station, Johnson's speech, 52–53

Marine battalions, Danang deployment, 15

McCarthy, Eugene, 48, 50, 51, 131, 151, 164, 166–67, 169–70, 172–73, 186

McCormack, John, 112

McGovern, George, 9, 162

McNamara, Robert: and Ball's dissenting opinions, 20; bombing halt recommendation, 92, 94–95; consultations about Johnson's withdrawal, 149; on 82nd Airborne deployment, 129–30; during Kennedy administration, 9; in McPherson's meeting notes, 61; at Senate hearings, 44; stabilization plan of, 24–25, 26; and Tet Offensive, 34; transfer to World Bank, 25, 43, 95; troop commitment considerations, 117, 120, 131

McPherson, Harry: on bombing halt expectations, 106; bombing halt suggestions, 93–94; and Johnson's withdrawal talk, 151–52; and Tet Offensive, 37

McPherson, Harry (March speech development): Alternate Drafts #1 through #5, 76, 77–85, 101, 109, 156; directive about war theme, 65–66; drafting processes, 67–68, 70; Drafts #5 and #6, 70, 73–75, 81; February meeting notes, 61; initial instructions for, 58; negotiations offers, 64–65; negotiations-oriented perspective, 62; Rusk's bombing halt proposal, 96; Tet Offensive arguments, 63; uncertainty/doubt theme, 61, 105

military advisors designation, during Kennedy administration, 8

Military Assistance Command, Vietnam (MACV), 28, 92

Mills, Wilbur, 141, 143

Minneapolis Tribune, 163

Moïse, Edwin E. (writing about): bombing halt illusion, 113–14; optimism campaign, 27, 39; Tet Offensive, 31, 36, 40, 41, 196n40; troop commitments, 117, 118; war critics, 35–36

morale messages, 15

Morse, F. Bradford, 112

Murphy, Robert, 55

Nashville Banner, 163

National Alliance of Businessmen, Johnson's speech, 52, 54

National Farmers Union, Johnson's speech, 52, 54

National Liberation Front for Southern Vietnam, formation of, 6

National Press Club, 29, 137

National Rural Electric Cooperative Association, Johnson's speech, 52

National Security Council, 18

NATO, in troop commitments argument, 127

Nebraska primary, 51

negotiations. *See* peace negotiations *entries*

New Hampshire primary, 48, 136

Newsweek, 51, 126

New York Times (article topics): bombing

halt, 108, 115; gold crisis, 143; Johnson's campaign, 152; March speech, 88–89, 103–104, 167; peace negotiations offer, 103–104, 107; San Antonio formula, 187; troop commitments, 47, 122, 127, 132, 135; war debate divisiveness, 67; war escalation, 36; war policy review, 47

New Zealand, 17

Nhu, Ngo Dinh, 8

Nitze, Paul, 48, 61–62, 83, 96, 101, 142

Nixon, Richard M., 22, 51, 57, 87, 137–38, 170, 186, 188–89

NLF, formation of, 6

North Korea, 34, 54, 118

nuclear weapons, public opinion, 42

nuclear weapons paradox, 2–3

Nugent, Luci Johnson, 87, 159

Nugent, Pat, 87, 159

O'Brien, Lawrence, 150

Office of Speechwriting, 57

Oglesby, Carl, 171–72

Okun, Arthur, 85, 143

Operation Flaming Dart, 14–15

Operation Rolling Thunder, 15

opinion leaders, war opposition, 19–20

optimism campaign, 25–30, 36–39

Oregon primary, 51

Osgood, Charles, 103

Otten, Alan, 48

peace negotiations: logistics-related obstacles, 111–12, 178; mutual demands problem, 18–19; North Vietnam's unexpected acceptance, 176; October 1968 announcement, 188–89; and optimism campaign, 28; public opinion, 11; responses to North Vietnam's offer, 111–14. *See also* bombing halt *entries*

peace negotiations, in speech development discussions: Alternate Drafts #1 through #4, 77–78, 81–82, 83, 84; arguments about, 63–65; Drafts #1 through #6, 68, 72–73, 75–76, 81; final version, 85–87

Pearson, Drew, 165

peroration. *See* closing peroration

perseverance emphasis, March speech, 62, 68, 70, 74

petroleum facilities, bombing of, 17

Philippines, in domino theory, 6

Pickle, Jake, 149

Pleiku attack, 14–15, 91

Poland, 18

policy reviews, after Tet Offensive, 43–44, 47, 54–55. *See also* Clifford task force, policy topics

Prados, John (writing about): bombing campaign's purpose, 10; Diem's leverage, 5–6; diplomacy's purpose, 92; Eisenhower administration actions, 4; government dissenters, 20–21; Johnson's mindset about antiwar movement, 23–24; March speech drafting, 76; Nixon administration, 189; October 1968 peace negotiations, 188; optimism campaign, 27, 29; peace negotiations obstacles, 18; resistance of allies, 17; Tet Offensive, 33; visual images, 39

presidential campaigns: Humphrey-Nixon, 187, 188–89; Johnson-Goldwater, 13, 14

primary campaigns, 48–49, 50–51, 108–109, 136, 150, 151, 152, 168–69, 186

Public Affairs Office, Defense Department, 41, 126

public opinion: about bombing halt, 163; as bombing halt motive, 106–107; changes in support, 12–13, 21, 29–30, 47; as diplomacy mission, 92; Gulf of Tonkin impact, 13; Humphrey's campaign, 187; Johnson's appeal to, 51–53; Johnson's communication dilemma, 11; of Johnson's war management, 160, 166; and March speech development, 67, 71; in McNamara's stabilization plan, 24–25; and meeting with Soviet ambassador, 87–88; after Nixon's November speech, 189; and optimism campaign, 27, 29–30; policy preferences, 11–12; primary campaigns, 48, 49, 51; reelection withdrawal announcement, 162–63; tax increase, 141, 163; Tet Offensive impact, 41–43; in troop commitment arguments, 124–25, 128; in Wise Men discussions, 25–26

Pucinski, Roman, 162

Pueblo, USS, 34, 58, 59, 118

Qui Nhon attack, 14

rainy season factor, in proposed bombing halt, 46, 96, 99, 107, 109, 114

reciprocity norm, 103

reserve troops, call up option: Clifford's task force, 45, 46, 133; resistance, 16–17; in speech Alternate Drafts #1 and #3, 79, 82–83; in speech development process, 60, 136–37; in speech Drafts #1 through #4, 68–69, 72; and Westmoreland troops request, 118, 120–22, 129

Roche, John, 150

Rockefeller, David, 145

Rockefeller, Nelson, 170, 172–73

Rolling Thunder operation, 15, 91

Rollins, James H., 168–69

Roosevelt, Franklin D., 1, 152, 171, 172

Roosevelt, Theodore, 148

Rostow, Walt: bombing halt recommendation, 92, 97–98; expectation of March speech, 178; interpretation of Tet Offensive, 33; October 1968 peace negotiations, 188; in optimism campaign, 27, 28, 37; troop commitment discussions, 120, 124–25, 128, 129, 133, 134

Rostow, Walt (in speech development discussions): Alternate Drafts #1 through #3, 76–77, 80, 82; briefing of McPherson, 59; Draft #6, 74–75; influence summarized, 104–105; initial hawkish perspective, 61; linkage to *Pueblo* seizure, 58; meeting with Soviet ambassador, 87–88; perseverance emphasis, 62; public opinion's role, 106

Rowe, James, 54, 150

run on the dollar, 47, 50

Rusk, Dean: air power directive from Johnson, 44; consultations about Johnson's withdrawal, 149; early peace talks perspective, 93; expectation of

March speech, 178; and Goldberg's bombing halt proposal, 98; interpretation of Tet Offensive, 33; and McNamara's bombing halt plan, 24, 95; monetary system concerns, 142; on North Vietnam's negotiations offer, 111; October 1968 peace negotiations, 188; proposed bombing halt, 46, 96, 97, 107; recommendations to Bunker about bombing halt announcement, 109; at Senate hearings, 47–48; Westmoreland's troops request, 120, 133, 136, 210n4

Rusk, Dean (in speech development discussions): Alternate Drafts #1 and #3, 76–77, 80, 82; bombing halt element, 64, 66, 98, 100–101, 105–106; Drafts #1 through #6, 69, 71–72, 74, 76; influence summarized, 104–105; initial hawkish perspective, 61; negotiations-oriented perspectives, 61, 64, 102–103; tour of duty extension proposal, 58

Russell, Richard, 22, 162

Saigon, during Tet Offensive, 31–32

San Antonio formula: and Clifford's task force, 45; elements of, 19, 93; and final bombing halt, 187; in March speech development, 72–73, 74, 82, 84, 86; and McNamara's stabilization plan, 24; and Tet Offensive, 43. *See also* peace negotiations

Sanders, Barefoot, 162

Schandler, Herbert Y. (writing about): bombing pauses and negotiations, 109, 114; Clifford's post-speech statements, 177; Clifford task force, 45; costs of war, 20, 142; logic of Vietnam policy, 1–2, 3, 9, 10; March speech influencers, 104, 105; public opinion influence, 47; Rusk's bombing halt proposal, 101; troop commitments, 120–21, 122, 137, 210n10

SEATO (Southeast Asia Treaty Organization), 5

Senate, Gulf of Tonkin response, 13. *See also* Congress, U.S.

Senate Foreign Relations Committee:

hearings, 21, 44, 47–48; Tet Offensive impact, 36; in Wise Men discussions, 26

Sherman, William Tecumseh, 170–71

Sixth Draft Alternative, 81, 82

Small, Melvin, 130, 189–90

Smathers, George, 112, 145–46

Smith, C. R., 162

Smith, Hedrick, 88–89, 103–104, 107, 108

Southeast Asia Treaty Organization (SEATO), 5

South Vietnam, U.S. recognition of, 5

South Vietnamese Army, 79, 86, 129, 137–39, 179

Soviet Union: invasion of Czechoslovakia, 173; Johnson's détente agenda, 11; during Kennedy administration, 7; and March speech development, 74, 82, 86, 87, 110; nuclear weapons, 2; response to reelection withdrawal, 110, 171

Special Drawing Rights, 143, 145

Speechwriting, Office of, 57

Spock, Benjamin, 168–69

stabilization plan, McNamara's, 24–25, 26

stalemate perception, public opinion, 11, 131

Stanford poll, 11

State of the Union address, 32, 39, 58, 150, 154–55, 219n32

Stockholm agreement, 143–44

stock market, after March 31 speech, 163

Supreme Court, 16

surtax: public opinion, 163; for war costs, 141

surtax, in speech development discussions: in Alternate Drafts #1 through #4, 79, 84, 85, 143–44, 145; in Drafts #1 through #6, 69, 70, 71, 72, 74, 75; in final version, 86, 145

Tan Son Nhut, 32

taxes. See surtax entries

Taylor, Maxwell, 55, 95, 119, 120, 128–29, 210n4

Temple, Larry, 162

Tet Offensive: overview, 40–41; attacks during, 31–32; intelligence failure about, 34–35; Johnson's policy response, 43–44; media coverage, 39–40, 196n40; misinterpretations of, 32–33; North Vietnamese motives, 32, 33–34; as presidential speech requirement, 57, 58; public opinion impact, 35–39, 41–43; in speech development discussions, 62–63, 68, 70, 76, 82, 86; troop commitment arguments, 116–17, 118, 123–24, 126–27, 130–31

Tet II, 179

Texas, Johnson's speeches, 52

Thailand, in domino theory, 6

Thieu, Nguyen van, 109, 139, 168, 177, 179, 188–89

Thompson, Llewellyn, 81, 86, 110

Times, London, 111–12

tours of duty, extension, 58, 133

troop commitments/requests: overview, 146–47; for air base protection, 15; Clifford's post-speech statements, 177; Clifford's task force, 44–45, 48, 97; decision postponements, 133–35; effectiveness arguments, 126–28, 129; gold market response, 142; Helms' perspectives, 119; during Kennedy administration, 8; leaked news report about, 47, 135–36; in McNamara's stabilization plan, 24–25; as negotiations obstacle, 18–19; Nixon administration actions, 189; opposition arguments listed, 125; public opinion arguments, 11, 124–25, 128, 129, 130, 131; Tet Offensive arguments, 116–17, 118, 123–24, 130–31; Westmoreland's statements about, 44, 117–18, 125–26; Wheeler's perspectives, 118–22, 132–33. See also Khe Sanh; South Vietnamese Army

troop commitments/requests, in speech development discussions: overview of debate arguments, 62–63, 65–66; Alternate Drafts #1 through #3, 78–79, 82–83; in Drafts #1 through #6, 73, 74, 75, 81; in final version, 86, 116, 136–37

truce signing, 190

Truman, Harry (and administration), 4, 7, 21, 148, 155, 160, 218n30

Tyler, John, 148

Udall, Stewart, 162
unification goal, North Vietnam's, 18
United Kingdom. *See* Great Britain
United Nations, 16, 100
unity motive, March speech, 154, 163, 178
US News and World Report, 150
U Thant, 50, 100

Vance, Cyrus, 55, 92
Vandiver, Frank E., 75, 111, 121, 177
Viet Cong, formation of, 6
Vietnam Information Group, 27
visual images, public confidence impact, 38–39
Voice of America, 16

Wallace, George, 170, 187
Wall Street Journal, 48, 62, 108, 111, 126, 146, 167, 172
Warden, Philip, 168
Warnke, Paul, 61, 80–81, 83, 101–102, 106–107
war of liberation, as communism threat, 10, 90–91
war protesters. *See* antiwar movement; critics of war policy, overview
Watson, Marvin, 150, 162
weather factor, in proposed bombing halt, 46, 96, 99, 107, 109, 114
Westmoreland, William: in Clifford task force directives, 131–32; discussion with Johnson about election withdrawal, 149; long-term strategy planning, 121, 123, 135; and McNamara's bombing halt plan, 95; in optimism campaign, 27, 28, 29, 133, 149; statements about troop requirements, 44, 117–18, 125–26, 135, 200n14, 210n4; and Tet Offensive, 31, 32, 33, 34, 37, 40; and Wheeler's troops perspectives, 118–19, 123, 210n10
Wheeler, Earle: expectation of March speech, 178; and Johnson's withdrawal from reelection, 149, 164; long-term strategy planning, 121, 123; on media coverage, 40; and reserves call up, 118,

120, 121, 129; and Tet Offensive, 33, 37; tour of duty extension proposal, 58; troop commitment perspectives, 134; troop commitment statistics, 122; visit to Vietnam, 44, 59, 96, 117–18, 120, 210n4, n10; on Westmoreland's troops request, 118–19, 123, 128, 132–33, 137
Wicker, Tom, 143, 149, 171
Willis, David K., 110
Wirtz, Willard, 162
Wisconsin primary, 51, 169–70
Wisconsin State Journal, 163
Wise Men meetings, 25–26, 54–55, 75
withdrawal from reelection, Johnson's: aftermath theorizing, 174–78; alternative scenarios, 170–73; disbelief responses, 148, 174; discussions/consultations about, 149–50, 151–53, 155–56, 218n30; draftings of statement, 84, 150, 155, 156–61; health considerations, 153; national unity motive, 154, 163, 178; notifications about, 161–62; political effects, 166–69, 175–76; responses to, 153, 161–65, 174–75; secrecy about, 148, 152, 153, 165, 217n1; skepticism about, 170–72; Soviet Union response, 110, 171; speculation about timing, 165–66; and State of the Union address, 150–51, 154–55, 156–57, 219n32
withdrawal from Vietnam, as option, 8–9, 12, 25, 87. *See also* antiwar movement
Woods, Randall B., 35, 121
World Bank, 25, 43, 95
World War II, 1, 32–33

Zablocki, Clement J., 169
zero-sum perspective, 3, 9–10. *See also* Cold War logic *entries*

CPSIA information can be obtained
at www.ICGtesting.com
Printed in the USA
LVHW031020080321
680848LV00001B/1